THE MAKING OF
THE MASTERS

CLIFFORD ROBERTS, AUGUSTA NATIONAL, AND GOLF'S MOST PRESTIGIOUS TOURNAMENT

DAVID OWEN

SIMON & SCHUSTER

For my father.

SIMON & SCHUSTER
Rockefeller Center
1230 Avenue of the Americas
New York, NY 10020

SIMON & SCHUSTER and colophon are registered trademarks
of Simon & Schuster Inc.

Designed by Maura Rosenthal

Manufactured in the United States of America

3   5   7   9   10   8   6   4   2

Library of Congress Cataloging-in-Publication Data
Owen, David, date.
The making of the Masters: Clifford Roberts, Augusta National,
and golf's most prestigious tournament / David Owen.
p.   cm.
Includes index.
1. Roberts, Clifford.   2. Masters Golf Tournament—History.
3. Augusta National Golf Club—History.   I. Title.
GV970.R63094   1999
796.352'66—dc21
[B]   98-55532
                                                         CIP

ISBN 0-684-85729-4

Masters is a registered trademark of Augusta National, Inc.

Contents

CHAPTER ONE
Benevolent Dictator   13

CHAPTER TWO
"I Just Figured Cliff Had Never Been a Child"   33

CHAPTER THREE
Beginning   49

CHAPTER FOUR
Augusta National Invitation Tournament   79

CHAPTER FIVE
"The World's Wonder Inland Golf Course"   101

CHAPTER SIX
Cattle, Turkeys, and Prisoners of War   141

CHAPTER SEVEN
General Ike   165

CHAPTER EIGHT
Television   183

CHAPTER NINE
Roberts's Rules   209

CHAPTER TEN
Inside, Outside   227

CHAPTER ELEVEN
Monuments   257

Acknowledgments   277

Index   281

Photo Credits   290

THE MAKING OF
THE MASTERS

CHAPTER ONE

Benevolent Dictator

THE MODERN GOLF season never ends, but it does begin. When the first contestant tees off at Augusta National Golf Club on Thursday morning during Masters week, golfers all over the world reset their internal clocks. The first page in a golfer's calendar is April.

For the world's best players, the Masters divides one season's aspirations from another's. Success at the highest levels on tour means recognition, money, autograph requests, endorsements, exemptions—and an invitation to Augusta. As the first full week of April draws near, players who have not yet qualified for invitations juggle their schedules to maximize their chances, and television commentators count down the tournaments remaining. When the Masters begins, every competitor has a theoretical chance of matching Bobby Jones's unduplicated feat of winning all four major tournaments in one year; when the Masters ends, the Grand Slam field has shrunk to one.

For tournament spectators, the Masters is an annual reunion where the passage of time is measured not in years but in the names of champions. The principal viewing areas have the settled feel of old neighborhoods; the course is as familiar as a friend's backyard. In countless gatherings beneath the pine trees, acquaintances are renewed and records are brought up to date: deaths, marriages, children, grandchildren, new houses, old jobs. The dogwood blossoms are compared with the dogwood blossoms of previous years. A rebuilt green is examined

and approved. Two veterans discuss the careers of Sam Snead and
Arnold Palmer—and then Sam Snead and Arnold Palmer walk by. A
guest once said, "I rode here in the front seat and will be in the back seat
going out so I can stay as long as I can."

For distant golf fans, the first glimpse of Amen Corner on TV is
proof that winter is gone. Northerners who haven't swung a club since
Halloween scrounge an old ball from the garage and roll a few wobbly
putts across the family room carpet during commercials. A swirling
gray New England sky stops looking like a vestige of December and begins to seem like a harbinger of spring. The hours crawl from Saturday
evening till Sunday afternoon. Meetings and social engagements are ignored or rescheduled; no avid golfer was ever married on Masters weekend. In 1987, two fans from Olympia Fields, Illinois, named their new
daughter Tori Augusta National.

For sportswriters, the Masters is the plum assignment of the year. It
is the first trip entered in a reporter's appointment book, and it is written in ink. Journalists take the Masters personally. Herbert Warren
Wind, *The New Yorker*'s incomparable golf correspondent for many
years, once stopped another reporter upon arriving in Augusta's airport
and anxiously inquired about the state of the greens: "Are they firm?" Senior golf writers postpone hip replacements and cataract operations
until just after the tournament, giving themselves a full fifty weeks to recover.

For nongolfers, the Masters is the one tournament of the year that
compels attention. Over breakfast on Sunday morning, a golfer's non-
playing spouse may suddenly offer an informed observation about the
chances of Faldo, Couples, or Woods—the result of an hour's seduction
by the sports page or the TV. The beauty of the setting makes one's love
for golf comprehensible to the game's antagonists. For four days, the
national flower is the azalea.

Gary Player once said, "The Masters is the only tournament I ever
knew where you choke when you drive through the front gate." The trip
down Magnolia Lane may be the most dreamed about entrance in
sports. Although the Masters is not ancient as golf goes, no contest runs
deeper in the imaginations of participants. Sam Snead says, "If you

asked golfers what tournament they would rather win over all the others, I think every one of them to a man would say the Masters." Late at night after Tiger Woods's record-breaking victory in 1997, Earl Woods looked in on his son and found him curled up in bed, asleep with a smile on his face, his arms wrapped around his green jacket.

The Masters is unique among major tournaments in that it is conducted not by a national golf organization but by a private club. Two dozen committees headed by club members assume responsibility for everything from the placement of the holes to the pricing of the barbecued pork sandwiches in the concession stands. A member who may squeeze in only a week or two of golf in Augusta for himself in a typical year may spend another week or two wrestling with parking allocations, entertainment for international reporters, or the placement of public telephones. The tournament shortens by a week an already abbreviated playing season, and it does so at the most beautiful time of the year. The course is closed from late May until early October, a period when summer heat threatens the turf, and it receives little play during January and February, months when the weather is chilly, wet, and unpredictable. In March, the members share the course with crews erecting scoreboards, spectator stands, concession tents, and television towers. In early April, they vacate their clubhouse and turn their dining room into a commissary. In late May, they surrender the course again, this time to tournament volunteers, club employees, caddies, and other friends of the club, who close the golf season with a week-long party.

The prestige of the Masters has made the club's green blazer the most coveted adornment in golf—so much so that a modern golf fan has difficulty imagining that neither the club nor the tournament was a foreordained success. Founded at the beginning of the Great Depression, the club faced financial ruin repeatedly during its first fifteen years. As the club was being formed in 1931, the first business plan called for 1,800 members, each of whom would pay dues of sixty dollars a year. Three years later, as the first Masters got underway, the club was 1,724 members short of that goal. The Masters, which began in 1934 as the

Augusta National Invitation Tournament, was recognized from the start as an exceptionally well-run event—*Time* that year described it as "a new golfing institution and a new competition, rivaling even the U.S. Open in importance, far surpassing it in atmosphere"—but it remained an economic burden for years. The club couldn't afford to pay the first winner, Horton Smith, or any of the other top finishers until seventeen members chipped in the purse. The winner in 1946, Herman Keiser, had to be told that his plaque would be along shortly, just as soon as the club could come up with the silver.

The club survived those early adversities because of the perseverance of its two founders: Clifford Roberts and Robert Tyre "Bobby" Jones, Jr. They were, respectively, Augusta National's first chairman and its only president. (In 1966, five years before his death, the club declared Jones "president in perpetuity," and no successor has ever been named.) They are commemorated by a pair of bronze plaques set in the ground at the base of the flagpole in front of the clubhouse. The modesty of the memorial, which is known as the Founders Circle, would have pleased both men: Jones loved Augusta National in part because for him it was a refuge from celebrity; Roberts was proud of what he and his friend had created but was an enemy of ostentation.

It is usually said that Jones conceived of the club and Roberts financed it, but one could argue that the roles were reversed—that without Jones's immense popularity the enterprise would never have attracted enough financial support to survive, and that without the vision and stubborn determination of Roberts the club would have folded and the Augusta National Invitation Tournament would never have grown into the modern Masters. Roberts said in later years that if he and Jones had known at the outset how long the Depression was going to last, they would never have had the nerve to proceed. He was not exaggerating. On several occasions, they came close to giving up. The final decision to build the course was made early in 1932 with deep trepidation and after months of wavering. By late 1935, eight months after Gene Sarazen had seemingly secured the future of the tournament by hitting "the shot heard round the world," his monumental double-eagle on fifteen, the club's situation was so dire that its lenders actually foreclosed.

In historical accounts of the club and the tournament, Jones has always overshadowed Roberts. That is as Roberts would have wished it; Augusta National, in his view, was Jones's club, and the Masters was Jones's tournament. But they were Jones's in large measure because Roberts made them that way. Jones was always involved in important decisions, especially during the early years, and his influence went far beyond consultation, since the easiest way to describe Roberts's conception of the Masters is to say that his goal was to put on a tournament worthy of its association with Jones. But Roberts was almost always the man behind the curtain, and he pursued the job with a dedication that sometimes gave others pause. In 1956, while hospitalized in New York after suffering a heart attack, he asked a secretary to send him a list of the previous year's Masters committee assignments. As the secretary later recounted with wonder in a letter to Jones, Roberts was bored and wanted to turn his mind to a subject that he said would relax him. Kathryn Murphy, who worked as his secretary on tournament matters from 1962 until he retired in 1976, kept a stenographer's pad next to the phone by her bed at home, because there was no telling at what hour Roberts might call to dictate a letter. Byron Nelson says, "This place was his bride."

The partnership of Jones and Roberts was as unlikely as it was successful. "They were as different as day and night," Sam Snead says, "but, you know, that's the type that get along." At the time of the club's founding, Jones was the most beloved athlete in the world. In 1930, at the age of twenty-eight, he had conquered what George Trevor of the *New York Sun* called "the impregnable quadrilateral of golf"—the British and U.S. Amateur championships and the British and U.S. Opens. He had been honored with two New York City ticker tape parades and had retired from competition. He was "the model American athlete come to life," according to Herbert Warren Wind, who wrote, "Everybody adored him—not just dyed-in-the-wool golfers, but people who had never struck a golf ball or had the least desire to. They admired the ingrained modesty, the humor, the generosity of spirit that were evident in Jones's remarks and deportment. They liked the way he looked, this handsome, clean cut young man, whose eyes gleamed with both a frank boyishness and a perceptiveness far beyond his years."

Roberts in 1930 was a pragmatic and frequently grim-faced thirty-six-year-old Wall Street stockbroker and speculator who had taken a beating in the Crash of 1929. He knew all about hardship, having grown up on the edges of poverty in a dozen small towns in Iowa, Kansas, California, Oklahoma, and Texas. His family moved so often during his childhood that Roberts in later years said he doubted he could readily name all the places where he had lived as a boy. "No sooner would I become acquainted with a few companions," he wrote in a letter in 1967, "[than] I would be moved to an altogether different place and sometimes quite a different one." His life was hard, but he met it squarely. At the age of ten, he walked home nearly four miles rather than work all day for fifty cents when he had been promised seventy-five. He dug potatoes for money to buy schoolbooks, and he helped care for his younger siblings when his mother—who suffered from a variety of ailments and eventually committed suicide—could not get out of bed. His last completed year of school was eighth grade. He farmed, sold dry goods, worked in an oyster house in Texas, took a three-week course in shorthand and other clerical skills, and managed a failing orchard. At the age of twenty-three, having worked for several years as a traveling salesman of men's clothing based in Kansas City, he went to New York to escape the world in which he had grown up.

Jones and Roberts met through mutual friends in the mid-twenties. Jones was already a celebrity and a hero, and Roberts, despite some growing success in the investment world, was still at heart an awestruck country boy. For Jones, Roberts was at first a congenial acquaintance—a friend of friends—who enjoyed sharing a drink and a funny story in a clubhouse grill. During at least one such gathering, Jones spoke of a wish to build in the South a golf course that would reflect his ideas about the game. Roberts one day suggested Augusta, Georgia—a city with which both men were familiar. Jones agreed to the plan, Roberts later wrote, "but with a stipulation that I agree to look after the financing."

Jones trusted Roberts with his idea because he believed that Roberts could carry it out. Roberts, despite his relative youth, exuded confidence and competence to an extraordinary degree. Byron Nelson says, "Of all the executives I have known, Cliff was the best. He listened, and he would take what people said and turn it over in his mind and decide whether or not it was a good idea. Then he would follow through and find the right people to get the job done." Herbert Warren Wind once called Roberts "a relentless perfectionist with one of the best minds for management and significant detail since Salmon P. Chase."* He was meticulous, methodical, and impervious to distraction. His secretary at the club would sometimes find him hunched over his desk on autumn afternoons, working in the gloom. She would flick on the lights, and he would straighten up in his chair but show no other sign of having noticed the change.

In the spring of 1931, through an acquaintance in Augusta, Roberts discovered a likely piece of property for Jones's course: a long-abandoned commercial nursery on the outskirts of town. Seeing the land for the first time was an "unforgettable" experience, Jones wrote in *Golf Is My Game,* which was published in 1960: "It seemed that this land had been lying here for years just waiting for someone to lay a golf course upon it. Indeed, it even looked as though it were already a golf course, and I am sure that one standing today where I stood on this first visit, on the terrace overlooking the practice putting green, sees the property almost exactly as I saw it then."

Jones was right about the appearance of the property: If you know the course today, you can look at a hundred-year-old photograph and mentally superimpose many of the holes. In fact, you can almost make yourself believe that the thirteenth fairway is already lying beside that small stream in the distance, and that the eighteenth tee must be just out of sight, beyond that line of trees to the left.

As for the founders, their outlines are harder to discern. Jones has

---

* Chase was Abraham Lincoln's secretary of the treasury and the sixth chief justice of the United States; Chase National Bank, the forerunner of Chase Manhattan Bank, was named in his memory.

been celebrated for so long and in such exalted terms that today he belongs as much to mythology as to the history of golf. Sportswriters have
maintained the pious tone established by O. B. Keeler—Jones's close
friend and adoring first biographer—who described his golf in biblical
terms, dividing his career into "seven lean years" and "seven fat years,"
and was reverent even in depicting his foibles, such as the temper that
had sometimes threatened to eclipse his promise. ("To the finish of my
golfing days," Jones himself once wrote, "I encountered golfing emo-
tions which could not be endured with the club still in my hands.") People who were close to Jones say that he really was the remarkable
gentleman that Keeler, Wind, Paul Gallico, Charles Price, Sidney L.
Matthew, and other writers portrayed him to be. But legends acquire a
power of their own, and no one today can hope to see past Jones's aura
to the man his drinking buddies knew. Even when he was a young man,
the myth must have been in the way: Jones viewed "Bobby" almost as a
stage name; he asked to be called Bob.

Roberts is equally hard to see clearly. Among sportswriters he has
been demonized to almost the same extent that Jones has been deified.
He is known today mainly as the villain in a handful of classic press tent
anecdotes—as a tyrant who ejected a player from the Masters for a triv-
ial infraction, sent members bills for course improvements they had
been rash enough to suggest, withdrew the memberships of men who
had dared to cross him, and administered nervous breakdowns to a succession of executives at CBS, which began broadcasting the tournament
on television in 1956. Most of the classic stories about Roberts contain
at least a kernel of truth—he could be hard to work with, especially for
anyone who wasn't used to dealing with a determined man who said exactly what he thought—but none of the stories begins to do him justice.
The more grotesque tales are invariably told by people who didn't know
him well, if they knew him at all; taken together, they add up to a portrait of a man who never existed.

The misperceptions were to a great extent his own fault. He seldom
spoke publicly about himself or any part of his life outside his responsibilities with the tournament and the club. In a letter to Jones in 1964, he
offered one explanation for his reticence: "I have repeatedly [taken] the

position that one personality, meaning yourself, was enough for any one Club." Because he nearly always turned the same blank face to the public, strangers have assumed that he was easy to comprehend. His forbidding manner, glimpsed during the tournament or on other formal occasions, invited hasty summarization: autocratic, domineering, stubborn, humorless, tyrannical, mean. All such terms obscured not only the real dimensions of his personality but also the true achievements of his life. The real Roberts is as hard to see as the real Jones.

In 1972, the great British golf writer and television commentator Henry Longhurst—who for many years covered the Masters from a television tower beside the sixteenth green—sent Roberts a copy of his latest book, which he had inscribed to the "benevolent dictator" of Augusta National Golf Club. In acknowledging the gift, Roberts, with characteristic contrariness, objected to both terms. "Ordinarily I would not want to be classified as being benevolent," he wrote, "and I also do not wish to be called a dictator." He was joking, mostly—he concluded by telling Longhurst that "just so long as you recognize my existence, I shall always be happy for you to call me any damned thing you like"— but he was also revealing something about himself. In pursuing what he believed to be the best interests of his club and its tournament, he behaved as though he knew that a reputation for malevolence had its uses. He often seemed to encourage his chilly image; in any event, he did little to contradict it. In the photograph of himself that he selected for the dust jacket of his history of the club, he wears an expression that only a relative or intimate friend could confidently identify as a smile. He looks stern, uncomfortable, and disapproving. He is leaning away from the camera—literally increasing the distance between his reader and himself. He seems annoyed. His legs are crossed and he holds a cigarette in his right hand, but his posture conveys the opposite of ease.

What is truly interesting about the photograph, though, is not the image it conveys but the one it conceals. The picture on the dust jacket shows Roberts only as he presented himself in public; to his friends, he turned a different face. His favorite portrait of himself—copies of which he sent to friends not long before he died—was a candid color photograph of a smiling face in profile. In it he looked like a kindly uncle. This was the Roberts his closest friends and associates knew. It was the Roberts for whom the wife of the club's steward baked pound cake, knitted an afghan, and made jars of stewed peaches. It was the Roberts who commandeered a member's private airplane in the middle of the night to transport the critically ill wife of one of the club's professionals to his own specialist in Boston. It was the Roberts whose death prompted Philip Reed, the chairman of General Electric Co., to resign his membership in the club. (Reed said he missed Roberts so much that coming back to Augusta would merely depress him.) It was the Roberts who baby-sat for and watched television with the young daughters of one of the club's employees. It was the Roberts who quietly but firmly intervened when Masters competitors underpaid their caddies. It was the Roberts who sometimes signed his letters to Jones "Much love, yours faithfully," and whom Jones remembered at Christmas one year with a homey gift of a pair of socks. It was the Roberts whom British golf writer Peter Dobereiner described in a tribute published when Roberts resigned as the chairman of the Masters Tournament Committee in 1976: "To a large degree Roberts is not the ogre he pretends to be," Dobereiner wrote in the *Observer*. "The style of the man, as an uncompromising dictator, hides a natural shyness and a generous spirit. He has helped many people, in large and small ways, but always by stealth, covering his traces so well that as often as not his benefaction is not even suspected. If this austere old man commands respect rather than affection, then that is by his own choice, a sacrifice he has made in the cause of his beloved Masters." And in the cause of his beloved club, which in Roberts's mind always came first. (Elsewhere in the same column, Dobereiner exactly captured what he called Roberts's "simple creed": "everything about Augusta National Golf Club and the Masters had to be the best, and if it was not the best then it would have to be improved every year until it was.")

For decades, sportswriters who wouldn't dream of quoting a baseball score without double-checking it have felt no compunction about repeating and embellishing even the unlikeliest tales about Roberts. Indeed, he has so often been portrayed as a conniving misanthrope that few stories about him today are automatically dismissed as too outrageous to be believed. But the cartoon that so often stands in for Roberts defies credulity. If he really had been the monster that the meaner tales make him out to be, Jones would never have associated with him, friends from all over the world would not have sought and cherished his company, some of golf's most celebrated names would not credit him with having helped to build their careers, Dwight D. Eisenhower would never have reserved a White House bedroom for his exclusive use, long-time members and employees of the club would not still speak wistfully of his death, and the Masters today would be nothing more than a long-forgotten artifact of the halting early years of American competitive golf.

The greatest human strengths and weaknesses are usually allied; they are sides of a coin. To know Roberts at his worst is easy, because he did not dissemble. To know him as he really was requires both effort and an open mind.

Roberts died in 1977. He was eighty-three years old and, like his mother more than six decades before, he was a suicide. Ill and enfeebled, he had made his way back to Augusta in a borrowed airplane so that he could end his life in the place he viewed, above all other residences, as his home.

Although he has now been dead for more than twenty years, he is still very much in evidence at Augusta National. He is still quoted at meetings, sometimes in the present tense. His book about the club—*The Story of Augusta National Golf Club*, published in 1976, the year before he died—is still the first source young staff members check when a question arises concerning the cracker barrel in the golf shop, the origin of the green jacket, or the location of the original bunker in the second fairway. Pictures at the club are still hung on two hooks, because crooked pictures drove him to distraction. The golf shop still makes change with brand-new currency, because he couldn't stand dirty bills. (He folded his bills in groups, by denomination, and he always carried enough of each kind so that no one would ever have to give him change.) He is still often referred to as *Mr.* Roberts, even by men who today are older than he was when he died.

You can still hear his voice at the club: There are members, employees, and caddies who do accurate impressions, and when they quote him in a funny story they inevitably adopt his glacier-slow delivery. Roberts spoke as though he were dictating to an engraver. He silently considered any question until he had thoroughly arranged his answer. The first sound out of his mouth was usually a cough, a clearing of his throat, or "Uh," a monosyllable he was capable of drawing to narrative length. ("Cliff could say 'Uh' for two days," a friend says.) Strangers sometimes interpreted his hesitation as deafness or an encouragement to restate the topic; his friends knew to wait. If Roberts was preoccupied with a club matter or a tournament detail, the wait could be considerable. A member who greeted him in passing on a sidewalk outside the clubhouse might hear his greeting returned, from a receding distance, many seconds later.

The menu at Augusta National still reflects Roberts's simple tastes. The dishes are mostly unadorned. The enormous canned olives that he loved are still passed around before dinner. James Clark, the club's chef, no longer burns the cornbread, as he did to please Roberts, but he still serves cornbread every day. Roberts always ordered the same lunch: consommé, a grilled chicken breast sandwich on white toast, tea, a homemade cookie, white nectar peaches. Although his lunch order was unvarying, he consulted a menu before making it, and his waiter wrote everything down. A friend, joining him for lunch one day, as a joke ordered exactly what Roberts always ordered. Without blinking, Roberts said, "That sounds excellent. I'll have the same."

The room in which Roberts usually stayed when he was at the club still looks much as it did when he was alive. It is named for him and is called a suite, but it is really just a single bedroom with a small bathroom at the far end. It looks like a hotel room, and the furniture looks like hotel room furniture. There is a bust of Arnold Palmer, who was probably Roberts's favorite golfer. (Officially, Roberts had no favorites, but in private his affection for Palmer was unsurpassed.) There is a closet in which Byron Nelson, another favorite, kept clothes between visits to the club. The only amenity is a fireplace, which Roberts was apt to light at the first rumor of a chill. (Although he loved fires, he was ambivalent about firewood; on his order, every log delivered to his hearth was first shorn of anything resembling bark.) In all weather, he kept his room warm—uncomfortably so, in the opinion of visitors. The room had two thermostats, and he would make minute adjustments in one or the other as conditions changed in ways that only he could detect.

Members who today are old men remember crouching outside Roberts's room when they were young, hoping to catch a glimpse of the chairman through the window. If Roberts was wearing a tie, they knew he could safely be approached; if he had taken off the tie, they knew to stay away. And the mood of the chairman was the mood of the club. When Roberts arrived in Augusta from New York, John Milton, the driver who picked him up at the airport, was under standing instructions from Bowman Milligan, the club's steward, to assess his state of mind—and, if possible, to improve it. Back at the club, Milton would report his findings to Milligan, who would send a message to the course superintendent. If Roberts was in a bad mood, the grounds crew would set up the greens with easy pin positions. If Roberts was in a good mood, the holes would be cut as though for Sunday at the Masters.

The main event each year for members of Augusta National is still the Jamboree, a springtime competition and party that Roberts viewed as more important than the Masters. He believed that the Jamboree and other members-only gatherings were the soul of the club, because they promoted a sense of fraternity without which he feared the club would not survive. He would often add members to the club's board of governors solely in the hope that the appointment would shame them into spending more time in Augusta. One such member was George B. Storer, of Miami, who didn't realize he was a governor until Roberts wrote to him in 1964 to chastise him for his failure to attend that year's meeting.

The true purpose of Roberts's board of governors was not to run the club—Roberts mostly handled that himself—but to provide a pool of likely participants for an autumn golf outing that happened to coincide with the board's superfluous annual meeting. The meeting seldom lasted very long. When Roberts, at the outset of one of them, asked Charles Yates, the club's secretary, what was on the agenda for the day, Yates replied, "Why, nothing at all." (At another governors meeting, Roberts asked Yates if he had the minutes, and Yates asked, "Do you

mean last year's, this year's, or next year's?") Meetings with Roberts
were always short. One day, a local member named William Fulcher was
summoned to give advice on a legal matter. On his way out, he stopped
by the bag room, which is still a good place to hear stories about
Roberts. "Well, that was a damned waste," Fulcher said to Fred Bennett,
the caddie master. "I could have stayed downtown."

"You had your meeting, didn't you?" Bennett asked.

"Yes," Fulcher said. "But when Cliff asks you a question, he answers
it, too."

On the second floor of the clubhouse is a comfortable library, which
in the old days served as the locker room. In a cabinet on one wall is a
small collection of objects associated with the former chairman. There
is a bronze bust, on which a pair of bronze eyeglasses sits slightly askew,
as Roberts's own glasses often did. The real glasses are in the cabinet,
too, and to old friends they recall their former owner as vividly as a photograph would. Near the glasses is a gold pocket watch, which may have
been Roberts's single favorite possession. He would slowly and conspic-
uously consult it whenever a member entered the club's dining room
after eight o'clock, an hour of arrival that he felt represented an unreasonable imposition on the staff. Attached to the watch chain is a gold
locket signifying his honorary membership in the most exclusive organization he ever belonged to: the Masters Club, whose members were the
Masters winners, Jones, and himself. Every year or so he would send the
watch back to Switzerland to be cleaned and adjusted, but he never let
go of the locket.

On a table in the library lies an old leather-bound scrapbook containing tournament photographs from 1951 and 1952. Each year, Roberts
sent gifts to a long list of friends who had helped to bring off the tournament, and the scrapbook was one of those gifts. Maintaining warm
relationships with supporters would help to ensure the long-term health
of the Masters, Roberts believed, and he devoted a great deal of time to
planning the gifts, generally beginning a year or more in advance.
Among the more notable items were a tool set, a pocket secretary, and a
first-aid kit, which Roberts believed to be the only decent one available
in America.

Roberts's attention to detail in planning the gifts could be dazzlingly minute. One of the gifts in 1966 was a pair of women's satin jewelry pouches. After studying prototypes in the spring of 1965, Roberts sent a detailed critique to an assistant who was handling negotiations with the manufacturer. Roberts had found problems with everything from the method of closure (satin strings) to the texture of the lining ("smooth" on one side, "soft" on the other) to the covering on the buttons. "Our best suggestion," he wrote, making figurative use of the first-person plural, "is that the manufacturer might cut down on the size of each container by making them three pockets instead of four pockets. Each pocket might be made just a little deeper and then constructed so that it would naturally fold in accordance with the depth of each pocket. The lady would then merely fold the bag twice and then button on the flap, assuming that buttons are the final decision, as a means of closing the jewelry bag. If the jewelry bag is fronted in accordance with the dimensions of the three slots, the bag would then close up properly in the same fashion regardless of whether the jewelry bag was filled with jewelry or only slightly filled. . . . Also, I think we should have three buttons instead of two."

The following year, the club's gift was an address book modeled on one that Roberts had used for years. Each address book was accompanied by a letter from Roberts containing instructions on how it might best be used:

1. You will find that about 20% of your friends will annually change their address or phone number, and then erasing becomes necessary; therefore, entries should not be made in your book except with a pencil. Always use sharply pointed, hard-lead pencils (No. 3) as soft-lead pencils will smear. You will need to list quite a bit of data in limited spaces so I'd advise you to print rather than write your entries.

2. All entries should be made by the same person; yourself, your wife or your secretary. Make a note about any new names to be entered in your book but do not make the entry until you are in your home or office where you are properly equipped.

3. Attached is a facsimile of a page out of your book with typical entries. The man's name goes on the full line in the first section and you can, if you wish, list the first name of his wife. In the second section, the letter "H" stands for home and "B" stands for business. . . .

4. The back section of your book contains 16 pages. . . . I find it handy to
list the principal persons I know, see occasionally, or have contact with
in certain cities such as San Francisco, Washington, D.C., Chicago,
London, etc. . . .

6. To me, the handiest place to carry an address book is in my left breast
coat pocket.

The address book was attractive (although the minuscule entry spaces
were designed around Roberts's agate-sized printing), but many of
Roberts's friends felt that the real gift was the letter. In a few paragraphs
it captured much of what was endearing and infuriating about his personality: his thoughtfulness, his attention to detail, his devotion to effi-
ciency, his innocent solipsism. Who else would have bothered to
recommend a grade of pencil lead, to explain what "H" and "B" stood
for, or to give examples of "certain cities" as though readers might otherwise have been confused about what he meant? *The New Yorker* reproduced Roberts's letter as one of its "newsbreaks," the humorous items
the magazine uses as filler.

Roberts himself was aware that his absorption with detail was potentially comical, as he acknowledged in his closing: "I hope you will
find the address book to be useful. If not, please do not hesitate to con-
sign it to the nearest trash can." Of the thousand or so recipients, there
can't be more than a few who still have the address book. But there are
many who still have the letter.

A portrait of Roberts hangs on a wall in the library. It was painted by
Eisenhower, who first visited Augusta National in 1948, became a member shortly afterward, and loved the club above all other retreats. In the
shape of the bald head in the painting there is a slight suggestion of self-
portrait—an allusion that, if he noticed it, must have pleased Roberts
immensely. He admired Eisenhower as much as he did Jones, and he was
a close friend and confidant for the rest of Ike's life. He was heavily involved in both presidential campaigns. During both terms, he was a valued behind-the-scenes adviser on a broad range of issues, and he spent

many nights at the White House. He managed the Eisenhower family's investments, tutored Ike in international finance, and invented what is now a standard American political accessory, the blind trust. Eisenhower named him an executor of his estate.

With Eisenhower as with Jones, Roberts's preferred position was in the background. He sought nothing for himself except the great man's friendship and trust. He might have pursued (and could have received) an appointment in the administration, but that was not the style of his ambition. Even at the club, where he eventually made nearly all the important decisions, he secured his influence first of all by making himself subordinate to Jones. That was how he attached himself to the world. His chosen place was always at the edge of any circle to which he belonged. He was a member of the club, of course, but his position as the chairman created what for him was a comfortable distance between himself and all but his closest friends. His table in the dining room stood in a corner near an outside door. When he played cards, he sat next to the wall. When he practiced his golf swing, he typically did so not on the driving range but at the end of what was then a field on the other side of Magnolia Lane. (On blustery days, he and a caddie would take a bag of balls to the eleventh fairway, which was protected from the wind, and he would practice there.) His bedroom was at the end of the residential wing on the east end of the clubhouse; his office stood beyond the farthest end of the farthest wing in the opposite direction, at one end of a building that in those days served as the tournament headquarters. His apartments elsewhere were almost always on the top floor or at the end of the hall. When he decided to spend his summers in North Carolina, the lot he chose for his condominium was on the end.

Roberts governed the Masters from the edges as well. He made occasional forays onto the course, usually in a golf cart, often in the company of Jones, but he spent most of every tournament either in his room or in his office. He received reports, gathered information, studied the broadcast on closed-circuit television, and issued instructions. When he appeared on camera at the end of the tournament on Sunday evening, he was an awkward presence; his only real role was to surrender the floor to Jones.

Even so, the easiest place to find Roberts, then as now, is in the golf tournament he conceived, nurtured, and ran for nearly forty years. More than two decades after his death, the Masters still operates largely as though he were at the controls. Hootie Johnson, who in 1998 became the fifth chairman of the tournament and the club, says, "Mr. Roberts was told once what a great tournament it was. And he said, 'Thank you, but we really never get it right.' We still feel that way." *

Others are less critical. The Masters is still viewed almost universally as the best-run golf tournament in the world, if not the best-run sporting event, and, as Roberts would have insisted, it has maintained its standing without acquiring the modern trappings of success. Spectators can still buy lunch for about what they might pay for a soft drink at any other tournament, because Roberts believed that anyone who had traveled two hundred miles to watch a round of golf ought to be able to buy a decent meal at a decent price. Teams of uniformed workers still intercept crumpled paper cups almost before they hit the ground, because Roberts felt that litter detracted from the beauty of the course and the dignity of the event. (The cups and sandwich bags are green, making them nearly invisible to television cameras—a major issue with Roberts.) Amateur competitors are still offered inexpensive accommodations in the clubhouse itself, because Roberts didn't want an invitation to the Masters to be a financial burden. Members still wear their green coats all week, as they have done since 1937, because Roberts felt that knowledgeable sources of information ought to be easily identifiable to spectators in need of assistance. There are no advertising banners or billboards pasted with corporate logos. The television broadcast is scarcely interrupted by commercials. There are no hole-in-one cars floating on the water hazards. Asked what they're playing for, the competitors still name not a sum of money but an article of clothing.

---

* Johnson believes that the four most influential figures in American golf in this century have been Bobby Jones, whose record as an amateur remains unsurpassed; Arnold Palmer, whose popularity as a player and a person marked golf's arrival as a professional sport; President Eisenhower, whose enthusiasm for the game helped broaden its popularity; and Roberts.

The Masters is still the competition by which other competitions are judged. That's a remarkable achievement, and the credit for it belongs largely to Roberts. He built the club and the tournament against what at first appeared to be insuperable odds, and in doing so he probably did as much as any other single person to shape what golfers and golf fans today think of as the world of competitive golf.

CHAPTER TWO

"I Just Figured Cliff Had Never Been a Child"

HERBERT WARREN WIND wrote in *Sports Illustrated* and *The New Yorker* that Clifford Roberts was born in Chicago. (He wasn't.) Ross Goodner wrote in *Golf World* that his real name was Charles D. Clifford Roberts. (Not true, although Goodner was close.) Frank Christian—a photographer and the co-author, with Cal Brown, of *Augusta National and the Masters*—wrote that Roberts as a child spent time in an orphanage. (He never did.) Charles Price, in *A Golf Story*, wrote that Roberts graduated from high school. (He didn't finish ninth grade.) Curt Sampson, in *The Masters*, wrote that Roberts made $50,000 in 1923 and used the money to buy a one-sixth partnership in an investment firm called the Reynolds Company. (Roberts made $2,441.63 in 1923; Reynolds & Co.—the correct name—didn't exist until 1931; Roberts went to work there in the mid-thirties; he became the firm's ninth general partner on May 1, 1941.)

All these errors, and many others, are understandable; Roberts was stingy with biographical detail, and he almost never talked about his early years, even among friends. Jackson Stephens, who was the club's chairman between 1991 and 1998 and was close to Roberts during the last fifteen years of his life, says, "I just figured Cliff had never been a child."

Time, as Roberts measured it, began the day he met Bobby Jones. But the years leading up to that encounter are in many ways as interesting as the years that followed it. They are the years that shaped the man who shaped Augusta National and the Masters.

Charles DeClifford Roberts, Jr., was born on March 6, 1894, on his mother's parents' farm near a tiny Iowa town called Morning Sun. He was known as Clifford from the beginning. For his first Christmas, he received "a toy chicken and a half interest in blocks and a monkey riding a goat mounted on wheels," his mother recorded in her diary. (The other co-owner of the blocks was his brother John, who was sixteen months older.) He was a good eater. For Christmas dinner he had pudding, popovers, grapes, cranberries, baked oysters, and squirrel.

Clifford was the second of five children. His mother, Rebecca Key Roberts, was twenty-five years old and pleasantly attractive. She had a cameo the size of a hen's egg which she wore at her throat. She was proud of her long brown hair, her clothes, and her skills as a baker. She owned a revolver, and she once fired it at a stray dog—"only scared it"—though she later traded the gun to an acquaintance. She had false teeth. She enjoyed the antics and enthusiasms of her children, and when Clifford, at the age of nine, became captivated by marbles, she sewed extra pockets in his pants so that he could carry more of them around. She was fond of ice cream. Her first diary petered out in 1898, but she started another in 1900—after giving birth to twins, named Robert Key and Dorothy—and kept it faithfully until 1911. "A Katydid jumped on Alpheus's dress," she wrote in 1905, when Alpheus, her fourth son and youngest child, was two. "He was so scared & called it a 'gog.' " The diary makes fascinating reading, especially if you know that in 1913, when Clifford was nineteen and Alpheus was nine, she committed suicide.

> 1902 Read nearly all day—very blue and discouraged. . . . I left John &
> Clifford to keep house while I went up town in evening. There had been
> a fight and shooting on the street. . . . Boys distributed some Rip Van
> Winkle show bills and so each got a free pass. . . . Tramp here for din-
> ner. . . . Boy here selling needles to keep from begging. . . . Still it rains.

The cover of a Fruitland Nurseries catalogue from 1888. Most of the flowering plants that bloom at Augusta National during Masters week are descended from plants listed in this booklet.

The back cover of the same catalogue. The picture shows the view north from the balcony of the old Redmond manor house, which today is the Augusta National clubhouse. Magnolia Lane, its trees a little more than thirty years old, is near the center of the photograph.

Members of the Berckmans family on the verandah of the manor house.

The Roberts family in 1907. From left: Charles, Clifford, Alpheus, Dorothy, Key, John, and Rebecca. At around the time the photograph was taken, the family went to see a show put on by a "hypnotist & mind reader" named Dr. Glick; Clifford volunteered to be a subject and, according to his mother's diary, "did funny things—picking strawberries from floor— peddling them—motioning a man across a tight wire, etc."

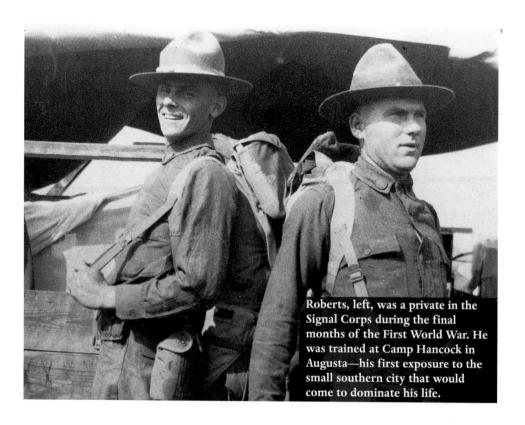

Roberts, left, was a private in the Signal Corps during the final months of the First World War. He was trained at Camp Hancock in Augusta—his first exposure to the small southern city that would come to dominate his life.

Morton Hodgson, Bobby Jones, Robert Woodruff, and Clifford Roberts at the "Boys Club" at Highlands C.C. during the early thirties. Woodruff was the president of the Coca-Cola Company, and Hodgson was an executive of the same company.

Bobby Jones (carrying a golf club) during an early Masters. The man on his right in the fedora and dark jacket is Grantland Rice.

Alister MacKenzie and his wife, Hilda, on the fifteenth green at Cypress Point.

MacKenzie's original watercolor sketch of his plan for the course. The holes in the sketch are numbered as they are today. MacKenzie would later switch the nines; after the first Masters, the club switched them back, because the current front nine thawed first on frosty mornings.

Mrs. Spencer Tracy and Marion Hollins, dressed for polo at Pasatiempo, the club she created in Santa Cruz, California. Roberts and Jones almost certainly borrowed a number of Hollins's ideas—including her decision to hire Alister MacKenzie.

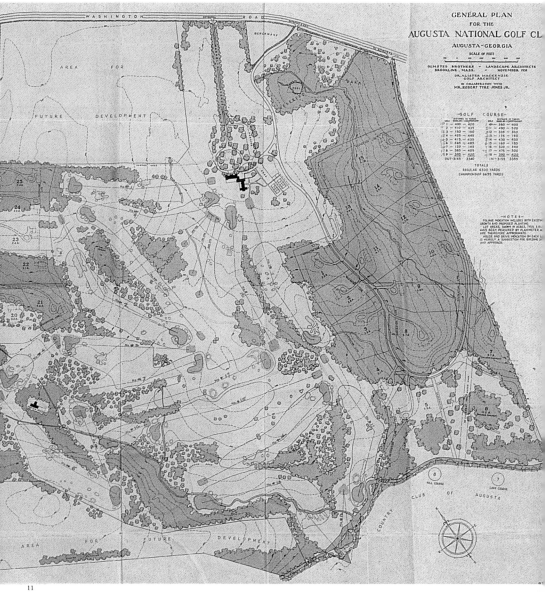

11

A subdivision plan for the club's property prepared by Olmsted Bros. in 1932. Proposed building lots are delineated and numbered on the east and west sides of the course. The footprint of the proposed new clubhouse is shown in black at the south end of Magnolia Lane. Note the two tennis courts (which were never built) to the east of the proposed clubhouse site.

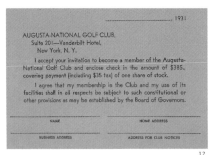

One of tens of thousands of membership forms distributed by Roberts and Jones in the early thirties. The initiation fee was $350, plus tax; annual dues were $60. All a recipient had to do was fill out the form and send it back, but the nation's economy was a shambles, and there were virtually no takers.

A souvenir first-day cover marking the official opening of the club. The Augusta National logo, near Jones's shoulder, has never been changed.

The circular driveway between Magnolia Lane and the front of the clubhouse, as it appeared in 1947 and as it appears today. Plaques commemorating Roberts and Jones are visible at the base of the flagpole. Note the dire condition of the yellow pansies in the earlier photograph.

Jones and Roberts in the mid-thirties.

16

The Augusta National clubhouse today.

An aerial photograph taken in 1932, shortly after the course was completed. The fifteenth green is visible near the upper left hand corner of the picture. The old sixteenth green is just to the right of the fifteenth, near the top of the picture. The eighteenth green is near the middle of the left hand side; note the fairway bunker, which in 1966 was replaced by two bunkers closer to the tee. The ninth green—which at the time was shaped a little like the head of a rabbit—is just to the right of the eighteenth.

Things floating in our cellar. . . . Boys have carpenter fever—new nails and nail apron and making twins a play house. . . . Boys cared for twins, cooked and swept and washed dishes—all in their boyish way. . . . Gone all day & sold only 1 bushel of apples. Brought new milk strainer, shoe polish, steel pens & school sponges. Clifford churned.

Rebecca was a sharp observer and had a sense of humor, and although her entries are telegraphic—"Twins fat and well. Hope they may not be kidnapped as Cudahys was"—they vividly describe what seems to have been a happy life for her children and a troubled life for her. The family had many joyful moments ("Husband & I read late & Clifford & Key 'had a spell'—they could not quit laughing & playing pranks until the lights were all out. Such merry times at our house"), but the underlying themes are of dislocation and despair. "I am very miserable—life almost a burden," she wrote in 1908, in a typical entry. Her husband was often absent, and he moved the family constantly. Rebecca had numerous ailments, among them severe headaches, back pain, "curvature of the spine," a miscarriage followed by months of hemorrhaging, pleurisy, "nervous chills," and a persistent melancholy that a modern reader does not hesitate to diagnose as depression. Winter was the hardest, and she often felt overwhelmed by her children. "I am hardly able to be out of bed," she wrote in 1904, "but must keep going to care for my numerous family." She took patent medicines—many of which would have contained narcotics along with a great deal of alcohol. (The most popular children's cough medicine of the period, Mrs. Winslow's Soothing Syrup, was based on morphine. One night, Rebecca used one of her own medicines to quiet baby Alpheus, who was colicky and had been crying.) She pursued electrical baths, osteopathy treatments, homeopathy treatments, hot water cures, and other fad therapies administered by a variety of practitioners. On many mornings, she was unable to get out of bed. At such times, she often left the housework and the care of the younger children to Clifford and John, beginning when Clifford was six and John was seven. The boys shouldered the burden cheerfully and with ingenuity. One day when Clifford was ten and his mother and John were late in returning by train from a visit to a doctor in another town,

Clifford dressed Dorothy, who was three, in a new red dress, "made her new garters when he could not find her suspenders," and took her with him to a party to which he had been invited. Rebecca was proud of her children for rising to the occasion, but she was unromantic about child-rearing, and she hired housekeeping help when she could afford it. "Ida Kellogg came to work," she wrote in 1907, "—measles still showing, has whooping cough & only 10 years old—*but willing.*"

Ill health was taken for granted. Clifford's father had gastrointestinal trouble, a rupture, and "heart failure palpitation." John, with whom Clifford shared a bed, stammered and suffered seizures that various doctors diagnosed as St. Vitus's dance, "worm spasms"—for which he was treated with "vermifuge tonic"—and (correctly) grand mal epilepsy. Clifford had trouble with his eyes, suffered from "malaria & biliousness," and endured devastating bouts with poison ivy. Days when everyone was well were rare enough to be noted in the diary. Clifford knew children who died of pneumonia, scarlet fever, smallpox, "brain fever," tonsillitis, typhoid, and tuberculosis. "Boys sent Chinese lilies," Rebecca noted in 1902, when a seven-year-old classmate of Clifford's was buried.

Charles DeClifford Roberts, Sr., was a restless small-time entrepreneur who tried his hand and failed at a broad variety of undertakings. "My father always was interested in seeing what was on the other side of the next hill," Clifford said with understatement many years later. Charles was apt to trade the family store on a whim for a farm in another state—then, after harvesting a single crop of wheat and oats, to trade the farm for a business somewhere else, and then to sell that business and invest the proceeds in another. He bought and sold everything from candles and thread to farm equipment and fur coats. He speculated in real estate and arranged the sale of other people's property. He once owned two fish-and-oyster houses in Texas. He bought bankrupt businesses and liquidated their stock. He sued hucksters who had cheated him. In 1906, in Oklahoma, he received a large rail shipment consisting of flour and shoes.

The hectic pace of Charles's wheeling and dealing suggests compulsion as much as enterprise. Few of his deals greatly improved the family's standard of living, which rose and fell within a narrow band at the lower limits of the respectable. Almost invariably, his first step after acquiring a new store or piece of property was to attempt to trade it for something else. Rebecca—who was never consulted—lamented most of these transactions. As soon as she had decorated a house to her satisfaction, it seemed, he put it up for sale. Charles's quixotic dealings didn't bring him happiness, either; he suffered from insomnia and sometimes paced the floor, terrified that his world was coming apart. He died in San Benito, Texas, in 1921, after being struck by a train, and his death may have been a suicide. At the time, he was suffering the effects of a stroke, and was supporting himself and what remained of his family with the help of regular checks from Clifford, who was struggling to make his own way in New York.

Charles and Rebecca's marriage was not desolate. They were often happy together when he was at home. He was loving with the children, gave expensive presents when business was good, wrote poetry in the evenings, and took Rebecca's illnesses seriously. But he worked long hours and traveled for weeks at a stretch. When the twins were young he had to be reintroduced to them upon returning. (On one occasion, they recognized him only after he had sung a song they knew; on another, they wouldn't let him hold them until after they had watched him eat breakfast.) He wrote home irregularly. He moved the family so often and on such short notice that a reader must study the diary carefully to detect when the locale has changed. The constant shifting took a heavy toll. At one point Rebecca wrote, "I can hardly bear to think of the tremendous task of moving—hardly able to live—even quietly." Other entries have a sardonic edge: "Charles's Texas fever is all gone & he is now confident that New Mexico will just suit us." In later years, Clifford often described his background simply as "Midwestern." In a letter to Eisenhower, in 1967, he wrote that he envied Ike's ability to remember "boyhood escapades," as evidenced by a recent article in the *Saturday Evening Post*. Much of his own childhood seemed to him a blur, or a blank.

In the fall of 1904, when Clifford was ten, Rebecca took the children to live with relatives of hers in California. She was acting on the advice of a doctor in Kansas, who had said that a trip and "a complete change" might improve her still mysterious condition. Not long before, she had written in her diary, "I am going down hill as rapidly as possible and there seems to be nothing to stop it." They made the journey by train and stayed for seven months, while Charles tended business interests elsewhere. (He wrote occasionally, sent fifteen dollars for Christmas, and sold most of the family's furniture—including the dining room linoleum—while they were gone.) For part of that period, Clifford lived not with his mother, brothers, sister, aunt, and cousins, but with his mother's parents, who lived in Lakeside, a train ride away. He made brief visits to his mother by himself every week or two, attended a different school from the other children, and seemed to enjoy, or at any rate not object to, his independence. Before returning to Kansas the following spring, the boys traded their schoolbooks for a checkers set, with which they occupied themselves on the long ride home.

John and Clifford both worked outside the house from early ages. They did odd jobs, raised and sold chickens and dogs, made deliveries for their father, served as clerks in the family's various stores, milked cows, raised pigs, caddied at local golf courses, and sold onions. They helped with the harvest when their father was farming. They worked to pay for their own schoolbooks and clothes. They sold calling cards and the *Saturday Evening Post*, played baseball for a share of the gate receipts, and, as they got older, accompanied their father on business expeditions. They inherited his entrepreneurial drive. One day, the brothers caught another boy selling trout from a line they had set in a stream. Instead of starting a fight—something they usually did when opportunities arose—they sold him the line and invested the proceeds in a new one. Shortly after the family moved from Kansas to Oklahoma in 1906, Rebecca noted that Clifford, now twelve, was "using his Spanish selling goods to Mexicans working on R. R." By then, Clifford was spending long periods working at real jobs for adult wages. He and his older brother both quit school before the end of ninth grade.

Clifford grew up fast. He got into fistfights, stole rides on freight trains, chewed gum at school, smoked, entertained poorly behaved friends at home while his mother was away, prompted one of his teachers to strike him, and shot pool—"such troubles as all boys make," according to Rebecca, who smiled at the shenanigans of all her children and was a gentle disciplinarian. In 1909 she wrote, without apparent alarm, "All schools having a war with rubber shooters & paper wads. Clifford sent home. Charles went back with him—may have special tutor." When the boys got into trouble, she seldom sided with their accusers—noting, for example, that Clifford's teacher had returned only thirty of sixty marbles she had confiscated.

Despite occasional forays into juvenile delinquency, Clifford was the member of the Roberts family who on Sunday mornings was the most likely to be found in church. "Clifford went alone to Sunday School," is a typical diary entry—this one from when he was seven. He won Sunday school prizes, went to Christian Endearment picnics, often followed Sunday school with a regular service at a different church, and escorted younger siblings to Sunday school on days when no one else was going. Shortly after the family moved to Oklahoma, he took his little sister, Dorothy, to a Baptist church—a novelty for both of them—then later went with his father and older brother to watch a group of recent converts being baptized in a lake. "Clifford went to Catholic Mass with Carl Lully," Rebecca wrote in 1908, when Clifford was fourteen and the family was living in Emporia, Kansas. "First time he had seen their service & quite impressed." His steady church attendance won him special privileges, including an invitation to a fancy social at the home of his Sunday school teacher. "A four course luncheon served," his mother wrote. "Everything of finest—finger bowl passed by maid. Brick ice cream, deviled eggs, angel food, candy, nuts, etc., etc."

Clifford appears to have had no trouble making friends. The diary mentions many playmates and overnight guests—including more than a few whom his mother considered "bad boys" or "roughs." Clifford enjoyed and was good at marbles, football, basketball, and baseball, and he and his older brother were always arranging games of one kind or another. Clifford's popularity may have been eased by the fact that he was strong and good-looking—although he was considered less handsome than John. His sharply arched eyebrows, which would contribute to a perennial look of alarm in his sixties and seventies, made him seem playful and mischievous when he was young. He parted his hair in the middle and had a strong taste for nice clothes. When he earned extra money, he often spent it on a tie, a shirt, or a suit. ("John & Clifford went shopping for Spats, sweater, cap & cruet tray," Rebecca wrote in 1909.) In eighth grade, he attended a school May Day celebration wearing a "silk hat & Knickerbockers," and in more than one family photograph he has the only pocket handkerchief. He began to meet girls. "Clifford went to dance—*to look on*—but he danced."

Maintaining friendships was hard, however. The children changed schools and neighborhoods constantly, and they seldom finished a year with the same companions they had begun it with. Many of the family's many moves were not only sudden—"Charles wrote for us to pack up & we commenced"—but also complete: Charles sometimes sold or auctioned much of their furniture rather than take it with them. All the moves were stressful, some more than others. ("Three moves is worse than a fire," was a nineteenth-century American proverb.) Two days after Charles sold the family's Emporia house—a showplace that he and Rebecca had scarcely finished fixing up—the new owners, along with their children and a maid, moved in with the Robertses. The two families shared a roof for more than two weeks, then Rebecca and the children went to stay with one of her sisters for another three weeks before setting out by train, at one o'clock in the morning, for yet another new life—this time, in a five-room house on a ten-acre "orange ranch" in Palacios, Texas, a small, dusty town on the Gulf of Mexico between Galveston and Corpus Christi. "Alpheus said, 'Mama, you look as though you did not know anything,' and that is just how I feel."

1909 Had to take one small dose of sleeping medicine—the last. . . . Am so sorry Dorothy & Key are to be disappointed again in not having a birthday party—but have neither money nor strength. . . . Received $50 interest on $1,000 note in Kansas. Boys could not have begun high school else. . . . John & Clifford sold $8.35 of fine figs—quite cheering. . . . Charles is worn to a sick shadow, nervous dyspepsia wreck. Is uneasy all day & night. Has sued F. M. Elliott for $4,220.00 & we are living as skimped as possible in a land of strangers. . . . Clifford saved life of a woman (in childbirth) by calling Dr. when her children did not know how. . . . My hair is nearly all coming out—am so very sorry—for it was my one beauty.

Late in the year, Charles received $15,000 for their old farm in Kansas and was able to pay off a number of debts. But the family's financial situation remained precarious, and a year later it took a sharp turn for the worse. On October 30, 1910, Clifford went to Sunday school at the Presbyterian church and then escorted his mother to the regular service. On the way, he realized he had left his gloves at home and ran back to get them. He lit a kerosene lamp in his and John's dark room—which the two boys had just begun to set up for themselves in the attic of the family's small house—and dropped a match on the floor, starting a fire that consumed the house. The twins sounded the alarm. "We got back to see its finish," Rebecca wrote in her diary, which someone had the foresight to rescue. Charles dragged the family's cherished player piano out of the house by himself. Almost everything else was destroyed, and there was no insurance. The local dentist, who had been doing dental work for Rebecca and Dorothy, "made us a Christmas present" of his fee.

The fire marks the beginning of Clifford's life as an adult. He promised his mother he would try to make up for his negligence by doing as much as he could to help out. He was sixteen years old and had left school for good the previous spring. He continued to work on the family's farm—which was failing—and to help his father with various business ventures. He began to work as a clerk in a dry-goods store in Blessing, a town several miles to the north. ("He actually sold more goods during their 10 days sale than any other clerk or the two owners themselves," his mother noted with pride.) In July, he went to Galveston for a three-week course in business skills. He talked about teaming up with an acquaintance to run a meat company in Blessing. His name began to appear less often in his mother's diary—which she continued to keep for another year and then abandoned—because he was now spending more time away from the rented house that had become the family's home.

In that house, not quite three years after the fire, Rebecca Roberts

rose quietly from her bed at four o'clock one morning, crept downstairs
without waking her husband or her children, walked behind the house
to a spot near the garage, and shot herself in the chest with a shotgun. It
was three days after her forty-fourth birthday. No one in the family
heard. Charles found her body when he awoke at five. "The coroner's
verdict was that the deceased came to her death by her own hand," an
article on the front page of the *Palacios Beacon* said. "Letters afterward
found written by Mrs. Roberts addressed to each member of the family
showed that the act was premeditated. Each of the letters was an expression of affectionate farewell." The letters, which were brief, were written in pencil in steady script on small sheets of lined notepaper.

> *Dear Dorothy —*
> *Mama's love goes on just*
> *the same & you must be a*
> *good girl & do as Papa*
> *says. Stay with friends*
> *I chose for you in life.*
> *Love Mama*

The tone seems chilling, especially when compared with the tender in-
formality of Rebecca's diary: "Dorothy often draws me to rocking chair
& when she's in my arms—then she takes up my fingers in left hand &
taps end of one with her small one—meaning that she wants me to sing."
    Rebecca's note to Clifford was equally restrained:

> *Dear Clifford*
> *I write to beg you to*
> *not grieve but be a*
> *man in time of trial.*
> *Papa will need you.*
> *   Be a sober upright*
> *son & all will be well.*
> *I know Ma wants you*
> *to come to her.*
> *Love Mama*

"Ma" in the last sentence is Maria Lyman Key, Rebecca's mother, with whom Clifford had lived during part of the family's seven-month stay in California nine years before. Clifford must have been considering a move or a visit, but there is no indication in the family's records that he ever went; Charles, with Rebecca gone, would have needed him close at hand. Maria Key died in early 1915, a little less than a year and a half after her daughter's suicide.

What a desolate experience it must have been to read those flat, emotionless notes on the morning of Rebecca's death. Since the fire, Clifford had felt a disproportionate share of responsibility for the family's misfortunes; Rebecca's brief note would not have lightened his burden. Late in his life, he commissioned a portrait of his mother based on an old photograph and hung it in his apartment in the Bahamas. In 1904, when he was ten, he had made her a small paper heart and inscribed it to his "dear Mama." More than fifty years later, Dorothy found the heart among their mother's things and sent it to him. "What a sweet person Mother was!" Roberts wrote back in wistful acknowledgment. "I'm glad to be reminded that at least on one occasion I let her know how I felt about her." The years in Palacios had become a void in his memory by then; once he left, he never went back.

In May 1915, a little less than two years after the suicide, Dorothy began to keep a diary of her own. She was fourteen years old. Her father had married a considerably younger woman, from Missouri, and had moved the family to Kansas City, where he continued to pursue a bewildering variety of ill-considered business ventures. Clifford's older brother, now called Jack, had married about a year before; he and his wife were living in Kansas City, too, but would soon move to California. Clifford made occasional appearances at home but spent most of his time selling men's clothing on the road in a territory that covered much of the Midwest. His salary in 1916 was $1.30 a month plus commissions, and he did so well that he frequently was able to make substantial gifts to members of the family—especially to Dorothy, who had long looked up to him as more of a father figure than her father.

At different times over the next decade, Dorothy, Key, and Alpheus followed Jack to California, and all eventually settled permanently on the West Coast. Only Clifford looked east. As he traveled around the Midwest and South selling suits, he was planning a new life for himself. He studied the biographies of wealthy men, hoping to learn the secrets of their success. He decided—as he later told a relative—that he would rather be a little fish in a big pond than a big fish in a little pond. He assessed the advantages and disadvantages of living in various cities, eventually deciding that he would need to move to New York because New York was where the money was. He invested much of his earnings in nice clothes for himself, because he had decided that in order to make his way in the big city he would have to look the part. He memorized information about leading colleges and universities, so that he would not embarrass himself when introduced to men who had been far better educated than he. With the same unblinking focus that would later characterize his planning for the Masters Tournament, he studied the life he wanted to lead and then set out to lead it.

Clifford's assault on New York was not an immediate success. In 1917, when he was twenty-three, he sold his share of some Iowa property that he and the other children had inherited from their mother's side of the family, and with that money as a stake he set out to make his fortune in the East. Before the end of the month, he was back in Kansas City again and probably close to broke. "Think Cliff is going to make some money real soon," Dorothy wrote. "Surely hope he does, for he has had so much hard luck."

Shortly afterward, he tried again, and this time he stayed. He rented a room in a small residential hotel, and by early April 1918, he was working for what Dorothy in her diary called "the Oklahoma-Wyoming Oil Company" and expecting "to make a small fortune." One month later, the draft intervened. He was trained as a private in the Signal Corps at Camp Hancock, in Augusta, Georgia—his first exposure to the small southern city that would dominate his life. He was shipped to France in October 1918, roughly a month before the Armistice, and was shipped home six and a half months later, following an entirely uneventful tour of duty. (He passed some of the time by learning French from a Canadian soldier.) He was discharged on May 7, 1919.

After his return, he at first divided his time between New York and Chicago, where he was involved in a variety of investment deals. None amounted to much. A little over a year later, in a Christmas letter to Dorothy, he wrote, "1920 has been a rather rough and terrible year for me—the stock market has been shot to pieces and general business badly upset." He was spending much of his modest income to help support various family members, including his father, who had suffered a stroke and would soon die. (Charles was buried in Kansas City. Of the five siblings, only Clifford and Alpheus—who was still living in Kansas City with their stepmother—attended his funeral. Dorothy scarcely noted the death in her diary.)

By 1922, Roberts was a principal in a struggling partnership called Roberts & Co., which that year had income of less than a thousand dollars. His net income the following year was a little more than $2,400. He made a little more than $7,500 in 1924.* By 1925, he was associated with a New York firm called Banta & Morrin and was calling himself a "financial negotiator" and "stock-and-bond broker." A nephew has said that Roberts in the early twenties put together an oil-and-gas deal that made him $50,000. That didn't happen, but the nephew may be thinking of 1929, when Roberts's tax return shows that he was paid a $55,000 commission by an investment banking firm called F. A. Willard & Co. That year, his total net income amounted to just under $70,000—by far his most successful year up to that point (and the most successful he would have for quite a few years to come).

Unfortunately, 1929 was a disastrous year in which to make a fortune. Roberts invested much of his windfall in securities that turned sour during the October Crash or in the dreary years that followed it; his 1929 tax return lists a number of stocks that he bought shortly before Black Thursday and sold at substantial losses shortly after. In 1930 and

---

* Adjusted for inflation, $2,400 in 1923 would be the equivalent of about $23,000 today, and $7,500 in 1924 would be the equivalent of about $70,000—although the world has changed so much that exact comparisons are impossible to make.

1931, trading losses more than wiped out all his other income, leaving him with a cumulative net loss for those two years of more than $21,000. By way of comparison, in 1931, the year the club was formed, Bobby Jones had net income of more than $140,000—far more than Roberts's total earnings during the fourteen years he had been in New York. The popular conception is that Roberts was rich and Jones was scarcely employed when the club began; in fact, the reverse was true.*

During that difficult period, golf was a part of the New York social milieu to which Roberts was striving to belong. He had first encountered the game as a youngster in California, where he and his brother had caddied for fifteen cents a bag. He taught himself to play as caddies always have, by hitting found balls with abandoned clubs during the idle hours between loops. When he started to make some money in New York, he joined Knollwood Country Club in Westchester County, and worked on his game and social connections there. At some point in the mid-twenties, he attended an exhibition at Knollwood in which Jones played—an exhibition that may have been the occasion of their first meeting. "Each time I saw Bob or read his public comments, I respected and liked him more," he wrote in his book about the club. "I watched part of the final of the 1926 USGA Amateur Championship at Baltusrol, in New Jersey, in which George Von Elm defeated Jones two and one. Shortly afterwards, I was one of some half-dozen who were having a drink with the loser and trying to think of something comforting to say to him." Jones's effect on Roberts was similar to that, two decades later,

---

* In his book about the club, Roberts wrote that Melvin A. Traylor—who was the president of the First National Bank of Chicago, a former president of the United States Golf Association, an important early member of the club, and a good friend of Roberts's—"warned me in the early part of 1929 to prepare for a storm. Mel is the only person I knew personally in a leadership position in banking circles who openly warned of the impending disaster." Several writers have hugely amplified this passage, concluding that Roberts "knew" the Crash was coming and got himself and his investment clients out of the market beforehand. But a record of his trading from 1929 shows that he was steadily buying stocks in the months before the Crash and that he sold most of his holdings at steep losses shortly after.

of Eisenhower, who also became a close friend. In an interview with a researcher in the Oral History Research Office at Columbia University in the late sixties, Roberts said of Eisenhower that "people just instinctively want to help him and to gain favor in his eyes by doing things that might please him." Roberts could as easily have been describing his initial attraction to Jones.

Jones in those years often spoke of his desire to build a championship course in the South. One day in 1930, Roberts suggested building the course in Augusta, where both men coincidentally had played winter golf while staying at Bon Air–Vanderbilt Hotel, which was run by a mutual friend. Roberts, after his stint in the army, had returned to Augusta for occasional golf vacations; he liked the city in part because it was warm in the winter yet far enough north to be easily reachable by overnight train from New York. Jones liked Augusta's mild winter climate and believed that a club there might afford him some privacy—a scarcity at home in Atlanta. ("It had got so that he couldn't even plan a weekday game without feeling like he was playing an exhibition," Roberts told the *Saturday Evening Post* in 1951.) They agreed to proceed.

The notion of engaging in any sort of continuing project with Jones must have held extraordinary appeal for Roberts. Not many years before, he had been selling clothes and living out of a suitcase in a territory that extended from Chicago to New Orleans. Now he was living in the biggest, richest, most exciting city in the country and helping to implement a dream of one of the most celebrated athletes in the world. Years later, Roberts reprinted for club members a chapter from the book *Farewell to Sport*, by Paul Gallico. The chapter, called "One Hero," was about Jones, and it was probably Roberts's single favorite text. He quoted from it again in his book about the club: "I am, by nature, a hero-worshipper, as, I guess, most of us are, but in all the years of contact with the famous ones of sport I have found only one that would stand up in every way as a gentleman as well as a celebrity, a fine, decent, human being as well as a newsprint personage, and who never once, since I have known him, has let me down in my estimate of him. That one is Robert Tyre Jones, Jr., the golf-player from Atlanta, Georgia. And Jones in his day was considered the champion of champions."

Roberts was, by nature, a hero-worshipper, too. He took enormous personal satisfaction from making himself indispensable to Jones (as he would again later with Eisenhower). Roberts's deep, genuine, and enduring commitment to the game of golf did not predate their friendship. He said himself in later years that if he had never met Jones he would never have been more than a weekend golfer. He adopted the ideals of his hero and made them his own.

The Augusta project must have had a further powerful appeal for Roberts: It gave him an opportunity to become acquainted with and make himself useful to a large group of lesser heroes, the successors of the pioneering capitalists whose lives he had studied as a young man. Some of those same men would later become investment clients of his, but any personal financial gain would have meant less to Roberts than the growing ease with which he was able to move within their once inaccessible world. The club was so time-consuming from the start that its net effect on his investment business was certainly negative. But he did not regret the loss. It was the life, not the money, that he wanted.

CHAPTER THREE

Beginning

MAGNOLIA LANE IS far older than the Masters or Augusta National. The trees that line the long driveway leading to the clubhouse were planted from seeds shortly before the outbreak of the Civil War. Lawrence Bennett—a part-time employee of the club as well as a high school history teacher—says that his grandmother, whose own grandmother had been a slave, remembered noticing the magnolias just after the turn of the century, when her family came to town in a covered wagon once a month to buy supplies. By 1931, when Roberts and Jones first visited the property, the magnolias were good-sized trees and the driveway was known locally as Magnolia Avenue. Because the branches were long and close to the ground, two cars could not pass side by side between the rows, and Roberts and Jones briefly considered placing the club's main entrance somewhere else.

Roberts loved the magnolias and worried about them, as he did about most of the trees on the club's property. If a loblolly pine on the golf course died, he wanted to know why it had died, and he wanted the tree removed immediately in case the thing that had killed it was catching. He didn't like deciduous trees, because in his view fallen leaves were a species of litter; he thinned oaks and maples in favor of half a dozen varieties of pine. He read scholarly articles about tree care and consulted forestry professors. When a contractor who was building a new tee ignored his warning to keep construction machinery away from some old trees that he was especially fond of, he ordered the contractor to leave the grounds.

One night in the sixties, Roberts and his wife had dinner in New York with another Augusta National member and his wife. They got to talking about the plantings on the club's property. The member asked how old the Magnolia Lane magnolias were. Roberts said they were a little more than a hundred years old, and that with proper care they ought to live another hundred or hundred and fifty years. The member's wife said, "Well, that certainly ought to be long enough."

Roberts turned on her the same fierce stare with which he pinned neglectful committee members to the backs of their chairs. "No," he said, after what to the wife seemed like the better part of the life span of a magnolia, "that is *not* long enough."

According to local legend, the site now occupied by the club was visited in the early sixteenth century by the Spanish explorer Hernando de Soto, who between 1539 and 1542 led six hundred men on a winding journey through the South in a futile search for treasure. Had de Soto and his men remained, they might have found a little of what they were looking for: A small spring among the trees between the thirteenth and fourteenth fairways is said to yield trace amounts of gold dust after heavy rains. James Edward Oglethorpe—an English politician and military officer, who founded the colony that became the state of Georgia, and who laid out and named (for the wife of the Prince of Wales) the city of Augusta—is said to have smoked a peace pipe with local Indians on the site in the early seventeen thirties. The meeting, if it occurred, may have taken place beside a spring-fed pond in an area now occupied by Augusta National's par three course. The pond had been a well-known meeting place for several centuries.

Someone built a tavern on the property around the time of the Revolutionary War. It stood on what is now Washington Road, not far from Magnolia Lane. The land beyond the tavern was farmland. For a brief period in the eighteen fifties, it was a plantation sown with indigo, a weedy plant whose berries were the source of a dark blue dye used in the manufacture of a newly popular article of clothing: blue jeans. A few scattered descendants of the old indigo plants were found in the woods during construction of the course; none are known to remain today.

The building that now serves as the clubhouse was built in 1854 as the home of Dennis Redmond, who had bought the plantation a year before. Redmond was, in addition to a planter, an architectural historian and an editor of an agricultural publication called *The Southern Cultivator*. His house had eighteen-inch-thick walls made of concrete, a material that before that time had not been used in residential construction in the South; Redmond called it "artificial rock." In 1858, he gave up on indigo and sold his property and house to a Belgian horticulturist named Prosper Berckmans, who turned the plantation into Fruitland Nurseries. It is said to have been the first commercial nursery in the South. In the company's 1861 catalogue, Prosper reported that his test gardens contained more than thirteen hundred varieties of pears, nine hundred varieties of apples, three hundred varieties of grapes, and a hundred varieties of azaleas—a plant that Berckmans was largely responsible for making popular in this country. Most of the flowering plants that bloom at Augusta National during Masters week are descended from Fruitland stock. The vast, gnarled wisteria vine that now engulfs the rear of the clubhouse is said to be among the first ever brought to this country. The club's monumental privet hedge is descended from ten plants imported from France around 1860 and was once referred to as the "Mother Hedge" of all privet hedges in the South.

Prosper died in 1910 and left the house and land to his widow and three sons. The nursery declined over the next few years; by 1918, it was defunct. In 1925, a Miami businessman named Commodore J. Perry Stoltz planned to build a golf course and a $2 million hotel on the site. He went bankrupt shortly after pouring concrete footings. The abandoned foundation, flanked by piles of excavated earth, was still an eyesore when Roberts and Jones first saw the property in 1931; it was buried during the construction of the course. In 1996, workers at the club uncovered the old footings while moving and rebuilding the practice putting green. The nuts on the threaded rods could be turned by hand.

Roberts was led to the old Berckmans property by Thomas Barrett, Jr., a member of a prominent Augusta family who had been cited for bravery in the gruesome Battle of the Argonne at the end of the First World War. He wasn't a golfer, but he had strong ties in the community and was the vice president of the Bon Air–Vanderbilt Hotel. He felt that the club, if successful, would boost the local economy by attracting well-heeled visitors from far away. Roberts felt the same way, and thought the club could help Augusta become a winter golf resort to rival Pinehurst, North Carolina. Barrett became the mayor of Augusta in 1933 and helped smooth the way for the first Masters in 1934. He died, at the age of forty, shortly after the tournament, apparently as a result of complications from wounds suffered during the war.

In January 1931, the Bon Air–Vanderbilt Company, acting for the benefit of the proposed club, paid $5,000 for a six-month option to purchase roughly 365 acres. To buy the property, a group that included Barrett, Roberts, Walton H. Marshall (who ran the Vanderbilt chain of hotels, including both the Vanderbilt Hotel in New York and the Bon Air–Vanderbilt in Augusta), Fielding Wallace (a local businessman), and Bobby Jones's father, Col. Robert P. Jones, created a real estate company called Fruitland Manor Corporation. Barrett was the president. In June, Fruitland acquired the land by paying $15,000 in cash and assuming roughly $60,000 of the previous owner's debt, most of it in the form of a first mortgage held by what was then the Georgia Railroad Bank. The cash may have came from Jones's father, who was given the honor of being the first stockholder in the golf club, a separate corporation formed at the same time. Fruitland later leased a little more than half the property to the club. The idea was that Augusta National would eventually buy the leased land, while Fruitland would recover the rest of its costs, and perhaps turn a profit, by selling or developing the remainder of the parcel. All that Roberts had to do was fill the club's rolls with dues-paying members.

American-International Golf Club, Georgia-National Golf Club, International Golf Club of Augusta, and Southern National Golf Club were among the names originally considered for the new club. Georgia-National was the early favorite. Jones had always been associated with the state, and Roberts believed that if Georgia was in the title "all of the people of that State should be inclined to support the Club." Augusta-National—the hyphen would later be dropped—was also on the list, and eventually it prevailed. Roberts, in his book, said Jones thought of that name—and he may have, although Roberts would have been likely to attribute the final choice to Jones regardless.

The earliest proposal for the club called for eighteen hundred members. (The club today has roughly a sixth as many.) The initiation fee was three hundred fifty dollars, plus tax. Dues were sixty dollars a year—fifteen dollars for wives and children—and Roberts planned to reduce the charge as soon as the club's financial position was secure. Jones had been impressed by the modest membership fees of the Royal and Ancient Golf Club of St. Andrews and other Scottish clubs, and he and Roberts wanted Augusta National to follow that model. They envisioned a membership drawn from all over the United States and from as many foreign countries as possible.

The initiation payments from a fully subscribed club would have yielded a fund of $630,000, of which Roberts expected to spend a little more than half on the construction of two eighteen-hole golf courses—a "Championship Course" and a "Ladies Course." The second course was to be built as soon as the membership passed one thousand. According to various versions of the plan, there would also be tennis courts, outdoor squash courts, an eighteen-hole pitch-and-putt course, a bridle path, a couple of dozen houses for members alongside some of the fairways, and, possibly, an on-site hotel to be operated for members and their guests by the management of the Bon Air. In addition, $100,000 was to be spent on a clubhouse.

A clubhouse was needed because the old Redmond manor house was going to be torn down—a plan to which Roberts, Jones, and nearly all the earliest members initially agreed. Unimaginable though it seems today, demolishing the old manor house would not necessarily have been a reckless act. Although the building looks imposing in photographs, it is quite small. Much of its apparent bulk comes from its

porches, which are nine and a half feet deep and run all the way around
on both floors, and from large wings added later on each side. In 1931,
the building had fourteen rooms, but most were cramped and dark, and
there was no kitchen, no electricity, and no plumbing. The ground floor
had been referred to by the builder as a "basement," and it looked like
one. A consulting engineer, after making an inspection, concluded that
most members "would probably be better satisfied in a modern building
with all modern conveniences." Few disagreed.

Roberts and Jones hired a local architect and developer named Willis
Irvin to draw plans for a new clubhouse, and a detailed rendering of the
design appeared in the *Augusta Chronicle*. The building was to have two
large wings, an exterior of whitewashed brick, a slate roof, several im-
pressive chimneys, and a vast neoclassical portico supported by four tall
columns. The most striking feature was to be an enormous men's locker
room containing four hundred lockers, some double and some single.
There were to be numerous nooks and corners where golfers could
gather before, after, and between rounds to play cards, eat lunch, watch
the action on the course through large bay windows, or converse. A separate wing was to contain similar facilities for women.

Not everyone was eager to tear down the old manor house. Harry M.
Atkinson, an Atlantan who was one of the club's earliest members,
wrote to Roberts in 1931 to say that he and his wife loved the building
and believed it should be renovated rather than razed. "We both were
greatly impressed with the avenue of magnolias leading up to the old
Berckmans residence and the planting around the house," he wrote.
"We think that all of that, including the house, ought to be preserved
carefully. It can be made a perfect gem, using the old house for a club
house. You could not reproduce what is there for any amount of money."
Atkinson also said that he felt "a great many golf clubs" had been ruined
by the construction of "club houses that are too elaborate and too luxurious." In response to Atkinson, Roberts wrote that nothing was likely to
be done in a hurry, but that the house would be hard to save. Early maps
of the proposed course included a "Site for Club House." As soon as
there was money to pay for it, construction would begin.

To come up with the money for the new clubhouse, as well as the money needed for the courses and all the other elements of the plan, Roberts undertook an ambitious campaign to sign up members, beginning in the spring of 1931. He obtained the names and addresses of thirteen thousand past guests of the Bon Air Hotel, believing that he would be able to enlist at least several hundred of those. He sent solicitation letters to clubs throughout Georgia. "When you figure that some 400 people came to New York and spent several hundred dollars each just to welcome Bobby home from England last year," Roberts wrote to William A. Willingham, the chairman of the Universal Leaf Tobacco Company, "it is pretty hard to estimate that there will be anything under 100 prospective members out of the City of Atlanta alone. Aiken [South Carolina] should certainly supply in the neighborhood of 100 members, and you well know that 'our own gang' can dig up another 100 members." Roberts hired a man named E. F. Griffen to build a mailing list based on the membership rosters of prominent clubs. Griffen spent May traveling by train to Pittsburgh, Cincinnati, Columbus, Cleveland, Detroit, Chicago, Milwaukee, Minneapolis, Buffalo, Toronto, and Montreal.

Using names and addresses compiled by Griffen and others, Roberts mailed thousands of invitations, each of which contained a map of the projected course and a message from Jones. "While my time is now largely devoted to the practice of law," Jones wrote, "golf will always be my hobby, and having retired from active competition, my ambition is to help build something that may be recognized as one of the great courses of the world. . . . In the future, Augusta will be my winter vacation headquarters and I expect to give liberally of my time to the Club." Each mailing included an index-card-sized membership blank. All the recipient had to do was fill it out and send it back, along with a check.

The results of the membership drive were monumentally disappointing. The national economy was a wreck, and the pool of golfers with disposable income was small and getting smaller. In mid-May, Griffen wrote to say that he had been unable to meet with a prominent business friend of Roberts's because the man had been "very busy owing to four bank failures here in Chicago in the last few days." William A. Willingham not only didn't deliver "our own gang" but also didn't join himself (although he did sign up two years later). By the end of April 1932, a full year after the membership drive had begun, Augusta National Golf Club had managed to sign up only sixty-six members. Another two years of continuous effort would add just ten names to the total.

Even today, flipping through Augusta National's old correspondence files conveys a deflating sense of what it must have felt like to open the club's mail in the 1930s. The folders are filled with terse letters of regret from men who had been invited to join but either couldn't afford to or didn't want to. Frank Bailey, of Brooklyn, wrote curtly, "In reply to your letter, I would not be at all interested in the membership of your club." Most of those who were asked to join didn't bother to respond at all. Many of those who did join had to drop out later, usually because of personal financial difficulties. One man joined in 1931 on the condition that the club sign up ninety-nine other members; when it failed to do so, he withdrew.

In recent years, a few writers have suggested that Roberts filled the club with friends from Wall Street, and that he was hostile to southerners and (especially) to friends of Jones's. That notion has no basis in fact. If member solicitation was concentrated anywhere it was concentrated in the South. Roberts and Jones both hoped to attract members from everywhere, but both believed that Jones's appeal would be strongest in Georgia. In 1932, Roberts engaged a man named F. S. Bachler for the sole purpose of selling memberships in Atlanta. (He had virtually no success.) Augustans did not rush to join, partly because of the Depression and partly, perhaps, because Augusta National, unlike Augusta Country Club—which adjoined Augusta National's property and had a substantial deficit of its own—would be open only half the year. But local members were eagerly sought and highly valued, as they are today, in part because most of Augusta National's year-round administrative duties inevitably fell to them. Members of the country club, for their part, viewed the arrival of Augusta National as a great boon for themselves, because they believed that the new club would bring more golfers to town and thereby increase revenues from the second of their two golf courses, which was owned by the Bon Air and managed by the club. In 1932, a group of influential members of the country club predicted that Augusta National would help the city become "the Winter Golfing Capital of America."

The *Augusta Chronicle* also staunchly supported the new club. Late in 1931, when Roberts and Jones were making their first big push for members, Thomas J. Hamilton, the newspaper's editor, published a rhapsodic editorial, which he hoped would stir up local interest in the membership drive. In it he quoted a long, ornate pronouncement of Jones's that Jones almost certainly never made: "I can picture young men and maidens of a yesteryear that is gone never to return, with the strains of the violin echoing through the magnolias while the gay occupants tripped the light fantastic," Jones supposedly said, in part. As quoted by Hamilton, Jones also managed to work in a weather report and an approximate airline schedule.

It is true that Augusta National's minuscule early membership contained a disproportionate number of New Yorkers. However, most of those New Yorkers came to the club not through Roberts but through Jones, whose connections in New York at that time were stronger and deeper than Roberts's, or through the sportswriter Grantland Rice, who was a member of the club's organization committee. Rice's help was crucial; Rice was probably the club's most consistently effective salesman in the early thirties. He was the country's most famous sportswriter and was a glamorous national celebrity. (His best-known contribution to American athletic vernacular is contained in the last two lines of a poem of his called "Alumnus Football": "For when the One Great Scorer comes to mark against your name, / He writes—not that you won or lost—but how you played the game.") Rice wrote a widely syndicated newspaper column called "The Sportlight," in which he frequently mentioned the new course, and he was the editor of the magazine *American Golfer*, to which Jones was a contributor. One day in late 1931 or early 1932, he and Roberts brought half a dozen of Rice's friends in a private train car from New York to meet Jones and see the course, which was still far from completion—and all six of them joined. Neither Roberts nor Jones ever made a catch like that on his own.

Though their membership efforts were less fruitful than Rice's, Roberts and Jones nonetheless went to extraordinary lengths to court

new prospects for the club. Roberts wrote hundreds of personal solicita-
tions, most of them to people he had never met. When he one day saw a
newspaper photograph of some golfers gathered outside a hotel in Man-
chester, Vermont, he wrote to the hotel's proprietor to ask for the
golfers' names and addresses so that he could invite them to join Augusta National. The proprietor complied but told Roberts not to get his
hopes up, since most of the golfers in the picture were "boys home from
school." Roberts also offered memberships to public figures, elected officials, and the presidents of universities—none of whom he had ever
met, and none of whom accepted. For several years in the early thirties,
he and Jones enthusiastically pursued a group of four dozen East Coast
retirees called the Red Lead Pencils, fifteen or twenty of whom took an
annual week-long golf trip to the South. The Pencils were flattered yet
somewhat baffled by the attention. In a letter to Roberts, one of them
pointed out that most of the group were elderly, and that almost all of
them, including himself, were "in the hopeless duffer class who throw a
party when they get under a hundred." Roberts replied, with less than
complete accuracy, that Augusta National had "no steep hills" and that
the Pencils would find the course "not too hard." None joined. A year
later, Roberts tried to sign up a foursome from North Carolina. When
they declined, he wrote to one of them to suggest a more economical
arrangement. "It occurs to me to suggest to you," he wrote, "that you
[alone] might purchase a share of our Club stock, which costs three
hundred and fifty ($350.00) dollars, and thereby qualify for membership,
and put you in a position of taking care of your particular foursome any
time they wish to come here. You might also consider splitting the investment among the foursome, likewise letting them underwrite the
dues." But even at less than a hundred dollars a head, an Augusta National membership seemed too extravagant; none of the four signed up.

To most golf fans today, the idea of throwing out an invitation to
join Augusta National seems inconceivable. But until the end of the Second World War, when the national economy rebounded and the Masters
began to make an impression on the public imagination, joining the
club was an attractive proposition to a vanishingly small group. Golfers
from out of town had to consider the difficulty and expense of getting

to Augusta in the first place. The course was widely admired, but it had not yet acquired anything like the aura it has today. Roberts spent years doing the equivalent of making cold calls to strangers, and in response he received only a handful of acceptances. Numbed by the refusals, he and Jones created a less expensive class of membership, for which the initiation fee was a hundred dollars. Even then, they had very few takers.

The club remained afloat, though just barely, through its protracted membership crisis because a small handful of wealthy men agreed to underwrite the club's initial obligations. The most important of these men were Alfred Severin Bourne, who was an heir to the Singer Sewing Machine fortune, and Walton Marshall, who had been part of the group that arranged the purchase of the Fruitland property. Each of these two men pledged $25,000. Bourne made his commitment with deep regret, telling Roberts that if he had been approached before the Crash, he might have paid for the entire project himself. The payments were theoretically five-year loans, on which the club agreed to pay interest at a rate of six percent a year, but the debts were never repaid.

In his book about the club, Roberts glossed over this period, giving the impression that the club's early finances came together very quickly. It is true that he signed up sixteen underwriters and thereby raised $120,000. But the original goal had been $250,000, a target that was later reduced to $150,000, and collecting the money took two years. "No great amount of capital is involved," Roberts wrote at the time, "but I have found my task no easier than I suspect Mr. Dawes has found his job of financing the proposed World's Fair at Chicago." The underwriting group included Jones, who in 1932 made two payments totaling $5,000, but not Roberts, whose finances were shaky. In fact, the club in those years paid Roberts a commission of thirty-five dollars for every new member he signed up; he was able to spend very little time attending to his own business in New York, and he needed the money.

In 1932, when construction of the course was under way, Roberts wrote to Henry P. Crowell, an underwriter from Chicago, seeking not cash but merely Crowell's signature on a document the club wanted to use in pursuing a new loan. In a later letter, Roberts listed reasons why more than half of the other underwriters could not be approached for the same purpose: one of them, he wrote, was so widely known to be broke that Georgia banks "would question his signature"; another was " 'up to his neck' at the banks"; another, "as you know, is dead"; another had "very recently lost his father" and thus no longer had a reason to visit Augusta; another had had a stroke "and the doctors say he cannot recover."

"I shrink from putting any more money into a venture of this nature," Crowell responded, "for it means that any money given to you must be taken from men or organizations that need it to care for the discouraged, sick, and suffering in their ever increasing distress. It wrings one's heart to know that money is going for pleasure, and not to lift up the fallen and broken spirited humans in their extremity." Roberts, in response, told Crowell that he knew of and admired his commitment to charity. But, he added, "I want to remind you that in helping the Augusta National you did more than you could ever accomplish by handing out alms. You helped to give an opportunity to the 140 workmen in Augusta to earn a living and at the same time keep their self respect. These same people, very largely, would otherwise have had to ask for charity. I know you will be interested in learning, too, that 118 of these workmen supported a family on the $1.00 a day wage we paid. At the present time we have 40 laborers, all family men, earning $1.00 per day."

Roberts's argument was self-serving, of course; he wanted the club to survive. But the case he made was also true. The club was a significant employer in Augusta, and when construction began it was one of few local enterprises that were hiring rather than letting workers go. It's not clear whether Crowell gave Roberts the signature he wanted. But he must have been satisfied by Roberts's argument, because he came to Augusta the following January for the official opening of the course, and for the rest of his life he was an important participant in the management of the club.

The meager response to the early membership initiatives was a torment to Roberts. The Depression notwithstanding, he had believed that the appeal of rubbing shoulders with Jones would be as strong for other golfers as it was for him. He had thought the club would have no trouble attracting at least six hundred members—the minimum subscription level, he calculated, at which the pledges of the underwriters would not be needed. (The original plan had been to take no money at all from the underwriters, but merely to use their guarantees as marketing tools in soliciting members.) After a year of trying, though, he had been able to sign up only a small fraction of that number. When Jones had first offered to join the underwriting group, in 1931, Roberts had turned him down, saying that Jones had already made a far more valuable contribution. (To boost the confidence of the underwriters at one point, Roberts and Jones considered insuring Jones's life for $50,000.) It must have been painful for Roberts to admit to Jones in 1932 that he now needed his money as well as his good name.

The failure of the membership drive, as grim as it was, greatly simplified planning for the club: Forget about a clubhouse. Forget about tennis courts. Forget about a second eighteen. Month by month, Roberts pared back his conception of Augusta National until little remained but Jones's course.

The United States Amateur Championship in 1929 was held at the Del Monte Golf and Country Club, which today is known as Pebble Beach. Earlier that year, at Winged Foot, Jones had won the Open. He tied for low score in the Amateur's qualifier and was the favorite to win the tournament, but he lost his first match, one down, to Johnny Goodman, and was eliminated. With nothing else to do, he arranged a friendly game (in a foursome that included Francis Ouimet) at a brand-new club just down the road. That was Jones's first look at Cypress Point, and he was deeply impressed. The next day, he played in the opening exhibition at Pasatiempo, a new course in Santa Cruz which had been designed by the same man. By the time he left California, he knew that if he ever got the opportunity to build his own course, the architect would be Alister MacKenzie.

MacKenzie was an English physician of Scottish ancestry. In the best known picture of him, which was reproduced in the program for the first Masters, he is wearing a kilt. He had bushy eyebrows and a thick mustache and not much hair on the top of his head. He had served his country in both the South African War and the First World War, and he had become a specialist in camouflage, a field that he believed had an application in course design. He began to dabble in golf architecture as a hobby just after the turn of the century, when he was in his early thirties. His work caught the attention of Harry S. Colt, who, among numerous other accomplishments, helped to design Pine Valley in 1914. Colt and MacKenzie were partners for a brief period following the First World War, but their relationship was tempestuous and they never truly collaborated. Cypress Point—a commission that MacKenzie received after the original architect, Seth Raynor, suddenly died—secured his reputation.

In 1931, MacKenzie agreed to take on Augusta National. He first visited the site in July. At that time, he explored the property and, accompanied by Jones, roughly staked out the tees and greens—a task that was made difficult in many places by the density of the undergrowth. He returned to Augusta in September and stayed into October, then went back to California, where he was involved in two other projects: the south course at Haggin Oaks, which is a municipal club in Sacramento; and a pitch-and-putt course outside San Francisco. Roberts told MacKenzie that he was foolish to let such insignificant layouts prevent him from "giving the very best of your time and talent" to Bobby Jones and Augusta National. But bad weather had slowed progress on both the California courses, and MacKenzie felt that the project in Augusta was adequately supervised. It was also stalled, since the club had not yet committed to proceeding. "Clearing and grubbing" of the property began in November, but the final decision to build had not yet been made. "We are to have a meeting just after January 1st," Roberts wrote to MacKenzie in December, "at which time we hope to have a majority of the interested parties on hand and we will determine at that time whether or not business conditions will permit us to finance and carry through the construction of the course." The outcome of the meeting was by no means certain.

The club's wavering disturbed MacKenzie. "I have little doubt the business depression in America is largely due to timidity in carrying out similar enterprises," he wrote to Roberts. "If everyone is fearful of embarking on new enterprises, the business depression will continue." He also pointed out that they might never again have an opportunity to build a golf course so cheaply.

Costs were certainly low. The going rate for unskilled labor in Augusta in 1931 and 1932 was fifty cents a day for men who worked from "can to can't"—from the time in the early morning when a man can see until the time in the evening when he can't. Roberts instructed the club's contractor to pay a dollar a day—double the going rate, but far below what he would have had to pay in happier times. (Roberts later learned that one subcontractor had paid his crew just fifty cents a day, a discount he regretted.) Other costs, though, were higher. Roberts had thought initially that the club might be able to offset some of the expense of clearing the property by selling the trees that were felled, but there were no buyers for firewood even at a dollar and a half a cord, and no buyers for mill-ready timber logs at six dollars per thousand feet. At the end of December, according to a report, the wood was still "standing around in everybody's way."

The correspondence between Roberts and MacKenzie (whom Roberts addressed as "Dear Doc") was affectionate but always lively—and it was made especially lively by the fact that the two men had very different temperaments. MacKenzie was an artist.* His drawings of the course were sometimes suggestive rather than explicit—because, as he explained to Roberts, many of the most important decisions, such as

---

* Golf architecture was not MacKenzie's only area of expertise. A 1932 press release from the club reads, "The guests at the Bon Air Hotel have been regularly entertained by exhibition dancing on the part of Doctor and Mrs. MacKenzie. It has been learned on the best of authority that this distinguished couple have entered and won the first prize at a number of leading dancing contests in high social circles. Further, it is a well established fact that the good Doctor and his accomplished partner regularly captured first honors in the dancing contest that takes place on TransAtlantic Liners."

those governing the exact shapes and contours of the greens, could not be made until picks and shovels were in hand. Roberts, in contrast, liked details. "What I want you to do," he wrote in December 1931, "is to give us something in the nature of your official map, everything to be drawn to an exact scale and all features put down as accurately as it is possible at this time." He told MacKenzie that he needed a good map to display prominently, as an advertisement, during Augusta's winter resort season—perhaps in the lobby of the Bon Air. He also needed to shore up the flagging convictions of the club's underwriters and other lenders.*

Once the club finally committed to building the course—as it did in February 1932—construction proceeded with astonishing speed. In just three months, 120,000 cubic yards of soil were moved in the shaping of the fairways, the contouring of the greens, and the installation of a Buckner Hoseless watering system ("Outstanding Results at Low Cost"), which used water purchased from the city of Augusta at a rate of three cents per thousand gallons. MacKenzie returned to Augusta in March to supervise the last of the contour work on the greens, fifteen of which had been built by that point. He remained until April. Late in May, between eighty and ninety acres were planted with eight thousand pounds of Bermuda grass seed. Mowing began on June 10. Jones played his first round in August—by which time the fairways had been cut eight times and the greens more than thirty times—and he sent Roberts a telegram in New York to let him know how pleased he was with the course.

"The construction period of 124 consecutive calendar days included 18 Sundays and 30 days lost because of wet ground," according to a flattering, unsigned account written by Theodore R. Kendall in the October 1932 issue of *Contractors and Engineers Monthly,* a professional journal based in New York. "The actual construction period was 76 working days from the start of surface construction to completion of seeding.

---

* MacKenzie was entirely capable of making precise drawings of golf courses. Copies of his exquisitely detailed map of the Old Course at St. Andrews, which he completed in 1924, can be seen in clubhouses all over the world. MacKenzie spent a year on the Old Course project and did all the surveying himself.

The course was in finished condition ready for play on Labor Day. . . . It is believed that, considering the volume of dirt moved, the foregoing 124 days constitutes an all-time record in golf course construction."

Not only that, but there were no significant cost overruns. The journal reported that "efficient management, favorable weather, and the low cost of labor" had enabled the club to come close to meeting its (significantly reduced) budget of $100,000 while adding $15,000 worth of additional features.

Although the club did come close to meeting its budget, it came nowhere near paying its bills. One of the biggest creditors ended up being MacKenzie himself. In February 1932, in hopes of moving the project along, he had reduced his fee from $10,000 to $5,000, but even that figure was hypothetical; the club was barely able to meet its weekly payroll, which was two hundred dollars. (Roberts always paid employees and laborers first.) Roberts haggled over almost every dollar. "What an infernal trouble you are!" MacKenzie wrote, mostly good-naturedly, when Roberts had questioned his accounting of his expenses. "I suppose the mere fact that you are making yourself a damned nuisance to me is an indication of your value to the Augusta National."

By late 1932, at which time the course had been in play for several months, MacKenzie had received just $2,000—a sum that didn't cover even his estimate of his expenses. In November, he wired an urgent request for $1,000, and he followed it with a letter. On the day after Christmas he wrote again, saying his situation was now dire: "I am at the end of my tether, no one has paid me a cent since last June, we have mortgaged everything we have and have not yet been able to pay the nursing expenses of my wife's operation. . . . Can you possibly let me have, at any rate, five hundred dollars to keep us out of the poor house?"

But there was no money to send. The membership drive was yielding almost nothing, and Roberts was just barely meeting the club's payroll with green fees collected from guests. Jones made a "Sportlight" sound movie at Augusta National in November, and Roberts hoped that the film would be "a good advertisement" for the club, but no new prospects had turned up yet. In late January 1933, MacKenzie wrote that he was now in danger of losing his electric service and his telephone, and that he was afraid the bank might foreclose on his house. "For some time," he added, "I have been reduced to playing golf with four clubs and a Woolworth ball." He noted, however, that he had been winning and that his net cost was therefore zero.

MacKenzie had no head for business, his wife later told Roberts, and in his letters he was sometimes apt to exaggerate his difficulties for humorous effect. But there is no doubt that during this period he and his family were in financial distress. Roberts, unable to send money, proposed that the club issue two short-term notes, each with a face value of $1,000 and a nominal interest rate of six percent. The club wouldn't be able to make the interest payments, but Roberts thought MacKenzie might be able to dispose of the notes at a discount and thus obtain some cash. "I must tell you frankly, however," Roberts added, "that it will be out of the question for you to discount them in Augusta"—where the club's paper would be known to be worthless. MacKenzie accepted, and he did manage to use one of the notes in California as collateral for a loan of four hundred sixty dollars. He later asked Roberts to find out whether Jones might personally lend him $1,000—a request that by the end of the same letter he had raised to $2,000—but either Jones declined or Roberts didn't pass the request along.

Augusta National was not the only golf club that owed MacKenzie money. St. Andrews, in Yonkers, New York, had "repudiated" his fees, he told Roberts, and two other clubs for which he had done design work had gone belly-up. (Roberts tried to help him get some money from St. Andrews, to no avail.) MacKenzie was writing a book, called *The Spirit of St. Andrews*, which he thought might bring him some income, but he never found a publisher.* He and his wife began cutting each other's hair to save money. They also scrounged fuel for their furnace in woods near their house—"but now all the family have got poison oak and the medical treatment has cost more than we saved. . . . The future is bright but we shall be sunk before we get to it unless you can come to our rescue."

Rescue never came. The club was still broke on January 6, 1934,

---

* The book was finally published in 1995. It has a brief foreword by Jones, and it makes fascinating reading for any student of golf course architecture.

when MacKenzie, after a brief illness, suddenly died, at the age of sixty-three. He had last seen Augusta National in April 1932, when the grass had not yet been planted. He had called Augusta National "my best opportunity, and I believe, my finest achievement." But he didn't live to play it or even to see it in its finished form.

One of the club's best hopes for raising money in the early years was to sell building lots on which members might construct winter homes. Roughly a third of the property was reserved for that purpose, and the lots were delineated and numbered on several early maps. (For the most part, the lots occupied areas west of the second fairway and east of the tenth and eleventh.) The club hired the landscape architecture firm of Olmsted Bros., of Brookline, Massachusetts, to plan the subdivision, and also to give advice on building a clubhouse and landscaping the entire property. Olmsted Bros. was the most distinguished landscape architecture firm in the country. The brothers in the title were the sons of Frederick Law Olmsted, whose most famous creations include the grounds of the United States Capitol, Atlanta's Druid Hills subdivision (where Jones's parents lived, and where Jones himself would later live), the campus of Stanford University, the village of Pinehurst, North Carolina, and New York City's Central Park. Olmsted had died in 1903, but his work was carried on by his sons.

In his book about the club, Roberts made no mention of Olmsted Bros. The omission is puzzling, because the firm's involvement was extensive and continued intermittently for about ten years. In advertisements that ran in the programs for the first two tournaments, Olmsted Bros. was described as one of the "three eminent designers" of Augusta National (the other two being MacKenzie and Jones)—wording that Roberts and Jones had approved. The explanation may be that two of the chores assigned to the firm—planning a new clubhouse and subdividing the property for homes—were ones that in later years Roberts was just as happy to forget. Olmsted Bros. had also advised against concentrating a particular type of plant on each hole, a practice that had been suggested by the club's beautification committee and that became one of Roberts's favorite features of the course.

Roberts in later years was especially sensitive on the subject of the building lots. In his book, he downplayed the idea: "It was beginning to become the custom at new courses to sell off any excess acreage as building lots," he wrote, "and we planned to do the same, limiting the sale to about a dozen quite large homesites, to be constructed in locations well back from any fairway. Fortunately, only one lot was sold—to W. Montgomery Harison, an Augusta member—before we had a change of heart and called off any further sale of lots."

This is essentially accurate, although it greatly understates the scope of the original idea. The plan called for roughly twenty building sites, not a dozen, and additional acreage was reserved for more. Furthermore, the club actively tried to sell those lots or others for more than twenty years. Boundary lines were cleared, access roads were built, lots were numbered with signs that faced the roads, and a major, continuing effort was made to stir up sales—all without success. W. Montgomery Harison was the only buyer. (He actually bought not one lot but three adjoining ones.) He built a huge, attractive mansion, which until 1977 was clearly visible just beyond the first green; the elder of his two sons built a much smaller house next door.

After the war, the club briefly considered leasing or renting the remaining lots. (Roberts suggested annual charges ranging from two hundred fifty to five hundred dollars a year for lots that were several acres in size.) When no enthusiasm for that idea was evident, the club gave up on the original subdivision and for four or five years pursued a more modest development plan in a different location. This new subdivision—which was to be called De Soto Trail—was situated just east of the area now occupied by the par three course. It consisted of twenty-four lots, most of them roughly a half-acre in size, and was targeted not at club members but at local middle-income families. To avoid the expense of building an access road and installing utilities, the club in 1949 offered the entire parcel to local real estate agents. There were no bids. The club then tried without success to sell the lots individually. Late in 1952, a local developer offered $18,000 for fifteen acres. Roberts viewed that figure as too low, and the club eventually abandoned the entire idea.

Today, it's almost impossible to conceive that Augusta National, in more than twenty years of conscientious effort, could turn up only one solid prospect interested in building a house near what today may be the most fabled golf course in the world. If the same lots were offered for sale today, the bids would undoubtedly be astronomical. The failure of the real estate projects underscores the immensity of the challenge that Roberts, Jones, and other early members faced in nearly every area of the club's operation. As late as the early fifties, Roberts couldn't get local real estate developers to return his calls.

It was only in the mid-fifties—when the tournament had securely established itself, and the club was on firmer financial footing—that Roberts began to view all development ideas as a mistake. A local club member named Julian Roberts (no relation) eventually bought Harison's property and later sold it back to the club. One of Clifford Roberts's last acts before taking his life in 1977 was to walk to the first tee with the help of a waiter so that he could look up the fairway and assure himself that the old Harison mansion had been torn down.

A minor contributor to the design of Augusta National—and one whose participation in the original project has not previously been documented—was Marion Hollins, a gifted and flamboyant athlete who had won the U.S. Women's Amateur in 1921. Hollins was a close friend and patron of MacKenzie's. Beginning in the mid-twenties, she had played much the same role in the founding and development of Pasatiempo, in Santa Cruz, California, that Roberts was to play in the founding and development of Augusta National. The parallels are remarkable: Hollins discovered the Pasatiempo property (while horseback riding), announced her intention to build "the greatest golf course in the world," arranged financing, engaged Alister MacKenzie as the architect, and hired Olmsted Bros. to landscape the grounds and plan an extensive residential subdivision—all well before Roberts and Jones had even seen the old Fruitland nursery. Jones knew Hollins, and played in a number of exhibitions with her. At MacKenzie's request, she also visited Augusta National shortly before construction began and reported back to him with her observations. It seems highly likely that some of Jones's and Roberts's ideas were adapted from hers.

Hollins was a commanding figure. "She was independent, cared lit-

tle for the niceties of fashion, and most often could be seen striding
about in rumpled tweeds," Rhonda Glenn wrote in *The Illustrated History of Women's Golf.* "She wore her hair in a severe bob and often
donned a cloche hat at a rakish angle for golf. She wore skirts but preferred them to have pockets in which she could thrust her large hands,
and she set off a look that can, at best, be called casual." She was stocky
and strong, and she hit the ball considerably farther than most of her
fellow competitors.

Hollins was born in 1893 and was thus an almost exact contemporary of Roberts's. Her father, Harry P. Hollins, was an investment
banker, a speculator, and a business associate of various Vanderbilts. In
the early nineteen hundreds, he built a great Gilded Age fortune—which
he later lost—and Marion enjoyed a childhood of exquisite comfort.
Champion in a Man's World, a biography of Hollins written by David E.
Outerbridge, contains a photograph of her reclining in bed and drinking
champagne aboard the luxury ocean liner *Lusitania* in 1910, when she
was seventeen or eighteen. She became an accomplished athlete in several sports and was a determined competitor from an early age. In 1913,
when she was twenty-one, she made it to the final of the Women's Amateur, in which she lost a close match to Gladys Ravenscroft, who had
won the Ladies British Amateur the year before at Turnberry. In the
1921 U.S. Amateur, she improved the qualifying record by four strokes
and won the final, 5 and 4, over Alexa Stirling, who had won the title in
each of the three previous competitions. In 1932, Hollins served as the
captain of the victorious American team in the first Curtis Cup Match,
which was played in England at the Wentworth Golf Club. She was also
an expert horsewoman and an occasional automobile racer. Samuel F. B.
Morse, the developer of Pebble Beach, once called her "the only good
woman polo player I have ever known."

In 1923, Hollins founded Women's National Golf and Tennis Club,
in Glen Head, Long Island. The club was financed entirely by women—
among them Eleanor Mellon and the wives of Harold Pratt, Howard
Whitney, and Childs Frick—and did not permit men as members. Its
course was designed by Devereux Emmet, with help from Seth Raynor,
Charles Blair Macdonald, and Hollins herself, and the clubhouse was re-

modeled by McKim, Mead, and White. The club's head professional was the legendary teacher Ernest Jones, whom Hollins had discovered in England in 1922 and brought to the United States. (Jones later divided his time between Women's National and Pasatiempo. He wrote several classic instruction books, including *Swinging into Golf,* which he dedicated to Hollins, and *Swing the Clubhead.*) Women's National survived as an independent entity for just eighteen years. The course today is part of Glen Head Country Club.

Hollins was one of MacKenzie's earliest champions in the United States, and she was largely responsible for creating the set of circumstances that brought him to the attention of Bobby Jones. In the early twenties, Samuel Morse—who had bought and was in the process of developing most of California's Monterey Peninsula—hired Hollins as his athletic director. The idea of building a course at Cypress Point was largely hers, and it was she who secured the original option on that incomparable piece of property and organized the club. Several years before, Morse had hired Seth Raynor to build several courses. After Raynor died of pneumonia in 1926, it was Hollins who suggested MacKenzie as his replacement for Cypress Point. She worked closely with him and was credited by him with the design of that course's most famous hole, the sixteenth, with its unforgettable tee shot over Monterey Bay. "To give honor where it is due," MacKenzie wrote in *The Spirit of St. Andrews,* "I must say that, except for minor details in construction, I was in no way responsible for the hole. It was largely due to the vision of Miss Marion Hollins (the founder of Cypress Point). It was suggested to her by the late Seth Raynor that it was a pity the carry over the ocean was too long to enable a hole to be designed on this particular site. Miss Hollins said she did not think it was an impossible carry. She then teed up a ball and drove to the middle of the site for the suggested green."* It was Hollins who invited Jones to play at Pasatiempo on

---

* *The History of Cypress Point Club,* which that club published in 1996, contains a more colorful but less reliable account of the hole's conception, suggesting that it was MacKenzie rather than Raynor who felt the tee shot was not feasible:
" 'Nonsense, Alister,' said Marion, clad in her customary tweed coat and skirt,

opening day in 1929 after Jones had washed out of the Amateur. On that day, the two played as partners in a match with Cyril Tolley and Glenna Collett (and lost by six shots). According to Robert Beck, who is Pasatiempo's historian, they were accompanied during the round by MacKenzie himself, who spent much of the time talking with Jones.

When Roberts complained late in 1931 that MacKenzie was spending too much time in California and not enough in Augusta, MacKenzie sent Hollins to look things over in his stead. "She has been associated with me in three golf courses," he wrote to Roberts, "and not only are her own ideas valuable, but she is thoroughly conversant in regard to the character of the work I like. I want her views and also her personal impressions in regard to the way the work is being carried out." Roberts wasn't mollified—"I can tell you," he wrote, "that Bob Jones is going to be displeased and most unhappy if there is any disposition on your part to allow anything to interfere with your being on hand"—and MacKenzie later felt compelled to defend Hollins in a letter to Wendell Miller, the engineer who built the course. "I do not know any *man* who has sounder ideas," he wrote. "Unfortunately you were not at Augusta when she visited the course. She was most favourably impressed with it."

Whether Hollins and Roberts ever met is not clear. If they did, they would have had much to talk about, because Roberts's conception of Augusta National was very similar to the plan of development that Hollins was already executing at Pasatiempo. Indeed, more than a few of Roberts's and Jones's earliest ideas—including the decision to hire Olmsted Bros.—were almost certainly borrowed from Hollins's project. A year before her visit to Augusta, Hollins had earned $2.5 million in a major oil investment deal that she had helped to put together with Walter Chrysler, Payne Whitney, and at least one other eastern tycoon, and she was now pouring her sudden fortune into her club. Her oil money enabled her to build a lavish clubhouse, bridle paths, tennis courts (with

---

who then teed up a ball in the dirt, swung her hickory shafted wood club and knocked her ball squarely to the center of what is now the present green with some comment to the effect that if she could do it there must be some men who could as well." MacKenzie's account is almost certainly more accurate.

clay imported from England and France), a swimming pool, a polo field, a steeplechase track, and numerous other amenities. She also sold quite a few building lots—something that Roberts and Jones never managed to do—including one to MacKenzie, who built a house alongside the sixth fairway. (When Augusta National, in 1933, issued MacKenzie the two $1,000 notes in lieu of part of his unpaid fee, it was Hollins who arranged for him to use one of the notes as collateral for a loan.) By the time Hollins visited Augusta, Pasatiempo had become a thriving and decidedly glamorous hangout, especially considering the state of the national economy. Among the prominent guests in those days were Mary Pickford, Charlie Chaplin, Will Rogers, Spencer Tracy, Joan Fontaine, and Claudette Colbert.

Unfortunately for Hollins, the broad scope of her investment would eventually leave Pasatiempo even more vulnerable to the Depression than Augusta National was. By the end of the thirties, she had spent both herself and her club to the brink of financial ruin. In 1941, the golf course—after changing hands twice in what were essentially foreclosures—was offered for sale at $45,000, payable over forty-five years. There were no takers, although later in the year a group of investors did buy the course for an undisclosed sum. It has been maintained as a public golf club since 1942.

The last years of Hollins's life were bleak. She was gravely injured in an automobile accident in 1937. (A drunk driver crashed into her convertible as she was driving home to take care of a sick pet parrot, and she suffered a severe concussion that was not properly treated.) Within a year, she was deep in debt. She vowed that she would compete again as a golfer, and she did, in 1940, after a long and arduous recovery. But she died just four years after that, apparently of illnesses unrelated to her accident, in a rest home in Pacific Grove. She was fifty-one. By the time of her death, she would have had little reason to hope that her beloved Pasatiempo—in which she had invested nearly all her time and money for more than a decade—would outlast the war.

Pasatiempo did survive, though just barely. (The few golfers who showed up during the war were asked to leave donations in a box by the first tee.) The course today looks very little like the course that she and

Jones played together in 1929, but it still bears powerful traces of its principal patron and her favorite architect. Today, the original clubhouse is a restaurant called Hollins House, and Pasatiempo remains one of MacKenzie's most highly regarded creations. And the old club can almost certainly be regarded as an early model for Augusta National.

Augusta National's official opening took place in January 1933. Roberts and Grantland Rice arranged for a private train to bring members and prospective members from New York City to Augusta for a long weekend of golf. For a hundred dollars, a participant received a Pullman berth, a room at the Bon Air, all meals, local transportation, and three days of golf with Bobby Jones and Francis Ouimet, who had agreed to be on hand. The outing was fully subscribed—the hundred participants consisted mostly of New York businessmen, a few of whom brought their wives—but the golf was a disappointment. An article in the *Augusta Chronicle* described the fairways and greens that weekend as "soggy" and said that a planned competition was disrupted by "near freezing weather which came in with a cold rain." On the first morning, some of the players returned to the hotel after playing just nine holes. Those who remained were served barbecued chicken and bootleg corn liquor in a cold, wet tent on the lawn near the old manor house, which was not yet fit for entertaining.

Roberts had had high hopes for the train party. Two months before, he had enthusiastically described the idea to a representative of Olmsted Bros. and asked if the firm might be able to help him obtain an additional train car, which would leave from Boston and join the train in New York. But the party didn't live up to his expectations. It didn't lose money—in fact, at the end there was a small cash surplus, which Roberts distributed as tips to the crew of the train—but it failed in its larger purpose, which was to drum up interest in the club. Only one of the guests, a New Yorker named Frank Willard, signed on as a member. Willard was the head of F. A. Willard & Co., the New York investment banking firm that had been the source of Roberts's breakthrough $55,000 commission in 1929. Willard joined the club largely as a favor to

Roberts, and, according to a club member who knew both men, he helped to support Roberts financially during Roberts's lean years in the thirties. Willard's firm merged with Reynolds & Co. in 1934. It was most likely through his acquaintance with Willard that Roberts went to work at Reynolds. Willard's three-hundred-fifty-dollar initiation check covered the club's operating expenses for about ten days.

The weather grew worse when the party ended, and so did the near-term prospects of the club. "At the present moment," Roberts wrote from Augusta the following month, "the trees are covered with ice and we might just as well be in Canada as far as playing golf is concerned." That meant, among other things, that until the weather improved there would be no revenue from guest fees. Nor was there any interest in the building lots, which couldn't be shown anyway, because the poor weather made it impossible to get to them.

Roberts had reshaped his entire career for the Augusta project, and he couldn't understand why it wasn't getting off the ground. The train-party crowd was generally well heeled—a newspaper reporter marveled that the club's secretary had had to send out for change because fifteen of the participants used hundred dollar bills to pay for purchases in the golf shop—but by 1933, golf had become a luxury that even corporate chairmen had difficulty justifying. In March, Roberts sent a gloomy letter to Jones from a hotel room in Augusta. "If we were able to dispose of some memberships we could apply the entire proceeds to the reduction of debts," he wrote, "but at the moment I do not see a chance of securing a single membership check. All available funds have been used up, and we are operating on a 'hand to mouth' basis. I mean by this that we are using the daily green fees collection to meet our labor payroll on a currency basis." On a good day, a dozen golfers with guest cards might drop by to play—producing total revenues of forty-eight dollars. If it rained, the revenues were zero.

"There is one other factor that it may be worthwhile to consider," Roberts continued. "I have devoted all my time to the interests of the club during the past two years, but after the close of this season, I do not see how I shall be able to continue to do so. I have just been checking over my personal records and I find that in addition to the cash that I have advanced the club, I have, since I started work on this proposition, used up personal funds to the extent of nearly thirty thousand dollars. The time has now arrived when I will need to busy myself with the task of replenishing my own bank account."

The $30,000 that Roberts had spent during the formation of the club represented essentially all the money he had managed to save since coming to New York. If he wasn't broke, he was close; the Depression had hit him very hard. (In contrast, Jones's income between 1931 and 1933 added up to nearly $300,000.) By early 1933, Roberts had made himself a stranger on Wall Street, where, admittedly, there would have been little for him to do. In a ledger, he kept track of expenses he incurred in the service of the club: thirty-six cents for pencils for the golf course; ten cents for a bellboy at the Bon Air; five dollars for his regular maid; a dollar and a half for postage; fifteen cents for (appropriately) a bottle of red ink. The club's prospects were steadily eroding, a dime and quarter at a time.

By late March, a full listing of the club's debts filled two and a half single-spaced typewritten pages, and Roberts was forced to prepare a grim letter to the creditors. "The Augusta National is embarrassed," he wrote, ". . . by current debts amounting to approximately thirty-one thousand ($31,000) dollars." Roberts believed that he had identified at least five hundred solid membership prospects, all of whom had played the course, but he said that he had no hope of signing up any of them soon, now that Augusta's brief playing season was drawing to a close. "The Augusta National is obligated on a sixty thousand ($60,000) dollar mortgage which covers the golf course, club house, and grounds," he continued. "If trouble is made by any owner of current obligations, this mortgage will be foreclosed, the enterprise wrecked, and the sponsorship of Mr. Jones will be lost. In the interest of all concerned, we propose to the creditors a Stand-Still-Agreement ending April 15, 1934."

This was, it should be noted, a form letter. The club's situation was so precarious that even small bills had long gone unpaid. (The club owed $5.85 to Augusta Grocery Co. for toilet paper and $1.37 to Stumpp & Walter Co. for hose nozzles.) Roberts explained to one of the club's more understanding providers that he had written the letter because he had wanted to avoid "the temptation to pay out any available funds to such creditors as are causing the club the most annoyance." Any new cash, he explained, would be disbursed on a pro rata basis. In December, he found two dollars on the floor, and the sum was duly entered on the credit side of the club's ledger.

Roberts was even grimmer in a letter to Jones. He confided that any one of the club's larger creditors could ruin the club simply by insisting on payment. "The only thing that discourages such action," Roberts wrote, "is the fact that these creditors would obtain nothing by bankruptcy proceedings."

The steady succession of setbacks must have been agonizing for Roberts. He can't help but have been reminded of his father's chain of disappointments and business failures, and he must have been tormented by a fear that he might not be able to deliver what he had promised to the early members, the underwriters, and Jones. After a brief triumph in New York, he now found himself trapped again in an economic crisis. The sole consolation must have been his knowledge that, whatever disasters might await him in the coming months, he had nonetheless accomplished the most important of his goals: he had managed to build a golf course for Bobby Jones.

CHAPTER FOUR

Augusta National
Invitation Tournament

In February 1933, one month after the train party, Prescott S. Bush—whose second child, George (then eight years old), would one day be elected president of the United States—played two rounds at Augusta National Golf Club. Bush was a Wall Street lawyer and the chairman of the tournament committee of the United States Golf Association, American golf's main governing body and rule-making organization, and the sponsor of the U.S. Open and Amateur championships. (His wife's father, George H. Walker, had been the president of the U.S.G.A. in 1920 and is the man after whom the Walker Cup was named.) Not long after Bush's round, Roberts, in a letter to a club member named Charles H. Sabin, wrote that Bush had "made the suggestion that [Augusta National] might be used for the U.S. Open Championship in 1934." In his book about the club, Roberts said that the idea of hosting the Open had first arisen in late 1932—a few months before Bush's visit. If that's the case, then Bush's "suggestion" may in fact have been suggested to him by Roberts, who had sent Bush a guest card in January and invited him to play. In any event, the club was interested.

By 1933, neither the Open nor the Amateur—the two biggest tournaments conducted by the U.S.G.A.—had ever been held farther south than Illinois. Jones had long wanted to redress that geographical imbalance, and his desire to do so was one reason he had wanted to build a course of his own. Augusta National had been conceived from the beginning as a venue where championships might one day be held. Bush later told Roberts that he would call a special meeting of the U.S.G.A.'s executive committee to discuss the matter. Roberts was delighted.

Under ordinary circumstances, Roberts almost certainly would have preferred to wait a few years before attempting to conduct a big tournament. The course had been playable for just six months, the layout still needed what Roberts optimistically called "finishing touches," and the clubhouse and other facilities were rudimentary at best. But hosting the Open might accomplish something that Roberts and Jones had thus far been unable to accomplish on their own: It might attract enough new members to keep the club alive. Roberts also hoped that the U.S.G.A. would put up some money for course improvements before the tournament, enabling the club to partly compensate MacKenzie for what it owed him by offering him additional design work. "I do not need to tell you," Roberts wrote to Sabin, "that the event would naturally benefit in every way the Augusta National Golf Club." A few days later, Roberts asked Grantland Rice to press the club's case with various U.S.G.A. officials. "I will also ask Bob to communicate with these people," Roberts wrote, "and if it becomes necessary, Bob and I will get on the train and go to see anyone that may be hesitant about the matter."

In later years, Roberts suggested that the idea of hosting the Open had been one that the club did not strenuously pursue. "Bob was intrigued with the idea," he wrote in his book, "but, after much thought and a number of meetings, it was decided that our club could render a more important service to the game of golf by holding regularly a tournament of its own." That account gives no sense of the intensive lobbying that went on; Roberts and Jones wanted the Open badly. In the end, though, the U.S.G.A. was not persuaded. On April 13, Herbert Jaques, the organization's president, replied by letter that "whereas we are all favorably inclined to this move in the near future, we do not think it is practical to attempt in 1934."

There were, indeed, numerous obstacles. An Open in Augusta would have to be held in late March or early April, when the weather was at its best and the local resorts still had guests. That was roughly three months ahead of the Open's usual dates. To accommodate the change, the U.S.G.A.'s system of sectional qualifying would have to be drastically revised. The Professional Golfers' Association—an organization of club pros and touring players—in those days sponsored a handful of tournaments in the Southeast in February and March, and Jaques acknowledged that Augusta would be a convenient stop for pros returning north after competing in those events. But he pointed out that a springtime Open in Augusta "would present difficulties to a Professional holding a berth at a Northern course, who did not go South, in that he would have to make some other arrangement about preparing his game and go to no little expense to do so." The professional tour in those days was not what it is today. More than a few pros—from the South as well as the North—had to turn down invitations to play in early Masters Tournaments because they could not afford to take time away from their club jobs at that time of year.

Roberts was deeply disappointed by the U.S.G.A.'s decision; he needed tournament headlines as soon as possible. Within a short time, though, he came up with a new idea: the club could hold a tournament of its own. A private event wouldn't have the automatic appeal of the Open, but it might still attract notice, bring in revenues, lure some new members, and help to extend the patience of the club's financial backers—an increasingly urgent necessity. In a letter seeking an emergency contribution from Alfred Bourne, who from the beginning had been one of the club's most generous benefactors, he explained why the U.S.G.A.'s rejection might eventually work to the benefit of the club. Augusta National didn't need the Open, Roberts wrote, because "the tournament we are planning will do a great deal more for our club, especially since it would be a regular annual event."

Roberts now devoted to the new tournament the same energy with which he had courted the Open. In the fall of 1933, he formally announced his plan to the P.G.A., which shortly afterward released its tournament schedule for the coming season. The schedule listed ten winter events, most of them in California, and described entry fees, prize money, and the availability of hotel rooms for competitors. (The richest of the events was the now long-defunct Miami Biltmore Open, which had a purse of $10,000 and paid an unheard-of forty places. More typical was the National Capital Open, held in Bethesda, Maryland, which paid just twelve places, including a first prize of six hundred dollars.) In a brief note at the end of the schedule, the P.G.A. mentioned a handful of other events, about which less information was available: "There are four tournaments already scheduled for the spring season," the release said, "at Columbus, Georgia, dates not yet set, and for Charleston, South Carolina, on March 15, 16, and 17, Augusta National Golf course, March 22, 23, 24 and 25, and the North and South Open at Pinehurst, March 27, 28 and 29. Details of these events will be given when completed." That brief notice contained the first official mention of the tournament that would become the Masters.

Although a private tournament would be highly unlikely to attract the interest that an Open would, there were several big advantages to Roberts's new plan. The biggest one, he quickly realized, was that Jones might be persuaded to play. With Jones in the field, the new tournament would instantly become the most talked-about golf event of the year.

There would have been no possibility of Jones's playing in an Open. In order to do so, he would have had to "turn professional" as a player—an idea he abhorred—because by U.S.G.A. rules he was no longer an amateur. At the time of Jones's retirement from competition late in 1930, Warner Bros. hired him to make instructional films, and shortly after that, A. G. Spalding & Bros. hired him to design and promote golf clubs. (Those business opportunities represented a powerful inducement to stop playing competitive golf. Jones's golf-related income in 1933, when the first tournament was being planned, was over $100,000; in contrast, Paul Runyan, who won nine events that year and was the tour's leading money-winner, had gross tournament earnings of less than $6,500.) Upon signing with Warner Bros., Jones had written, "I am not certain that the step I am taking is in a strict sense a violation of the amateur rule. I think a lot might be said on either side. But I am so far convinced that it is contrary to the spirit of amateurism that I am prepared to accept and even endorse a ruling that it is an infringement." This had been a potentially inflammatory issue in 1930, and he did not want to visit it again.

There was probably a touch of snobbery in Jones's antipathy to being called a professional; in a letter to Roberts many years later, he described the typical pro as "an uneducated club servant"—a point of view he might well have formed in the days when only amateur competitors were accorded the honorific *Mr.*, professional golfers often weren't allowed to set foot inside clubhouses, and tournament organizers distinguished between "gentlemen" and "players." He wrote in 1960 that he had no contempt for what he called "an honest professionalism," thereby conveying nearly the opposite message. "So long as I played as an amateur, there could be no question of subterfuge or concealment," he wrote. Roberts purposely dodged the issue by making no distinction between amateurs and professionals in program listings and pairing sheets—a distinction that was invariably noted elsewhere.

Would Jones have played in the club's tournament if the club had been compelled to label him explicitly as a professional? Roberts said in later years that he suspected Jones probably would have played regardless, in order to help the club. But he was uncertain enough that he never raised the matter with him, either then or later. (In *Golf Is My Game*, Jones wrote that to give up his amateur status would have been "like giving up part of myself.") The club today, in its tournament records, treats Jones as an amateur, but at the time no one did. The Associated Press and other news organizations listed him with the professionals. Even O. B. Keeler, who had built his sportswriting career by celebrating Jones's amateur achievements, took it for granted that Jones was now a pro; he described Charles Yates, who finished three strokes behind him in the inaugural tournament, as the low amateur. (Yates is one of several distinguished amateur players who have been members of Augusta National. He won the British Amateur in 1938, and he competed in the first eleven Masters Tournaments. He and Jones became close friends, and used to play matches for a "willy rock"—their own term for a dollar bill. Yates is the last surviving Augusta National member who joined before the Second World War. He is believed to be the only person who has been present at every Masters since the beginning.)

Jones had another reason for not wanting to play: His game was, quite understandably, less sharp than it had been at the pinnacle of his career. He hadn't competed since the 1930 Amateur, and he didn't want

to disappoint his fans with mediocre play. He told Roberts in no uncertain terms that he would like to leave the golf to others and serve the
tournament merely as an "official."

But the tournament absolutely had to have Jones in the field. Attracting top players to a small new tournament would have been far harder, if
not impossible, without his participation, and so would selling tickets.
Revenues at the 1930 U.S. Open, the third leg of Jones's Grand Slam, had
been double what they were the following year, after Jones had quit the
game. At the 1930 Amateur, which was held at Merion, U.S.G.A. officials
had entreated Jones to play a practice round the day before the competition—something he ordinarily didn't like to do—so that they could sell
more tickets and thereby further replenish their treasury, which had
been ravaged by hard times. Without Jones, a new tournament in a
small city in Georgia in the spring of 1934 would not have had a chance.

In the end, Roberts later wrote, the argument that persuaded Jones
was one that Roberts himself advanced: "he simply could not invite his
golfing friends to play on his course and then decline to play with
them." That may be true, although it seems equally likely that the ulti-
mately unanswerable argument was an economic one: no Jones, no
tournament, no club. Once Jones agreed, Roberts left no room for him
to change his mind: He sealed the commitment by giving Jones his own
paragraph in the announcement he sent to the P.G.A. "Bobby Jones has
agreed to make this tournament the one exception to his rule against
further participation in tournament golf," Roberts wrote. "He does this
with the thought of helping to establish a new golfing event that is
hoped may assume the proportion of an important tournament."

Jones's participation was a huge relief as well to the P.G.A., which
was suffering the effects of the Depression and hoped that the return of
the game's biggest star would add some luster to the entire tour. The
low state of the tour in those days was clearly reflected in the events that
constituted it. One official tournament was held on a nine-hole course
in an impoverished coal-mining town called Hazard, Kentucky. The
sportswriter Herb Graffis, in an official history called *The PGA,* which
was published in 1975, wrote, "The event had been sponsored by an
Ohio company that owned the mines there, and the prize money

[$5,000] was more than many of the miners would be paid all their lives working underground. The small gallery watched the tournament just as the wail of hymns came from the small church built on a ledge of the hill, where burial services were being held for some miners killed in an explosion. As the mourners silently followed the coffins along the narrow bridge over the river, the golfers stopped complaining about the poor condition of the greens." Robert Harlow, who was the manager of the P.G.A.'s tournament bureau, suggested to Roberts that he make the most of Jones's participation by hiring a local sportswriter to supervise publicity for the event. Roberts did him one better by getting Grantland Rice to announce Jones's return in one of his syndicated newspaper columns.

"It all happened in this fashion," Rice wrote, exercising considerable dramatic license with the details. ". . . When the matter was put up to Bobby Jones he promptly agreed to play, 'if,' as he expressed it, 'I happen to be one of the best fifty or sixty golfers named by the committee. I've been out of action so long I may not belong in this group.' " Rice—who did not mention in his column that he would be the honorary chairman of the new tournament—went on to portray the contest as a long-awaited rematch between Jones and the rest of the world. (In Rice's formulation, Jones was both the underdog and the favorite.) "The interesting feature of this 72-hole contest," he continued, "will be to see just how the record-holding Georgian can stand up after a long absence from the tournament ranks—how the four-year vacation will affect his game under such heavy fire."

At the time of the tournament, some people speculated that Jones had decided to play in order to boost his own earning power and that the tournament, in the words of Alan Gould, of the Associated Press, had been partly "calculated to aid some of the eminent Georgian's business enterprises," by putting him back in the public eye. That seems unlikely. Jones was keenly interested in his various business dealings, and both he and Spalding stood to gain from the fact that he would be using his own new line of steel-shafted clubs—the first steel-shafted clubs he had ever used in competition—but in his early correspondence with Roberts he sounds genuinely ambivalent about the whole event. He

quickly came to love the tournament, and his initial reluctance to participate soon disappeared. But his early letters convey no sense that he
pushed the idea forward in order to advance himself or anyone else.

The Masters today gives the impression of having existed forever, but in
fact it is the youngest of the four majors. The British Open is seventy
four-years older, the U.S. Open is thirty-nine years older, and the P.G.A.
is eighteen years older. Exactly when the Masters became a major tournament, as opposed to when it was first held, is a matter of debate.
Some commentators—among them, the correspondent from *Time*—
moved it immediately to that select list. Some have identified Gene
Sarazen's victory the following year as the pivotal event. Others have
claimed that the critical tournament was the last Masters before the
wartime hiatus, in 1942, when Byron Nelson beat Ben Hogan by a stroke
in an eighteen-hole playoff that is still celebrated as epochal. By 1947,
Leonard Crawley, the golf correspondent of the *London Daily Telegraph*,
believed that there were two American majors, the Open and the Masters. Herbert Warren Wind felt that the Masters became a major seven
years later, in 1954, when Hogan lost a second monumental playoff, also
by a stroke, this time to Sam Snead.

The youngest major tournament is also the oldest modern one.
Many key features of professional golf tournaments were introduced in
Augusta. Regular tour events in those days were far less well run than
even a modern country club's annual member-guest tournament, and
against that background the Masters set a hugely influential example.
"Once a spectator had left the clubhouse area and made his way onto
the amphitheatrical course below," Herbert Warren Wind wrote in
1978, "he could stay out watching the golf the whole day. All his needs
had been anticipated: There were many refreshment stands (where the
prices were kept reasonable), and excellent picnicking grounds were
provided, as were lavatories. The Masters was the first golf tournament
at which there was room for ten thousand autos to be parked on the
club grounds. It was the first tournament that spared spectators from
having to lug a bulky program around; daily pairing sheets with a dia-

gram of the course on the reverse side were supplied gratis." The Masters was the first seventy-two-hole tournament to be scheduled for four days. It was the first tournament played on terrain that was routinely reshaped to provide better sight lines for spectators. It was the first golf tournament to be covered live on nationwide radio. It was the first to use bleachers—which Roberts preferred to call "observation stands." It was the first to systematically rope galleries and to allow only players, caddies, and officials inside the ropes. It was the first sporting event to employ private detectives to handle ticket sales, security, and other chores (and in doing so it invented what today remains an important business for Pinkerton's, Inc.). It developed the first on-course scoreboard network, in which scores were gathered over dedicated telephone lines as they occurred. It introduced the now universal over-and-under scoring system, in which the standing of the players is represented not by cumulative totals but by the number of strokes above or below par. Although it was not the first golf tournament to be televised, it has had a larger impact than any other single event on the form, content, and technology of modern golf broadcasts. In innumerable small and large ways, it has helped to establish the high standards and restrained atmosphere that continue to distinguish competitive golf.

For all of that, the great tournament began very modestly. Because the club had several members "who do not wish to be deprived of an opportunity to use the course during four days of the best portion of the winter season," Roberts wrote in his announcement to the P.G.A., the field would be kept small enough so that no competitive rounds would have to be scheduled for the mornings, when tee times would be reserved for members. Actually, there was never much danger of the field becoming too large. Roberts, Jones, and Rice planned for an event of modest size in part because they weren't sure how many of their invitations would be accepted. The club, furthermore, didn't have facilities for a large number of players. The clubhouse was still a mess, and other conveniences were minimal. To ensure that spectators would have enough places to sit, Roberts borrowed sixty-six chairs from two local funeral homes.

The idea of leaving the course open for members during the mornings was later dropped, possibly because of Rice. He pointed out that the fans would have nothing to do until after lunch, at which point most of them would try to follow Jones, thereby causing bottlenecks on the course. The solution, Rice said, was to send the golfers out in two waves, one in the morning and the other in the early afternoon. Jones would play in the first wave, and the fans who followed him would be able to follow someone else when he had finished. This was done. On Saturday, for example, the featured pairing was Jones and Walter Hagen, who teed off at 10:42. (A starting time was left empty before and after, to accommodate the crowds). Scheduled to begin roughly three hours later—the period of time in which two players were expected to comfortably finish eighteen holes in those days—were Leo Diegel and MacDonald Smith, Henry Picard and Al Watrous, Paul Runyan and Willie MacFarlane, and several other celebrity pairings, which could be expected to pick up Jones's fans as soon as he had dropped them off.

Seventy-two-hole tournaments at the time of the first Masters were invariably scheduled for three days, with a thirty-six-hole final on Saturday—an accommodation to the nation's blue laws. It was Jones who thought of expanding the schedule. "My idea in stringing out the medal play over four days," he wrote in a letter to Roberts not long before the tournament, "was to give time for special events to be sandwiched in between." These events included an optional alternate-shot match, an approach-and-putt contest (to be held on the practice putting green), an iron contest (to be held in the old practice area, which can still be seen between the ninth and eighteenth fairways), and a driving contest.

Roberts liked the four-round idea, in part because it eliminated what he believed to be a disadvantage for players who were "unable to do their best scoring if forced to play thirty-six holes in one day." He also liked the fact that the schedule would enable the club to sell four days' worth of tournament round tickets instead of just three. (Tournament round tickets sold for $2.20, including tax; practice round tickets were $1.10; series tickets, good for all week, were $5.50.) Roberts had initially wanted the driving contest and other special events to be scheduled alongside the practice rounds—on Sunday, Monday, Tuesday, and Wednesday—partly because he hoped they would increase practice round ticket sales, and partly because he thought a long schedule of activities might make the tournament seem more substantial to local hoteliers and merchants, whose support would be needed both that year and in the future.*

Jones didn't like that idea at all. He told Roberts in a letter that too few players would be on hand early in the week to make the special events worthwhile, and he expressed a fear that the tournament was being over-sold to the public. He must have been unsettled by the fact that the event, which was still nearly three months away, was being treated in the press—thanks in part to the efforts of his good friends Rice and Keeler (whom the club was paying for his promotional efforts, in golf privileges, accommodations, and cash)—as the Second Coming of Bobby Jones. He didn't want spectators' expectations to be raised beyond the point where he and the club would have a realistic chance of meeting them. It was in the same spirit that he objected strenuously to Roberts's suggestion that the tournament be called the Masters, a name that Jones felt was immod-est. Because of Jones's misgivings, the event for five years was officially called the Augusta National Invitation Tournament, although Roberts's preferred title was no secret and was picked up from the beginning by the press, the players, and the public. In 1938, Jones himself gave in; the name Masters became official for the tournament in 1939.

---

* Roberts loved the special events, and he helped to create many of them. One year, he arranged an exhibition for local children, who were given free practice round tickets; he scheduled the exhibition late in the afternoon so that it would not conflict with school. Another year, he devised a competition in which the pros took turns trying to repeat Sarazen's double-eagle shot from the fifteenth fairway. (None succeeded.) For the 1942 Masters, he wanted to hold a complex "ringer score contest" in which the seven tournament champions would com-pete against the rest of the field during the four practice rounds. The contest was never held, but not for lack of support from the chairman. (Among other things, he wrote, the competition would "give the newspaper boys something to write about" during the first half of the week.) According to one spectator from that era, "The contests were fun, because the pros were always so relaxed and having such a good time."

An additional source of revenue during the first tournament was an attractively printed program, which also served as an unofficial prospectus for potential members. The program was forty-four pages long and contained a map of the course, descriptions of the holes (written by MacKenzie), photographs of the clubhouse and other points of interest, historical information about the property, photographs of most of the members of the club, and several dozen advertisements. It sold for twenty-five cents. Overrepresented among the advertisers were the club's numerous creditors, who had been offered space in lieu of payment.

The Masters has always been a tournament to which players are invited. For the first tournament, the decision to send invitations may have been influenced by a fear that too few distinguished players would sign up if they weren't asked directly. (The tournament was also unusual at that time in that it neither charged an entry fee nor required competitors to qualify—further inducements to play.) In order to build a solid field, Roberts and the other officers of the club tried to contact every player directly "and to look after his individual comfort."

Invitations to active players are seldom declined nowadays, but that was not true in the beginning. Willie Klein, who was the professional at La Gorce Golf Club in Miami Beach, wrote two weeks before the first tournament to say that "it will be impossible for me to get away to play in the Masters Open"—a name that he had picked up not from the invitation but from the newspapers. (In 1950, Roberto de Vicenzo, through his manager, accepted his invitation to compete in "the Annual Teacher's Competition"—a mistaken retranslation from a Spanish version of his invitation.) Klein explained that his club was having "a fairly good season" and he therefore couldn't get away. Other pros had similar problems. Olin Dutra, who had won the P.G.A. in 1932 and would win the U.S. Open at Merion later in 1934, declined because he couldn't take time off from his job at Brentwood Country Club in Los Angeles. "My duties at my home club compel me to remain at home," he wrote, in a formal style of his own creation, "and you may rest assured that I must and do rescind your kindly invitation with reluctance. My very best wishes go forth at this time for the success of your tournament. Kindly extend my personal regards to Bob Jones Jr. at your convenience." Dutra's brother, Mortie, did play; he tied for eleventh and won a hundred dollars.

Gene Sarazen wrote in February that he was "very glad to accept" the invitation, but he backed out shortly before the tournament in order to embark on a series of foreign exhibitions with Joe Kirkwood, an Australian professional, who had also been invited. Sarazen and Kirkwood worked during the winter for the Miami Biltmore Hotel. Kirkwood had once proposed to Sarazen that they travel abroad together, and Sarazen had suggested South America. Kirkwood scheduled their departure for a week before the Augusta National Invitation, and their plans could not be changed. Sarazen deeply regretted missing Jones's tournament. (He says a caddie in Fiji told him, "We no hear of Mister Sarazen in Fiji, but we hear of Mister Jones.") He made certain that he would be available for the second Masters.

In recent years, Sarazen has often said that he skipped the first Masters because the invitation came not from Jones but from Clifford Roberts, whom he had never heard of, "and what the hell do I want to play in a tournament sponsored by a Wall Street broker?"—as he said in a telephone interview in 1997. He has also said that he threw out the first invitation because it had a Wall Street return address and he figured it must be some sort of financial promotion. Those are funny stories, but they aren't true. The invitations in both 1934 and 1935 came from Alfred Bourne, who was the club's vice president. On both occasions, Sarazen wrote very nice acceptance letters to Bourne. He withdrew in 1934 only after finding that Kirkwood had already made their South American travel plans and that their departure was going to conflict with the tournament.

Jones arrived in Augusta nine days before the tournament in order to get his game into shape. In his first practice round—which he played with Roberts and two other members—he shot 71. (During an earlier visit, he had shot 65.) The *Augusta Chronicle* reported that his score would have been lower except for "excessive grass" on the greens. "This condition," the *Chronicle* explained, "resulted from [the] decision of the keeper to mow it gradually so as to have the greens in perfect shape for the tournament." Jones's score may also have been affected by the absence of Calamity Jane, his legendary putter, which he had donated to the Royal and Ancient Golf Club in St. Andrews. (After two rounds in the tournament, he sent home for an old putter of his mother's, and putted better with that.)

Despite pronounced putting problems, Jones remained at or near the top of almost everyone's list of favorites—until Thursday afternoon. "So there you are," Keeler wrote in the *Atlanta Journal*, "and there was Bobby Jones, playing the first round with Paul Runyan before a simply magnificent gallery, and working steadily and hard, and bearing down at all times, and employing all the craft gained in fifteen years of major league campaigning—and betrayed by his putting and flaccid work about the greens into a 76 which ordinarily should have been a round in par or better." He followed his 76 with 74, leaving himself eight strokes behind Horton Smith, the eventual winner. He finished with two rounds of even par and ended up in a respectable tie for thirteenth (along with Hagen and Denny Shute, who had won the British Open the year before).*

Jones had never been a factor, and by the end of the tournament he was reasonably sure that he would never contend in a tournament again. But perhaps he was pleasantly surprised to discover that his fans didn't seem to mind, and that his gallery on the last day was larger than his gallery on the first. He had been embarrassed initially by the state of his short game, but by the time he finished on Sunday he was already looking forward to playing again the following year. Twenty-five years later, he was able to write, "Even though some of my playing experiences in the tournament have not been altogether rewarding, at this

---

* The first cut at the Masters was imposed in 1957, after thirty-six holes. Ben Hogan, Gene Littler, and Moe Norman were among nine players who missed it by a stroke.

point I have no hesitancy in saying that the Masters Tournament has provided one of the most truly wonderful aspects of my life with the associations and excitement it has brought and with the satisfaction we have felt in the development of the tournament and the golf course."

Up until his death two and a half months before the tournament, Alister MacKenzie had been hoping to be on hand in Augusta. He had told Roberts that if he could somehow come up with round-trip train fare he would be happy to camp out in the clubhouse—truly roughing it, given the condition of the building at that time. After he died, his widow, Hilda, wrote to Roberts to wish him luck with the tournament, concluding, "I know you will all wish Alister were there."

A couple of weeks after the tournament, Roberts wrote to Hilda with a report. "The Tournament was really a great success," he wrote, "despite cold weather and despite Bob's bad putting. We have definitely decided to hold this tournament as a regular annual event, provided, of course that we are able to hold this club together. I might mention in this regard that we were able to secure some eighteen or twenty new members and that we were likewise able to show a small net profit from the tournament. All in all, the Club now has a better chance of being a success." He added that he hoped to be able to send her some money soon.

Roberts's cheerful description of the tournament's financial results did not quite jibe with the actual accounting. The club had sold $8,011 worth of tickets. That was an excellent showing by the standards of the day—attendance had been comparable to that of the most recent U.S. Open—but the sum did not cover all the costs. One of Roberts's innovations (suggested by Jay R. Monroe, a member from New Jersey, who had served as the tournament's "advisory chairman") had been to use paid workers instead of volunteers for most tournament chores—a practice that the club continues to this day.* Doing so gave Roberts and Monroe better control over their workforce but added to the expense. The

---

* In 1998, the Masters Tournament employed more than two thousand paid workers and approximately one thousand volunteers.

course, the clubhouse, and the grounds had required numerous expenditures (among them, $90 for two new bunkers, $50 for a pond, $115 for grass seed for the greens, and more than $500 for fertilizer and fungicide), and the club had had to make an initial investment in scoreboards, signs, manila rope, trash barrels, furniture, rest rooms, and other infrastructure. Through a formal loan set up at Citizens & Southern National Bank, the club had borrowed $1,500 from six members in order to buy rye grass seed for the fairways. The city of Augusta, at the request of Mayor Barrett, had appropriated $10,000 to help defray expenses, but the tournament still finished in the red. (Roberts spent the bulk of the city's appropriation on the course; the city made appropriations of $7,500 in each of the following two years but held back a third of the money to cover the club's unpaid water bills.) The tournament in those days paid just the top twelve finishers—first prize was $1,500, and twelfth was $100—but even with that small purse Roberts had to pass the hat among the membership before he could hand out any of the prizes. Most important of all, Roberts believed that any unspent revenues from the tournament should be reinvested in the course or in new amenities for spectators and players.

The tournament's real contribution to the club's financial health came not from ticket sales but from memberships. The "eighteen or twenty new members" whom Roberts had mentioned produced more than $6,000 in new initiation fees along with a twenty-five percent increase in annual income from dues. With that infusion of cash, Roberts was able to send a year's interest to the club's creditors, pay down five percent of the mortgage balance, and set aside a fund to cover the club's pared-down operating costs for one more year.

Despite the marginal financial results, Roberts was now convinced that the Masters held the key to the club's success or failure. Jones's tournament had given both the club and the course an allure that Jones's name alone had not. The Depression was now more than four years old and surely couldn't continue much longer. For the first time in a long time, Roberts began to feel reasonably optimistic about the future.

It was a feeling that would not last.

In 1976, while discussing the early years of Augusta National, Roberts said that Gene Sarazen's double-eagle in the second tournament had "put the Masters in business." Sarazen in 1935 was considered by most to be the best golfer in the world, and his miraculous victory over Craig Wood gave the club a huge wave of publicity at a time when things looked very dark for both it and the tournament. (Among the spectators at the tournament in 1935 was Hootie Johnson, who today is the chairman of the club. He was accompanied by his mother, who had decided to go, he says, "as a novelty." He was four years old.) But the effect of Sarazen's victory, while real, was less immediately dramatic than Roberts suggested forty-one years later. Ticket sales had been down in 1935, and they were down again in 1936. What really put the Masters in business was the resurgent economy and sudden interest in golf that followed the end of the Second World War. Sarazen's contribution was to help keep the tournament and the club from collapsing before good times returned.

A telling measure of the fragility of the Masters during those years is the steadily decreasing size of the field. Seventy-two players competed in 1934, sixty-five in 1935, fifty-two in 1936, forty-six in 1937, forty-two in 1938, and forty-six in 1939 (the year the tournament was first officially called the Masters). The pool of players receiving invitations was not shrinking in those years; in fact, it was growing substantially. In both 1936 and 1938, the club made significant additions to the list of automatic qualifications—adding, among others, the first thirty finishers from the U.S. Open, the top two players from the P.G.A.'s winter circuit, and the finalists, semifinalists, and quarterfinalists from the most recent P.G.A. Championship. But the acceptance rate dwindled steadily, and by the end of the decade the tournament was just two-thirds its original size.

The decline in the field partly reflected golf's tenuousness as a profession during the years following the Crash, and partly reflected challenges that were unique to the club. Only a very few players in those days won enough money on tour to cover even their travel expenses.

The purse for the Masters didn't increase until 1946, the first year after the war, and cash prizes continued to be awarded only through twelfth place. For more than a few golfers who might otherwise have entered, a trip to Augusta was a costly luxury that offered little prospect of a pay-off at the end. Once the excitement of Jones's return had faded, fewer players chose to bear the expense of accepting an invitation, and the club had to confront many of the same grim considerations that had led the U.S.G.A. not to hold the Open at Augusta in 1934. Despite the appeal of Jones and Sarazen, the Masters was still a small tournament at a small club in an out-of-the-way city at an inconvenient time of the year.

The expense of conducting the tournament, though relatively modest in dollar terms, exacerbated Augusta National's general financial difficulties, and at the end of 1935 the club, under pressure from its bankers, took a drastic step. For some time, several of the people who had helped to initiate and finance the project had been telling Roberts that the club should declare bankruptcy. As Roberts wrote in a letter in 1934, "Colonel Jones and others were advocating that we turn the property over to the first mortgage bond holders, and then reorganize by giving all our members a new share of stock in a new Company." That sentence is in the past tense because it was written shortly after the first tournament, and at that time Roberts believed that the danger had passed. But a little over eighteen months later, the club did exactly what the Colonel had recommended. In a letter to the club's "underwriters and creditors" late in 1935, the club's attorney explained that "the holders of the bonds of the Fruitland Manor Corporation, through the Georgia Railroad Bank & Trust Company, as Trustee for the Bondholders, exercised their right of foreclosure and brought the entire property of the Fruitland Manor Corporation to sale under the powers contained in the trust mortgage." The bank for some time had been pressuring the club, which was more than a year delinquent in making interest payments. After the foreclosure, the bondholders bought all the assets of both the old club and the land company, and reconstituted themselves as Augusta National, Inc.* The purpose of this maneuver was to preserve

---

* Curt Sampson, in *The Masters,* wrote that "Cliff and the others may have realized they'd blundered royally by failing to incorporate from the start. Under the

the investment of the bank—which held the $60,000 first mortgage—by protecting the club from roughly $25,000 in construction-related debts (among them, the unpaid balance of the charges by Olmsted Bros.) and from the vastly larger unmet obligation represented by the original underwriting. The bank's only chance of being repaid was to keep the club in operation until better times returned.

As Roberts planned for the third Masters, the club's financial condition must have increased his conviction that the tournament was essential. What other hope was there? The tournament had given the club a national reputation, and it was the only significant variable in the equation. Many years later, Roberts said that the hospitality for which the Masters is legendary had been the product of necessity. To sell enough tickets to cover costs, the club had to pamper spectators. The price had to be low, the food had to be good, the views had to be unobstructed, the course had to be perfect, the bathrooms had to be clean. Roberts built the Masters in the same way successful entrepreneurs have always built businesses: by focusing on the needs of his customers.

In his quest for improvement, Roberts accepted suggestions from every quarter, and he did so with an enthusiasm that belies his reputation as an autocrat. Many of the tournament's amenities were suggested by outsiders, whose letters Roberts not only welcomed but often answered in detail. In 1956, for example, a spectator wrote to complain that the club's on-course scoreboards—a Masters innovation—were impossible to read while attendants were updating the scores; why not use the type found in ballparks, on which scores were adjusted from behind? Roberts liked the idea and immediately replaced all the existing scoreboards. The following year, he explained his thoughts about innovation in a lengthy letter to a spectator who had written to protest the tourna-

---

loose partnership used to found and build the club, Roberts, Jones and the rest could each have been sued for debts or for hospital bills and lost income from a mule kick or a shovel accident. The beauty of a corporation, of course, is that none of its owners bears any personal liability." This passage, like many others in Sampson's book, is unrelated to the facts. The old club (along with the new club and the old Fruitland Manor Corporation) had been not "a loose partnership" but a legally chartered corporation.

ment's imposition of a cut. "Any time our studies indicate that the present policies can be improved, we will be quick to act," he wrote. "And
please believe me when I say that letters such as the one you wrote are
very helpful. Many of the changes adopted in the past were suggested
by our loyal and keenly interested patrons." Roberts always referred to
spectators as patrons, a term that perfectly expressed his conception of
the relationship between ticket buyers and the tournament they financed. Few recommendations from patrons or others were automatically dismissed as outlandish. For more than a year, Roberts considered
the possibility of assigning to each twosome a scorekeeper who would
wear a large hat that would serve as "a device which would show
scores." In 1961, an executive of a fire hydrant manufacturing company
in Birmingham, Alabama, suggested that the television broadcast of the
tournament be shown on closed-circuit TV sets situated on the course
itself, to make it easier for spectators to follow the action of the more
popular players—an idea that Roberts liked and implemented, although
the images on the screens were hard to see outdoors. In 1970, Roberts
received a letter suggesting that the tournament's runner-up be
awarded a green vest, and another suggesting that all competitors be required to wear "a green knitted shirt, stockings, and knickers." Roberts
responded with gracious letters in which he politely deflected both
ideas.

Roberts's obsession with detail helped to create an extraordinarily
agreeable experience for the small group of people who in those years
encountered the tournament at first hand, whether as spectators, competitors, or correspondents. The sportswriter Herbert Warren Wind
didn't attend his first Masters until 1947—when the tournament had
grown far beyond what it had been before the war—but the scene he
later recalled evokes the earlier period as well. "It was the prettiest
course I had ever seen," he wrote in *The New Yorker* in 1984. "In those
days, its Bermuda-grass fairways were overseeded with an Italian rye
grass that gleamed a lovely shade of green in the sun. . . . There
couldn't have been more than two thousand people on the course on
Thursday and Friday. On Sunday, five thousand at the most were on
hand for the final round. It was a treat to be there. . . . [T]he players

The first hole today.

The first green as it appeared during the early years, in a photograph from a commemorative yearbook that the club published shortly before the second tournament, in 1935. The bunker on the left was later removed, and a greenside bunker was added.

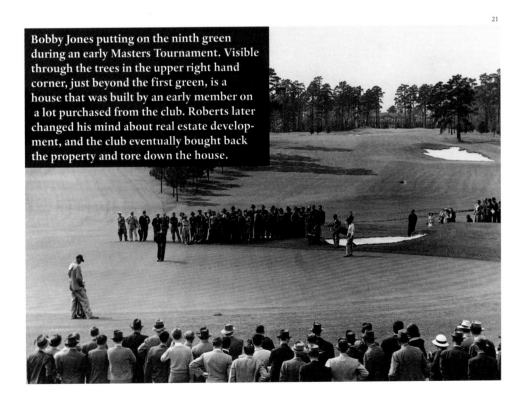

Bobby Jones putting on the ninth green during an early Masters Tournament. Visible through the trees in the upper right hand corner, just beyond the first green, is a house that was built by an early member on a lot purchased from the club. Roberts later changed his mind about real estate development, and the club eventually bought back the property and tore down the house.

The second green in 1935, when it had just one bunker.

The second hole today, viewed from just past the fairway bunker on the right side. The seventh green, surrounded by bunkers, can be seen just beyond and to the right of the second green.

The second green in 1948.

The third hole viewed from behind the tee, looking toward the green.

The third green in 1935. This green has been changed less than any other green on the golf course. MacKenzie felt that the hole was close to perfect.

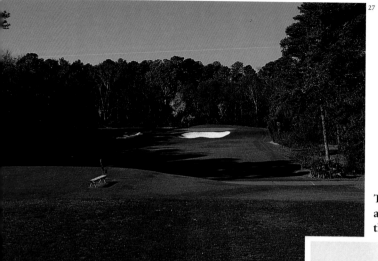

The fourth hole today
and in 1935. Note how
the trees have grown.

The fifth hole today. MacKenzie felt that the
fifth was descended in spirit from the seventeenth at the Old Course—the immortal
Road Hole. Jones initially disapproved of the
fairway bunkers on the left, and they
weren't added until well after the course had
opened for play.

The fifth green in 1935.

31

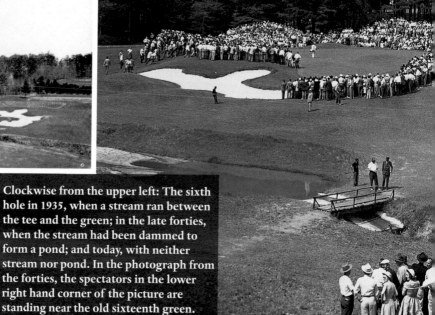

Clockwise from the upper left: The sixth hole in 1935, when a stream ran between the tee and the green; in the late forties, when the stream had been dammed to form a pond; and today, with neither stream nor pond. In the photograph from the forties, the spectators in the lower right hand corner of the picture are standing near the old sixteenth green.

32

33

The seventh green in a sketch from the 1934 program (when it was the sixteenth green) and today. The green was rebuilt and the bunkers were added in 1938, at the suggestion of Horton Smith. The change —which cost $2,500—was paid for by Lewis B. Maytag, a member.

The seventh hole, shot from just beyond the tee, in 1948 and today. The hole was slightly longer and the fairway was considerably less narrow in the forties.

The eighth hole today, looking back toward the tee, in a photograph taken from a helicopter.

The eighth green in 1935. A longtime member estimates that the restored mounds today are "about ninety-five percent the same" as they were originally.

The eighth green in 1956, shortly after the greenside mounds had been removed in order to improve sight lines for spectators. Removing the mounds came close to ruining the hole, in the opinion of Jones and many others; the mounds were restored in 1979 under the supervision of Byron Nelson.

41

The ninth hole today, viewed from the fairway. The flat landing area Roberts asked the original contractor to create for himself and other short-hitting members—still referred to as the Roberts Plateau—is visible in the foreground of this picture.

The ninth green in 1935. The "false front" for which the green has always been famous (on the right side of the putting surface) was even more pronounced than it is now.

42

The ninth hole during the 1949 Masters, showing a greenside bunker that was later removed. The tall grass in the foreground is several times the height of any rough on the course today.

43

were courteous and approachable. The spectators knew their golf. The pimiento sandwiches at the refreshment stands were fresh and exotic. The clubhouse, an elegant ante-bellum manor house wrapped in wisteria, overlooked the course, and let you know you were in the Deep South as explicitly as did the mockingbirds' song and the abundant flora."

People sometimes laughed in later years when Roberts worried that slow play might drive away his beloved patrons, or that lifting a regional television blackout might hurt ticket sales, or that the sudden appearance on camera of a crumpled paper cup might lead a television viewer to conclude that golf was a game unworthy of respect. But his anxieties were honestly earned, and his perfectionism was deeply rooted in his character. Virtually all the major events of his life—the traumatic moves, the debts, the fire, the suicide of his mother, the Crash—had taught him that success is ephemeral, that happiness and security can evaporate at any moment, and that good things happen only through unremitting effort and imperviousness to repeated failure. The Depression hit him hard, but for him it was nothing new: It was just the most recent confirmation of his lifelong experience of the way the world worked. At the time of the first Masters, he was forty years old and had never known an extended period of certainty, stability, or prosperity. His youth had been punctuated by dislocation and tragedy. His education had been sacrificed to the needs of his family. His career in business had stalled, soared, and stalled again. He had gotten the club under way only to see it continually threatened by dissolution. It should not seem surprising that he now managed the tournament with the same focused sense of purpose that had carried him through the first four difficult decades of his life.

CHAPTER FIVE

"The World's Wonder Inland Golf Course"

IF THE MASTERS seems older than it is, that's largely because the tournament, alone among the majors, is conducted year after year on the same course. Every important shot is played against a backdrop that consists of every other important shot, all the way back to 1934. Every key drive, approach, chip, and putt is footnoted and cross-referenced across decades of championship play. Every swing—good or bad—has a context.

The history of the tournament is so vivid in the minds of the competitors and spectators that it almost has a physical reality on the course. The four-wood shot that Gene Sarazen holed in the second Masters is as much a part of the fifteenth hole as the pond in front of the green. Players standing by their drives can't help but think about Sarazen's two as they plan their second shots, whether they go for the green or not—and the same is true for ticket holders and television viewers. The double-eagle is more than just a notable moment in Masters history; it is woven into the fabric of the course.

At the eleventh, no player aims at the flag without recalling that Ben Hogan once said, "If you ever see me on the eleventh green in two, you'll know I missed my second shot." At the twelfth, no player watches a tee shot roll down the bank in front of the green and into Rae's Creek without remembering the final round in 1992, when Fred Couples's tee shot rolled down the bank in front of the green—and stopped. When the hole is cut on the back right of the sixteenth green, no player lines up a long putt from below without thinking of Seve Ballesteros's four-putt in 1988. (Ballesteros, when asked what had happened, explained: "I miss. I miss. I miss. I make.")

When Tiger Woods turned a nine-stroke lead into a twelve-stroke victory on the final day of the Masters in 1997, he conquered not only Jack Nicklaus's thirty-two-year-old scoring record but also his own knowledge that in 1996 Greg Norman had turned a six-stroke lead into a five-stroke loss over the same eighteen holes. For Woods, Nicklaus's triumph and Norman's collapse were both parts of the terrain. And now, for every other player who ever competes in the tournament, Woods's record finish will be, too.

The original design work at Augusta National was done primarily by MacKenzie, who more than once referred to his creation as the "World's Wonder Inland Golf Course." He conceived the routing, positioned the bunkers, and blocked out the greens. Jones is sometimes given equal billing, or even first billing, but his role was more nearly that of a junior associate. (As Jones himself wrote, "No man learns to design a golf course simply by playing golf, no matter how well.") Still, the two men had similar ideas about golf course architecture, and Jones's contributions were significant.

Roberts was apt to emphasize Jones's role in the early days, because he knew that in the minds of most people at that time Augusta National was Jones's course, not MacKenzie's. In October 1931, before construction began, MacKenzie wrote a lengthy description of the holes, and Roberts asked him to supplement it with "two or three paragraphs detailing the fact that Bob collaborated with you on all phases of the plans and due to the fact that Bob had studied civil engineering, and due also to the fact that he is of a studious nature and studies carefully each course that he plays on, he was of very genuine and very practical help to you. You might also add that he contributed several ideas that were distinctly original." Roberts may genuinely have felt that MacKenzie hadn't given Jones sufficient credit, but his first concern was probably that Jones's name be firmly attached to any piece of publicity the club might generate. At any rate, MacKenzie happily—and effusively—complied, writing that Jones had made "most valuable suggestions in regard to almost every hole and I am convinced that from no one else in America or elsewhere could I have obtained such valuable help and collaboration."

Roberts's contributions to the original design were minimal, but he nonetheless played a real role in the creation of the course. In his critiques of MacKenzie's plans, which were sometimes lengthy, he was observant and exacting. He noticed, for example, that a promised bunker on what is now the tenth hole had been left out of a subsequent drawing, and that particular clumps of trees did not appear to be accurately positioned. MacKenzie responded to such comments with varying degrees of good humor and alarm. One result of Roberts's insistence on detailed explanations was that MacKenzie spelled out much more of his design philosophy than he might have if his employer had been more compliant. Regarding a plan for the short, treacherous par-three that was then the third and is now the twelfth, for example, Roberts had questioned whether the green had been drawn to scale, since it appeared to him to be disproportionately shallow and wide. MacKenzie, in his response, explained that the unconventional dimensions were the key to the hole's design—as has been borne out in every Masters ever held. MacKenzie's exchanges of letters with Roberts, along with Roberts's correspondence and conversations with Jones, provided Roberts with an education in golf course architecture. He took those lessons to heart, and, as the years went by, he became an able guardian of the ideas of the two men who had first conceived the course.

The most important idea behind the Augusta National design—and one to which MacKenzie, Jones, and Roberts agreed from the beginning—was that the course should be demanding for the expert player yet not intimidating to the average golfer. It was to be, in MacKenzie's words, "a course pleasurable to all." Jones, in a 1931 interview with O. B. Keeler, said, "We are in perfect agreement that a good golf course can be designed and constructed which will be an exacting test for the best competition, and at the same time afford a pleasant and reasonably

simple problem for the average player and the duffer. . . . Dr. MacKenzie
and I believe that no good golf hole exists that does not afford a proper
and convenient solution to the average golfer and the short player, as
well as to the more powerful and accurate expert." Jones addressed the
same idea in his book *Golf Is My Game*: "We want to make bogies easy if
frankly sought, pars readily obtainable by standard good play, and
birdies, except on par 5's, dearly bought."

Jones once said that one of the great strengths of Augusta National
was that while pros there were always in danger of succumbing to disaster, average members and their guests might well shoot some of their
best rounds ever—that an inveterate 90 shooter, for example, might have
a good day and shoot 85. That is still true—even, surprisingly, when the
course is in tournament condition. (Members and their guests are allowed to play through the Sunday before the tournament, and their
scores at that time seldom differ very much from their scores during the
rest of the playing season.) The reason for the seeming paradox is that
the kind of trouble which tends to defeat an average player is less severely penalized at Augusta National than it is on other demanding
courses: the fairways are generous, the trees are widely spaced, the
bunkers are few, out-of-bounds is seldom a danger, and the short rough
is (for an average player) as likely to be a comfort as a catastrophe, since
it can cause a ball to sit up a little higher than it would on a closely
mown fairway.* The greens are difficult, of course—but all greens are
difficult for an average player. For a twenty-handicapper, three-putting is
close to the norm on any course, and the particular perils of Augusta's
greens are offset by the reduced likelihood of losing a ball off the tee or
hitting into an unplayable lie.

---

* Average players sometimes have more trouble with Augusta's fairways than
with its greens. During the Masters, the fairways are cut to just 0.39 inch, and
they are kept at close to that height all spring. For a golfer who occasionally
makes less than perfect contact with the ball, such naked lies can lead to a discouraging number of fat shots. For the pros, Augusta's short rough is more of a
peril than it may appear, since it usually prevents players from generating enough
backspin to hold the firm, undulating greens.

MacKenzie's and Jones's ideas about course design were revolutionary, and they were squarely opposed to the dominant American design
philosophy of the time. That philosophy was perhaps most clearly em-
bodied by Oakmont Country Club, near Pittsburgh, which had been
built in 1903 and 1904 and was (and still is) viewed by many as the ar-
chetypal American championship course. The Oakmont ideal had been
summed up neatly in a single sentence by William Fownes, whose father, Henry C. Fownes, had designed and built the course: "A shot
poorly played should be a shot irrevocably lost." The fairways were narrow, the rough was thick and deep, and every hole offered numerous
unique opportunities for turning moderately wayward shots into disaster. When Tommy Armour won the Open at Oakmont in 1927, his
score for seventy-two holes was 301—a total that has been beaten by
every Open champion on every Open course since then. (Armour won
his title by shooting 76 in an eighteen-hole playoff with Harry Cooper,
who shot 79.)

MacKenzie and Jones both believed that such ruthlessly penal design
made the game unpleasant for ordinary players and obscured the differences between great golfers and merely good ones. If a course's perils
are so severe as to leave no reasonable possibility of escape, the two
men believed, then a skilled player's advantage over a less skilled player
is greatly reduced. One of the most famous shots Jones ever hit was a
blind mashie to the green after driving his ball into sandy scrub to the
left of the fairway on the seventeenth hole at Royal Lytham & St. Annes,
during the British Open in 1926. Had Jones driven instead into one of
Oakmont's bunkers—which in the early years had deep, triangular fur-
rows that were meant to prevent players from advancing their balls—he
would have lost the chance to compensate for a poor drive by playing a
spectacular recovery. MacKenzie and Jones both felt that Oakmont and
other adamantly punitive courses rewarded straight, conservative shooting at the expense of the game's most thrilling elements. A good golf
course, they believed, is one that consistently supplies situations in
which superior players can demonstrate their superiority. (Houdini
thrilled his audiences by escaping, not by being trapped.) On Open
courses today, the best players in the world sometimes feel compelled to

leave the best parts of their games at home: They hit long irons instead
of drivers from many tees, have few opportunities to demonstrate fi-
nesse around the greens, and can resort only to brute strength and good
luck when they stray into the rough.

MacKenzie and Jones's model, once again, was the Old Course at St.
Andrews. In his book *Golf Architecture,* which was published in 1920,
MacKenzie suggested that the one golf hole in the world that came closest to perfection was the Old Course's eleventh—a par-three measuring
just over a hundred and seventy yards. "Under certain conditions," he
wrote, "it is extremely difficult for even the best player that ever
breathed, especially if he is attempting to get a two, but at the same time
an inferior player may get a four if he plays his own game exceptionally
well." MacKenzie said that adding a cross bunker in front of the green—
as had sometimes been suggested—would ruin it, by making the hole
"impossible for the long handicap man" without increasing the challenge for the expert. This same philosophy guided the design of Augusta
National, and it has guided alterations ever since. (It is eerily appropriate
that MacKenzie should have chosen the Old Course's eleventh as his
epitome. On that hole in 1921—one year after *Golf Architecture* was published—Bobby Jones, who was then nineteen years old, took five shots to
reach the green and angrily withdrew from his first British Open. Jones's
mature career is sometimes measured from that burst of temper.)

Another feature of the Old Course that appealed to MacKenzie was
the absence of clearly defined boundaries between many of the holes.
On the Old Course, the area potentially in play for a given shot is often
enormous. Players almost always have distinct options to consider, depending on their level of skill and degree of ambition, and they can usually choose among very different routes to the green. MacKenzie's
original hope was that the divisions between fairways at Augusta would
be similarly vague. The course as constructed did not quite satisfy him
in that regard; while work was still under way, he objected (on the basis
of photographs) that the boundaries defining some of the fairways had
been cut "too straight." But the lines were softened as construction proceeded, and the course has continued to evolve in the same direction. As
a result of increased maintenance budgets and improvements in equip-

ment, even more of the course is now maintained as fairway than was true in the early days. Many greens can be approached—either on purpose or by accident—from reasonable lies in very different parts of the course. The latitude isn't nearly what it is on the Old Course—and never could be, since the two courses occupy entirely different pieces of terrain—but the theme is sustained. Indeed, first-time visitors to Augusta are often struck by the broad expanse of uninterrupted green that extends from the back of the clubhouse very nearly to Rae's Creek, at the far end of the course. The property looks more like a vast park than like a succession of individual holes cut through trees. That is exactly what MacKenzie and Jones had in mind.

Identifying meaningful similarities between the Old Course and Augusta National may seem far-fetched, since on first consideration the two courses seem antithetical. The Old Course is ancient, ragged, treeless, and so irregular as to seem entirely undesigned, while Augusta National is young, manicured, and almost defiantly artificial. Still, the British golf correspondent Leonard Crawley, after playing at Augusta for the first time in 1947, detected a powerful kinship and deduced correctly that MacKenzie and Jones had been deeply influenced by St. Andrews. "They have not copied one single hole on those maddeningly difficult and infinitely fascinating links," Crawley wrote a few weeks after his round, "but they built eighteen great holes, every one of which is perfectly fair and provides a problem. It seems to me that each one demands that a player shall firstly and foremostly use his brains and not merely his physical and, in these days, his almost mechanical ability to hit a target from a particular range. It restores the ideas of some of the old original golf links which furnished the world with those great players upon whose methods and tremendous skill the modern game is now based."

More than sixty years after the first tournament, MacKenzie's and Jones's ideas about golf course design continue to define the Masters in ways that modern golf fans may not fully appreciate. During the closing holes of a U.S. Open, a player can often ride a narrow lead to victory by pursuing a conservative strategy based on avoiding disaster. The same approach has never worked at Augusta, where the final nine holes offer so many birdie and eagle chances that a bold player can make up a wide deficit with brilliant play—or self-destruct with a handful of poorly struck iron shots or miscalculated putts. That possibility has been an integral part of the course from the beginning. "We have always felt that the make-or-break character of many of the holes of our second nine has been largely responsible for rewarding our spectators with so many dramatic finishes," Jones wrote in the early fifties. "It has always been a nine that could be played in the low thirties or the middle forties." The dual nature of those holes increases the pressure on an early leader, who, with an eye over one shoulder, can begin to worry that no number of birdies could possibly be enough. As a result, the Masters seldom turns into a war of attrition; the winner is often the player who is bold enough to gamble at the very moment when human nature is urging him to protect what he already has.

That a course can be extraordinarily demanding while yielding tantalizing opportunities for scoring is an idea that many have found difficult to accept. But it is the essence of Augusta National. In 1998, Greg Norman was quoted in *Sports Illustrated* as saying that the course was approaching obsolescence. ("It's getting close," he warned.) Yet Norman's own performance in the Masters less than two years before had demonstrated the opposite. Over and over during the final round in 1996, which he had entered with a six-stroke lead, he failed to meet the challenge of the course and in doing so turned what had appeared to be an easy victory into the tournament's most devastating defeat. He didn't lose because of the speed of the greens—which sports page pundits often refer to as the course's only remaining "defense." He lost because under the pressure of the final round he mishit or misjudged a succession of crucial iron shots—virtually all of them struck from perfect lies—leading him to play Augusta National's allegedly easy and outdated second nine in four strokes over par. (Two of his poorest shots—his tee shots on twelve and sixteen, both of which he put in the water—were hit under the most benign of circumstances: from tees, with short or medium irons.) Meanwhile, Nick Faldo was brilliantly managing both the course and Norman, who was playing with him, on the way to a virtually flawless 67 and a five-stroke win. It was exactly the sort of epic finish that the course had been designed to provide.

Augusta National is viewed as sacred ground by many golfers, who sometimes assume that the holes have remained inviolate for decades, if not since the beginning of time. But the course is not and never has been a museum. In fact, it has almost certainly undergone more significant changes over the years than any other important golf course in the world. Revenues from the Masters, along with substantial contributions from individual members, have financed a steady stream of alterations, some of them monumental. Almost every summer, greens are regraded or rebuilt, tees are moved, hazards are added or eliminated, new trees are planted in strategic positions, and mounds are reshaped, raised, flattened, moved, created, or carted away. Since the very earliest years of the club, the only thing sacred about the course has been a belief that it must continually be modified and improved. Roberts always viewed the course as a work in progress, and so did Jones.

Changes to the course over the years have had numerous designers. From the beginning, the club has been receptive to—and has steadily solicited—suggestions from players, members, guests, spectators, sportswriters, television viewers, television commentators, distinguished architects, and others. Even as early as the early fifties, Jones could say with accuracy that the course was "truly of national design." He viewed that miscellaneous heritage as one of the course's greatest strengths, and his assessment became still more apt in subsequent years, as increases in tournament revenues expanded the scope of what the club could afford to try.

Two of the most notable early alterations cost no money at all: the ordering of the nines. In MacKenzie's original conception, the holes were numbered as they are today. His thinking changed in 1931, before construction began, and in later drawings the nines were switched, so that the current first hole had become the tenth. Several writers have attributed the change to Jones, but contemporary documents make it clear that the idea was MacKenzie's. (His intention was probably to provide a better view of the finishing green to members who might be lounging near the big picture windows in the locker room of the planned new clubhouse.) The club switched the nines again in 1934, between the first tournament and the second. This time, the reason was that the shady area near the current twelfth green, which lay at the lowest elevation on the property, was the last part of the course to thaw on frosty mornings. By playing the other side first, golfers could tee off earlier. The new arrangement also made for more stirring Masters finishes, a fact that was recognized at the time.

One way to get a sense of the evolution of the course is to consider some of the most significant ways in which each hole has changed over the years. The following account is drawn from club records, old correspondence, and the recollections of older members and players. The original yardages for each hole are taken from the first tournament program and should be viewed as approximations—in some cases, fairly wild ones. (Even at the time, the club had doubts about many of them.) Incidentally, yardages at Augusta National have always been represented in increments of five, because Roberts felt that to suggest a greater degree of precision was ridiculous, especially since the exact tee and hole positions changed from day to day.

First Hole—Par Four

Oʀɪɢɪɴᴀʟ Lᴇɴɢᴛʜ		Cᴜʀʀᴇɴᴛ Lᴇɴɢᴛʜ	
Mᴇᴍʙᴇʀs	Mᴀsᴛᴇʀs	Mᴇᴍʙᴇʀs	Mᴀsᴛᴇʀs
380	400	365	410
Eᴀʀʟɪᴇsᴛ Nᴀᴍᴇ		Cᴜʀʀᴇɴᴛ Nᴀᴍᴇ	
Cʜᴇʀᴏᴋᴇᴇ Rᴏsᴇ		Tᴇᴀ Oʟɪᴠᴇ	

The first hole (which was originally the tenth) is roughly the same length that it was when it was built, but there have been many subtle changes. The tee was moved closer to the golf shop, making the slight dogleg more pronounced, and the fairway bunker was enlarged and moved closer to the green. A second large bunker, which used to sprawl across the left side of the fairway roughly a hundred yards from the green, has been removed. (Augusta National once had several such bunkers; in the thirties, they were sometimes likened to the sandy waste areas at Pine Valley.)

In the early years, a small creek ran across the fairway at the bottom of the hill, less than a hundred yards from the tee. The carry over the ditch was so short that few players even noticed the hazard, but a member named Clarence J. Schoo—who ran a boxboard manufacturing company in Springfield, Massachusetts, and was a close friend of Roberts's—drove into it so often that it came to be known as Schooie's Gulch. After topping yet another drive into the creek one day, Schoo said to Roberts, "I wish you'd fill in that damn ditch." Roberts did fill in the ditch, during the summer of 1951—and sent the bill to Schoo.

(That, at any rate, is how the story is usually told. The real reason for eliminating the ditch was that the club wanted to replace its old press tent with a Quonset hut, on a site to the right of the first fairway, and the ditch was in the way of the planned foundation. The ditch also constituted a maintenance headache that Roberts wanted to do away with. To fill it, he used dirt from the northwest corner of the property, an area that had been leveled to create a parking lot for Masters patrons. Schoo, who later became a vice president of the club, did gladly pay for part of the alteration, but he almost certainly wasn't surprised when he opened his bill.)

Schoo was such a poor golfer that when he one day made a natural birdie, Roberts decreed that he should be paid the same cash pot that was ordinarily given to golfers who made holes-in-one, on the theory that Schooie was never going to come any closer. Another time, while playing the seventh hole in a foursome that also included Roberts and Eisenhower, Schoo hit a dreadful drive that traveled just a few yards, into a clump of pampas grass to the left of the tee. Schoo said, "Well, in all the years I've been playing here, that's the first time I've done that." That summer, the grounds crew cut back the pampas grass and found several balls with his name imprinted on them. On another occasion, Schoo declared with exasperation that he must be the worst golfer in the club. His caddie, who had been around long enough to have heard stories but not long enough to recognize individual members, said, "No, sir. The worst golfer in this club is Mr. Schoo."

Second Hole—Par Five

ORIGINAL LENGTH			CURRENT LENGTH	
MEMBERS	MASTERS		MEMBERS	MASTERS
490	525		500	575
EARLIEST NAME			CURRENT NAME	
WOODBINE			PINK DOGWOOD	

In the earliest years, the second hole had a vast, ragged bunker in the fairway, not far from the tee. A more subdued version of the bunker survived into the mid-sixties, when it was replaced by a smaller bunker farther down the fairway and to the right. "The players all complained when Roberts put it in," Gene Sarazen, who suggested the change, says. "But it didn't mean a thing when you complained to Roberts. He had his own mind made up." Among the players who complained was Ben Hogan, whose fade made the sand a genuine annoyance. According to Sam Snead, "Hogan said the bunker should have been placed on the other side, so you couldn't cut the corner." But the left side of the fairway was already well guarded, as it is today, by a grove of pines and a deep ravine with a creek at the bottom of it—one of the few spots on the course where a player can hit a truly unrecoverable drive. (Gardner Dickinson once suggested that the tournament's airline office—a Roberts innovation that enables players and spectators to make last-minute changes in their travel plans without leaving the property—should be moved into the ravine, on the theory that any player unfortunate enough to drive his ball down there on Thursday or Friday might as well book a flight for Friday night.) During the summer of 1998, the Masters tee was moved back twenty-five yards in order to bring both the bunker and the ravine back into play for long hitters.

Third Hole—Par Four

Original Length		Current Length	
Members	Masters	Members	Masters
335	350	340	350
Earliest Name		Current Name	
Flowering Peach		Flowering Peach	

The third hole has probably undergone fewer changes than any other hole on the course. Its principal feature today, as was true in the beginning, is a treacherously shaped green that sits on a tilted natural plateau. Dropping off from the shallow left end of the green is a deep bunker from which pars can be excruciatingly difficult to save. The green is hard to hit and harder to hold, and approaches to it are complicated by the fact that the putting surface is invisible from the fairway.

In a letter to MacKenzie in 1933, Roberts raised the possibility of adding a deep cross bunker in the face of the plateau directly in front of the green. "It was my understanding," Roberts wrote, "that the deep-face trap located in about the center would make this a definite drive and pitch hole; that is to say, a well struck pitch would be required in order to hold the green and the trap would make it impossible to play a run-up shot." MacKenzie was vehement in vetoing that idea—which Roberts had admitted Jones didn't support—and his response contains so much of his thinking about design that it is worth quoting at length:

I am delighted that Bob agrees that the [third] with the one trap is all right. This confirms my impression that Bob knows more about golf and its sound principles than any man I have ever come across.

My own opinion is that a cross bunker would convert it into an ordinary stereotyped hole and would nullify all the subtleties of the undulations of the approach to which we gave so much time and thought.

Consider the many problems which face a golfer approaching the hole. In the first place he can play safely to the right and rely on a long putt going dead to get his four. If he elects to go straight at the flag he must play a perfect pitch or else his ball would hit the bank and come back or run over the green. On the other hand if he tries to run up from the right his shot must be played perfectly as a half hearted run up shot will inevitably run into the bunker on the left, which appears to me to be absolutely perfect both in regard to its position and its construction.

At this hole the super golfer, like Bob, has a most fascinating problem, as to have a reasonable chance of three he will have to attack the hole from the left, where all the slopes help him towards the hole. It is here that the tee-shot bunker comes in as he must make up his mind to play round it with a pulled shot from right to left or a fade from left to right, or, when a strong wind is in his favour, to play over it.

If the approach to this hole is maintained as hard and as true as the green it will make the most perfect hole of its length in the world of golf and any additional bunker would ruin it.

It is holes of this description that keep up one's interest in golf year after year, stimulate players to improve their game and prevent golf becoming stale.

Jones did not think as highly of the third hole as MacKenzie did; his favorite par-fours almost all required long-iron or fairway-wood approaches, at which he excelled. But MacKenzie's conviction has been borne out over the years. Of all the architects who have worked on the course, none has yet made a persuasive case for a major improvement. (The single original fairway bunker became a cluster of four fairway bunkers in 1983, but the impact on tee shots didn't change.) The third hole remains the shortest par-four on the course—along with the seventh, which measures about the same length, depending on where the markers are placed—yet it was one of the few holes that consistently gave Tiger Woods trouble during his record victory in 1997. (On Friday, he hit a bullet-like drive to within fifteen yards of the green, yet made a bogey.) In fact, the experience of Woods and other long-hitting players suggests that one effective way to "Tiger-proof" a golf hole may be to shorten it.

Fourth Hole—Par Three

ORIGINAL LENGTH	
MEMBERS	MASTERS
175	190
EARLIEST NAME	
PALM	

CURRENT LENGTH	
MEMBERS	MASTERS
170	205
CURRENT NAME	
FLOWERING CRAB APPLE	

One of the club's first member committees was called the beautification committee. It consisted of Alfred Bourne, Henry Crowell, and Louis Alphonse Berckmans, who was one of the three sons of Prosper Berckmans, the late owner of Fruitland Nurseries. (Louis had joined the club, although he was in his seventies and didn't play golf. His younger brother—Prosper Jr., who was known as Allie—served as the club's first general manager.) The committee's first report, which it presented to Jones in 1932, recommended "concentrating in the vicinity of each hole a massed profusion of a distinctive variety of trees or plants that bloom during the winter season." That was probably Berckmans's idea, and it was he who decided which plants should go with which holes. The featured plant on the fourth hole was originally the palm tree; five different varieties, among them three varieties of wild date palm, were planted on the hole. Just one of those trees remains today. (It is situated in front and to the right of the green.) The hole is now named Flowering Crab Apple.

The fourth hole today looks and plays much as it did in the early years, although the greenside bunker on the left is now closer to the putting surface. The biggest change has nothing to do with the hole itself. In the early years, some residential power lines were visible beyond the green. In 1966, Edwin Hatch, who was the chairman of Georgia Power Co., was asked to join the club. In one of his first rounds as a member, Roberts arranged for the two of them to play together. When they reached the fourth tee, Roberts commented that the hole's only flaw was the unsightly power lines, which he said ruined the view. Hatch said nothing, but not long afterward a crew from the power company arrived to lower the wires.

Fifth Hole—Par Four

ORIGINAL LENGTH	
MEMBERS	MASTERS
425	440
EARLIEST NAME	
MAGNOLIA	

CURRENT LENGTH	
MEMBERS	MASTERS
405	435
CURRENT NAME	
MAGNOLIA	

The fifth hole is the centerpiece of what has sometimes been called Augusta National's other Amen Corner. It is seldom seen on television—and when it is, the cameras can't do justice to the dramatic topography of both the fairway and the green—but it is ranked by more than a few players as the second best par-four on the course (after the tenth). MacKenzie felt that the fifth was descended in spirit from the immortal Road Hole, the seventeenth at the Old Course. The main similarity may be in the difficulty of the approach shot, since balls hit short invariably stay short, while balls hit long occasionally disappear for good in the trees and shrubbery beyond the green. The perils of the green make Jack Nicklaus's achievement during the 1996 Masters seem all the more astonishing: he eagled the fifth twice, in consecutive rounds.

The two large, steep bunkers on the left side of the fairway are characteristic MacKenzie hazards. (Equally characteristically, Jones initially felt that they were superfluous, and they were not built until after the course had opened.) They are more of a visual hazard than an actual one, since even in the early years players didn't have much trouble driving over them or playing safely to the right. But they make the hole's wide fairway appear narrow, and they force players to think twice before playing their drives along what is actually the shortest route to the green. (They also often aid less skilled players, by stopping pulled or hooked drives that might otherwise have run down the steep hill and out of play—as Wendell Miller, the contractor, predicted they would in May 1933 while making an unsuccessful attempt to interest Jones in adding the bunkers then.) MacKenzie, throughout his career as an architect, made frequent use of course features that were essentially optical illusions: seemingly narrow fairways that were ampler than they appeared from the tee; seemingly ample fairways on which the ideal landing areas were narrow and precise; large greens that seemed to provide huge targets but were contoured in such a way that reasonably simple putts could be earned only with brilliant approaches—and bunkers that looked threatening from a distance but were easy to carry. He felt that easily avoided fairway bunkers were good for a player's self-confidence and sense of achievement.

The fifth fairway caused problems for many years. Buried stones continually worked their way to the surface, where they were a threat to golf swings and mower blades. Finally, in 1962, the club resurfaced the fairway (and also the seventh) with new topsoil. When the job was complete, Roberts devised a characteristically simple method of testing the results: he asked Johnny Graves, a club employee, to drive a golf cart up and down at full speed and report back on the smoothness of the ride.

Sixth Hole—Par Three

ORIGINAL LENGTH		CURRENT LENGTH	
MEMBERS	MASTERS	MEMBERS	MASTERS
160	185	165	180
EARLIEST NAME		CURRENT NAME	
JUNIPER		JUNIPER	

The same tributary of Rae's Creek that runs in front of the thirteenth green and along the left side of the thirteenth fairway used to run also between the sixth tee and sixth green. The stream ran so far short of the green, though, that it virtually never came into play. In 1955, the club dammed the stream to create a more formidable hazard. But the new pond was still thirty yards from the front of the putting surface, making the water a nearly irrelevant peril even for high-handicap players. (It couldn't even be seen from the tournament tees.) In 1959, the pond was removed and the stream was buried.

Seventh Hole—Par Four

ORIGINAL LENGTH	
MEMBERS	MASTERS
320	340
EARLIEST NAME	
CEDAR	

CURRENT LENGTH	
MEMBERS	MASTERS
320	365
CURRENT NAME	
PAMPAS	

The seventh wasn't much of a hole in the early days. (The consensus, as described by Roberts, was that it was "the only weak hole out of the eighteen.") MacKenzie likened it to the eighteenth at St. Andrews, but the resemblance was superficial. Both holes were short, and both had large greens and no bunkers, but in comparison with the venerable and surprisingly difficult closing hole of the Old Course, the seventh at Augusta was a pushover. More than a few players today would have been able to drive it.

In a letter to MacKenzie in 1933, Roberts wrote, "I think the real criticism . . . is that it lacks character. Ed Dudley [the club's first professional] made a suggestion which appealed very much to me. He proposed putting a bunker in the middle of the face of the green and letting it wedge into the green. In other words, his thought is to partly develop this green into two sections, the same as is true of one of the greens at Lakeside, California. Bob did not have very much to say about this proposal, but I do not think he was much impressed by it. I think, in truth, that Bob is really hesitant about making any alterations or incidental refinements till you can come here and see the layout."

Nothing significant happened until 1938, when Horton Smith—who had won the first and third tournaments—suggested elevating the green and fronting it with several deep bunkers. He also suggested moving the green twenty yards back and to the right. Jones and Roberts both approved. The design work was done by Perry Maxwell, an Oklahoma banker-turned-architect, whose best-known course is probably Tulsa's Southern Hills. Maxwell had been a partner of MacKenzie's during the final years of MacKenzie's life. (Their last joint project, completed in 1933, was Crystal Downs, in Frankfort, Michigan.) The transformation of the seventh green, which cost $2,500, was paid for by Lewis B. Maytag, who was one of the club's earliest members and was the head of the Maytag Company. In addition, the driving area was tightened through the addition of a grove of pine trees on the left side of the fairway. (There were already trees on the right.)

Maxwell made several less dramatic changes in other greens— among them the first and the fourteenth, to which he added pronounced undulations. Such undulations were his trademark and were known as "Maxwell rolls." MacKenzie was no longer alive at that time, but he undoubtedly would have approved: He loved dramatic contours. In *The Spirit of St. Andrews,* he wrote wistfully about the early greens at Machrihanish, a legendary course, designed by Old Tom Morris, on the Kintyre peninsula in western Scotland: "Some of the natural greens were so undulating that at times one had to putt twenty or thirty yards round to lay dead at a hole only five yards away. These greens have all gone and today one loses all the joy of outwitting an opponent by making spectacular putts of this description." For the disappearance of such features, MacKenzie blamed a preoccupation with the elimination of "unfairness"—a word that he also placed in quotation marks.

Eighth Hole—Par Five

ORIGINAL LENGTH		CURRENT LENGTH	
MEMBERS	MASTERS	MEMBERS	MASTERS
475	500	460	550
EARLIEST NAME		CURRENT NAME	
YELLOW JASMINE		YELLOW JASMINE	

When the eighth green was built, it looked very much the way it does today, with tall, steeply contoured mounds on either side. In 1956, though, Roberts had the mounds removed. "That's the only time I can really remember Mr. Jones getting mad at Cliff," Phil Harison, a long-time member, recalls. "But he removed the mounds for a reason. They blocked the view of the spectators at the tournament, and once they were gone the spectators could see a lot better. But Mr. Jones got awfully upset about that. He really did, because without the mounds the hole was much less interesting, and the green didn't look like any other green on the golf course."

Roberts never thought that removing the mounds improved the hole—and, indeed, the new green was dreadful. It was featureless and vaguely hourglass-shaped, and it could be approached without trepidation from almost any angle. But Roberts felt strongly that spectators ought to be able to see. Not long before he died, though, he decided that the sacrifice had been too great and that the mounds should be restored. The change was finally made in 1979, not quite two years after his death. Byron Nelson led the project, along with Joseph S. Finger, an architect who, among other accomplishments, had played golf at Rice University in the thirties on a team that was coached by Jimmy Demaret. In restoring the mounds, Nelson and Finger relied heavily on photographs taken during the thirties and forties. Harison—whose father was Montgomery Harison, the early member who built the house that used to stand just beyond the first green—consulted on the project as well. During the Second World War, when the course was closed, he had often ridden a motorbike over the mounds, and he says that he retained a sort of physical memory of their shape.

Harison has belonged to the club for more than fifty years, although he is only in his early seventies. Jones and Roberts used to ask him to fill out groups in the Jamboree beginning when he was thirteen, and he and a partner won the event in 1941, when he was sixteen. He didn't officially become a member until 1946, when he turned twenty-one, but at that time, he recalls, Jones and Roberts kidded him by saying, "Oh, you've been a member for years." For more than fifty years, Harison has been the official starter of the Masters. It is he who announces each player on the first tee.

Ninth Hole—Par Four

Original Length		Current Length	
Members	Masters	Members	Masters
390	420	380	430
Earliest Name		Current Name	
Carolina Cherry		Carolina Cherry	

Roberts liked to say that he made only one contribution to the original design of the course. During the construction of the ninth hole, he persuaded the contractor to create a level landing area in the steeply tilting fairway at the distance he normally drove the ball. "The engineer was not at all enthusiastic about accommodating me," Roberts wrote in his book about the club, "but finally agreed to bring back a tractor and do the job." Roberts later told friends that he had requested the change because he didn't want any of his matches with Jones to be decided by his luck at hitting a fairway wood to an elevated green from a downhill, sidehill lie. (The current ninth hole was then the eighteenth. Jones customarily either gave Roberts nine strokes or allowed him to begin their matches with a nine-hole edge.*) Of course, Roberts's difficulties with the second shot on the ninth hole were shared by most of the club's other members, who, like him and unlike Jones, weren't long enough off the tee to come close to the ideal driving area, at the bottom of the hill. Incidentally, neither Jones nor MacKenzie was at all disapproving of Roberts's modification: In consultations among the three, Roberts's role was to supply the viewpoint of an average golfer, and Jones and MacKenzie both solicited his views. Roberts's landing area is still visible in the ninth fairway, and it still receives plentiful use from grateful members and their guests.

Tenth Hole—Par Four

ORIGINAL LENGTH		CURRENT LENGTH	
MEMBERS	MASTERS	MEMBERS	MASTERS
410	430	450	485
EARLIEST NAME		CURRENT NAME	
CAMELLIA		CAMELLIA	

It is easy to understand how Augusta National's routing could once have begun at what is now the tenth hole. The view from the tee is one of the most enticing in golf—the sort that can coax a smooth swing from a hurried player who hasn't taken time to loosen up. The drop in elevation to the ideal landing area is more than a hundred feet—enough to make a thinly struck drive seem solidly launched. The fairway runs down and left and out of sight through a bending corridor of pine trees. The slope

---

* Augusta National doesn't use the U.S.G.A.'s handicapping method. It has its own simple system, devised by Roberts, which is based on the number of pars a player ordinarily shoots, with a small adjustment for birdies. (If you make six pars, your handicap is twelve.) The Roberts system works well, is easy to compute, and allows daily modification. The club also uses Roberts's method, rather than the U.S.G.A.'s, for allocating handicap strokes: The sole criterion is yardage.

rewards any player who can work the ball from right to left, yet there is ample room on the right for those who can't. Golfers leave the tee feeling that they are descending into a different world—an appropriate emotion for players entering the most celebrated second nine in golf.

The tenth hole originally measured forty or fifty yards shorter than it does today, and it seemed shorter still, since both shots played downhill. (MacKenzie, in a note in the program for the first tournament, called the hole "comparatively easy.") The green until 1937 was situated well in front of and below where it is today, in the damp hollow to the right of the sprawling fairway bunker. That bunker seems anomalous to modern players, because even well-struck drives don't reach it and even poorly struck approach shots usually miss it. But in the early years the bunker embraced an otherwise defenseless green. (Even without the green nearby, the bunker has remained a hazard that MacKenzie would have liked: it *looks* as though it's in the way, even though it's not.)

Moving the green was the idea of Perry Maxwell, the Oklahoma architect who one year later would also redesign the seventh hole. Maxwell pointed out that moving the tenth green to higher ground would not only solve its drainage problems but also markedly strengthen the hole. The change turned a breathtaking but mediocre short hole into one of the greatest par-fours in the world.

Eleventh Hole—Par Four

Original Length		Current Length	
Members	Masters	Members	Masters
390	415	345	455
Earliest Name		Current Name	
Dogwood		White Dogwood	

The eleventh, twelfth, and thirteenth holes—which are laid out near Rae's Creek and one of its tributaries on the southeast side of the course—were sometimes referred to by early members as "the water loop." In 1958, Herbert Warren Wind, writing about that year's Masters in *Sports Illustrated,* called the same stretch Amen Corner. His inspiration was a jazz recording called "Shouting at Amen Corner," by the band of a Chicago clarinetist named Milton "Mezz" Mezzrow. Wind felt that the decisive moments in that year's tournament—which Arnold Palmer had won by a single stroke over Doug Ford and Fred Hawkins—had taken place on those holes, and the nickname has been a part of American golf lore ever since.

The championship tee on eleven was originally positioned above and to the right of the tenth green—on the same line as the members' tee today, though farther from the hole. As is still true for members, the hole ran steadily downhill from tee to green and so played considerably shorter than its measured distance. In fact, from the members' tees today the green is theoretically drivable, although the shot is blind and calls for a powerful fade.

The hole changed dramatically in 1950, when the club built a new tournament tee, positioned below and to the left of the tenth green. The change was suggested by Roberts and endorsed by Jones, and its purpose was both to lengthen the hole and to eliminate a gallery bottleneck between the tenth green and the eleventh tee. "Under the new arrangement," Jones wrote at the time, "the spectators will have ample room on the high ground to the right of the fairway to observe play, all the way from tee to green, without going on to the fairway at all. It will be substantially the same arrangement as is provided at number 13, where everyone can get a clear view of all shots played without following the contestants down the fairway." During the summer of 1997, the tournament tee was shifted a few yards to the right, a subtle change that has made the hole play longer by preventing players from hitting hard, running hooks down the tree line on the right-hand side of the fairway, which had been made vulnerable by the death of a large pine. The change is so subtle as to be nearly invisible, but it has greatly strengthened the hole.

The eleventh hole's most conspicuous feature is the pond to the left of the green. Roberts, in his book, wrote that the pond was his idea;

Byron Nelson remembers it as having been his own. "There was already water behind the green," Nelson says today, "because Rae's Creek ran back there. But not many people went over the green. So I told Cliff that I thought he ought to dam up the creek and let the water make a pond to the left of the green." (Nelson's memory that the creek passed only behind the green is not quite correct. The water also looped near the front left, almost as close to the green as the pond is today.) The dam was built in 1951, and it was rebuilt most recently in 1998. The slope and shape of the green, along with the precipitousness of the bank, make the little pond especially punishing. One measure of the treacherousness of the hole is that no sudden-death playoff in Masters history has lasted beyond it.

A small pot bunker was originally positioned in the center of the eleventh fairway at roughly the distance of a reasonable drive. The bunker, which could not be seen from the tee, was Jones's idea. He had wanted the course to have a hazard that could be avoided only with good luck or local knowledge—the sort of seemingly arbitrary booby trap that is plentiful on the Old Course. Jones's father, Colonel Bob Jones, drove into the hidden hazard during his first round on the course, in 1932. When the Colonel found his ball in the sand, he shouted, "What goddamned fool put a goddamned bunker right in the goddamned center of the goddamned fairway?" or words to that effect. His son, who was playing with him (along with Roberts), had to answer, "I did." The bunker was eventually filled in, though not till many years later.

The Colonel was one of the club's most colorful personages. Roberts, in his book, wrote, "When I first knew the Colonel, he could play to a handicap of about eight. When he played worse than that it was the fault of the ball, the way some green had been mowed, a divot hole, an unraked bunker, or some bad luck demon. On such days he was prone to express his feelings with swearwords; not just the usual kind of swearing, but original, lengthy, and complex imprecations that were classics. Numbers of people who were regular companions felt disappointed when the Colonel played well, as they always looked forward to a prolonged blast of cussing that they had never previously heard." On a trip to Philadelphia for the 1934 U.S. Open, Roberts and Bobby Jones lost track of the Colonel in the hotel where they were staying. After a lengthy search, they found him in the ballroom. Roberts wrote, "The Colonel, baton in hand, was directing the orchestra, and at the same time singing the words for the music that he was conducting." The Colonel died in 1956.

Twelfth Hole—Par Three

ORIGINAL LENGTH		CURRENT LENGTH	
MEMBERS	MASTERS	MEMBERS	MASTERS
130	150	145	155
EARLIEST NAME		CURRENT NAME	
THREE PINES		GOLDEN BELL	

The twelfth hole is a one-hundred-and-fifty-five-yard par-three that has just about the closest thing on the course to a flat green. Depending on the wind, the tee shot can call for anything from a pitching wedge to a six-iron. Nevertheless, Jack Nicklaus once called it "the toughest tournament hole in golf"; Lloyd Mangrum once called it "the meanest little par-three in the world"; and Rick Reilly of *Sports Illustrated* once called it "a hellacious, wonderful, terrifying, simple, treacherous, impossible, perfect molar-knocker." During the first two rounds of the Masters in 1980, Tom Weiskopf played the twelfth in twenty strokes—fourteen over par.

The twelfth was the hardest hole on the course to build. When an engineer saw that the plans called for a bunker in front of the green, he thought that the drawing must be in error, because the slope was so steep. The green was created by covering an exposed rock ledge with five thousand cubic yards of earth, which had been excavated on the opposite side of the creek. During that process, two tractors and eight mules became stuck in the mire and had to be pulled out with long ropes drawn by all the other tractors.

The twelfth green has always been shallow and treacherous; in the early years it was even more so. The right side of the green, where the hole is usually cut for the final round of the Masters, was enlarged in 1951 because, Jones explained, the hole had been "possibly a little too exacting." (The front right corner of the green had settled toward the creek, exacerbating the problem.) "I think we should build this up so as to provide the maximum level putting surface," Roberts explained in a letter at the time. "To do it right, logs should be used the same as when we extended the front of the left side of the green. While we are about it, we might provide another yard or two of depth. When the pin is on the right the hole is too damn tricky for fair tournament play especially since that area is subject to gusty winds. Also, we can never eliminate the bad feature of the damp bank back of the green in which a ball will bury. A good shot that is only a shade too short or too strong means a 2 stroke penalty—not one. Now that #11 is exacting such a surprising toll [because of the new pond] I wouldn't mind easing up a trifle on the boys at #12 green."

The creek in front of the twelfth green was a factor in a match played by Roberts, Ed Dudley (the club's pro), Jerome Franklin (a local member), and Dwight Eisenhower shortly after Eisenhower had been elected president. Eisenhower's tee shot landed short of the green, and his ball ended up on a sand bar next to the water. "You can play that ball off the sand bar," Roberts said as they walked to the green. Eisenhower climbed down the bank to his ball and sank past his knees in what turned out to be quicksand. Two Secret Service agents jumped in after him and pulled him out by the arms. The match was delayed while the president went back to his cottage to change clothes. When he returned, he told Roberts that he would never again take his advice on any matter concerning golf.

The twelfth hole was also the site of a memorable ruling. In the early years of the Masters, the club sometimes had trouble finding knowledgeable volunteers to serve as rules officials. "On one occasion," Roberts wrote in 1970 in a letter to Lincoln Werden of the *New York Times*, "the shortage was such that we appealed to Bob Jones for suggestions as to whom we might enlist. Bob said that we might in a pinch request his dad." The Colonel was accordingly posted to the twelfth hole on the final day of the tournament. There had been a great deal of rain during the night, and the course was very wet. One player hit a poor shot that landed in a soggy area near the creek. The player spotted the Colonel, called him over, and asked whether he was entitled to relief from casual water. The Colonel asked him where he stood in relation to par. "Eighteen over," the player said. The Colonel demanded, "Then what in the goddamn hell difference does it make? Tee the thing up on a peg for all I give a hoot!"

Thirteenth Hole—Par Five

ORIGINAL LENGTH		CURRENT LENGTH	
MEMBERS	MASTERS	MEMBERS	MASTERS
455	480	455	485
EARLIEST NAME		CURRENT NAME	
AZALEA		AZALEA	

The thirteenth hole is one that MacKenzie more nearly discovered than designed. When he first walked the Fruitland property in 1931, he found a field where much of the fairway is today and immediately recognized the makings of a great hole. Virtually all that had to be done was to build a green at the appropriate distance on the far side of the stream. He later said that the thirteenth bore a strong resemblance to a hypothetical ideal hole described by Charles Blair Macdonald in his book *Scotland's Gift: Golf.* (Macdonald's best-known courses include National Golf Links of America, on Long Island, and the Greenbrier Golf Club, in West Virginia.)

For many years, a tributary of Rae's Creek also ran directly across the thirteenth fairway roughly a hundred and fifty yards from the tee. An often told story (with several dozen versions and a shifting cast of participants) is that Roberts ordered the stream to be buried after one day driving into it. Something like that may have happened, although the change was undertaken with greater deliberation than most versions of the story suggest. That portion of the stream had long annoyed older members, and getting rid of it had no effect on the way the hole played during the tournament.

Fourteenth Hole—Par Four

ORIGINAL LENGTH		CURRENT LENGTH	
MEMBERS	MASTERS	MEMBERS	MASTERS
405	425	380	405
EARLIEST NAME		CURRENT NAME	
SPANISH DAGGER		CHINESE FIR	

Today, the fourteenth is the only hole on the course without a bunker. (The current fifth, seventh, fifteenth, and seventeenth were bunkerless when the course was first built.) Through the Masters in 1952, the fourteenth had a large bunker, which sprawled along the right-hand side of the fairway. It was so close to the tee, though, that its effect—like that of the steep fairway bunker on the fifth hole and the later abandoned left-hand fairway bunker on the second—was primarily visual (except for older members, who hated it). The bunker caused players to favor the left side of the fairway with their drives, even though the green usually was (and is) more easily approached from the right. After the Masters in 1997, a large mound just short and to the left of the green was also removed.

Sportswriters and television commentators often describe Augusta National as a course that favors players who typically draw the ball, or work it from right to left, over those who fade the ball, or work it from left to right. Like many pieces of conventional wisdom about the course and the club, this one does not stand up to examination. Although it is true that several holes on the course have fairways that bend to the left and therefore seemingly favor players who can draw the ball off the tee—the second, fifth, ninth, tenth, thirteenth, and fourteenth holes immediately come to mind—the matter is not so simple as it may at first appear. (And it doesn't help to explain the Masters success of Hogan, Nicklaus, Faldo, and Woods, to name four notable faders.) One usually overlooked fact about Augusta National is that all of its notable right-to-left holes, including the fourteenth, have wide-open landing areas on the right but severely punish shots that are hit too far to the left. In the final round at the Masters in 1998, Fred Couples derailed his round by hooking his drive on the thirteenth hole into the trees to the left of the creek that runs along the fairway. Had he played his customary fade from the tee, rather than trying to shorten his second shot by drawing his drive around the corner, he would have been far less likely to get into a position from which he had little chance of making par. He violated a cherished piece of local knowledge: Play away from the doglegs. On all the holes that seemingly favor players who can work the ball to the left, the only sure way to get into hopeless trouble off the tee is to hit a hook.

On holes where draws are seemingly favored from the tee, the greens often demand approach shots that move in the opposite direction. On the second and tenth holes, for example, right-to-left approaches that land to the left of the center of the green are unlikely to hold. In fact, many pin positions on many greens are most accessible to players who can hit high, soft fades. More than anything else, Augusta National requires careful positioning off the tee and a high degree of ball control on approaches. The most successful players tend to work backward from each day's pin positions in the hope of setting up approach shots that will leave reasonable chances of making birdie. A hole that calls for a draw on one day may favor a fade the next, and the actual target is always smaller than the entire green. As Roberts said in the fifties, "From the edge of some of our greens, three putts is par."

Fifteenth Hole—Par Five

Original Length		Current Length	
Members	Masters	Members	Masters
465	485	455	500
Earliest Name		Current Name	
Fire Thorn		Fire Thorn	

It is often said that the par-fives at Augusta National are in danger of becoming obsolete, since all four of them can be reached in two shots by players who hit good drives. But critics seldom realize that the holes were designed from the beginning to play relatively short. In 1933, Wendell Miller, the contractor who built the course, told Jones in a letter that golfers were telling him that the fifteenth hole was too easy to reach in two, and he added that by moving the tee he could lengthen the hole by ten yards. Jones's reaction is preserved in a marginal notation: "Bob say no." The possibility of having a relatively short second shot to the green was a feature of the original design, and Jones insisted that it be retained.

Jones had explained his ideas about par-fives to O. B. Keeler in 1931, before construction of the course began. "I am not among those who believe that a par-5 hole, so called, must be so extremely long, or must have some peculiarity of design or construction, that it cannot be reached in two shots," he said. "There are a good many of these holes in our championship courses nowadays, and some people appear quite proud of them. But in competition, it means simply that the man who can hit two really great shots is no better off than the man who can hit two good shots; his third is a bit shorter; that is all. Not by any means a fair chance for the expert to invest his superior skill and range in the picking up of a stroke." Over the years, all the par-fives at Augusta have been lengthened and otherwise tinkered with in order to make them play longer—but they have never been altered with the intention of making them unreachable in two. The idea has always been to keep them current while preserving the defining feature that MacKenzie and Jones built into them: a tantalizing scoring opportunity for better players.

Of course, most golfers' perceptions of length and difficulty are determined almost entirely by par designations. If the thirteenth and fifteenth holes were called par-fours, players would perceive both holes—and probably the course itself—as brutally long and excessively difficult, even though no feature of either hole would have changed. MacKenzie was never overly concerned about par designations. He was far more interested in shot values and strategic possibilities. The true measure of a hole, he felt, is the golf that it inspires in those who play it.

The bunker to the right of the green was added in 1957 (at the suggestion of Ben Hogan) and enlarged seven years later. At around the same time, a couple of good-sized mounds were added just beyond the green; they were removed in 1963. Removing the mounds made the green look from the fairway almost like an island, since their absence brought the pond on the sixteenth hole into play for approach shots hit long. The change also effectively lengthened the hole, by introducing a new level of risk into second shots played at the flag. In fact, in the final round that year, Jack Nicklaus hit a fairway wood approach that most likely would have ended up in the water if the slope beyond the green hadn't been soggy from the previous night's rain. He received relief from casual water, made a somewhat wobbly par, and went on to beat Tony Lema by a stroke.

Mounds were added to the right side of the fairway in 1969. Charles Yates recalls, "Cliff got hold of me, Jack Stephens, and several other members, and said he was thinking about putting in some mounds, because the pros were playing the ball with a big hook and getting a tremendous roll down that hill. He didn't want the hole to become too easy, so he called a meeting and asked us to come down and see whether he ought to put in the mounds or not. When we got there, a bulldozer was just topping off one of them. Jack said, 'Cliff, I thought you wanted us to help you decide whether these mounds would be a good thing to have.' And Cliff said, 'I just wanted you boys to be here so that if it didn't work out I'd have somebody to blame.'" The fairway mounds were substantially lowered in 1998, after a consensus had developed among the membership that they no longer served a purpose in the tournament—the longest pros were simply driving over them—and that they looked out of keeping with the rest of the course. In addition, new trees were planted on the right side of the fairway in order to narrow the ideal landing area.

Sixteenth Hole—Par Three

ORIGINAL LENGTH		CURRENT LENGTH	
MEMBERS	MASTERS	MEMBERS	MASTERS
120	145	145	170
EARLIEST NAME		CURRENT NAME	
RED BUD		RED BUD	

MacKenzie modeled the original version of the sixteenth hole on a short par-three that he believed to be the best hole on one of his favorite courses, Stoke Poges, in England. The early members liked the sixteenth, and MacKenzie felt that it was "probably a better hole" than its British inspiration. But the hole was far too easy for Masters competitors, who were more likely to view it as a feeble imitation of the incomparable twelfth, which it superficially resembled.

As the sixteenth was originally designed, the tee was situated directly beyond and to the right of the fifteenth green. Players hit across a tributary of Rae's Creek to a green at the base of the steep slope below the sixth tee. In 1947, Bobby Jones suggested moving the tee well to the left and the green well to the right, and damming the creek to create a pond between them. The architect Robert Trent Jones (no relation) executed that conception. The result is a demanding short hole that has produced nearly as many thrilling and decisive moments as the twelfth.

Even at its new length, the sixteenth—like the sixth and the twelfth—is still relatively short by modern tournament standards. That has been true of Augusta National's par-threes since the beginning. "None of these one-shotters [calls] for brassie or driver," Jones told O. B.

Keeler. "My idea of the proper place for the display of talent with the brassie or the spoon primarily is on a second shot—not from a tee." A par-three, Jones felt, should be a test of precision, not of strength. MacKenzie agreed.

Seventeenth Hole—Par Four

ORIGINAL LENGTH		CURRENT LENGTH	
MEMBERS	MASTERS	MEMBERS	MASTERS
380	400	350	425
EARLIEST NAME		CURRENT NAME	
NANDINA		NANDINA	

In the program for the first tournament MacKenzie wrote, "Until players have learned to play the desired shot this will undoubtedly be one of the most fiercely criticized holes." At that time, the hole had no bunkers. "It will be necessary to attack the green from the right," MacKenzie wrote, "and it will be essential to play a run-up shot if par figures are desired. We hope to make the turf of such a character that an indifferent pitch will not stop on the green."

Run-up shots are no longer feasible. The green is defended today by two large bunkers. For most pin positions, the best angle of approach is still probably from the right. The green looks easy to hit from head-on, but the putting surface slopes away so severely on the left that many perfect-looking shots end up running long.

The hole's most conspicuous feature is a large pine tree that grows on the left side of the fairway a hundred and twenty-five yards from the members' tee. (A small creek used to cross the fairway between the tee and the tree; it was buried in 1951.) Masters competitors seldom notice the tree—most of them simply drive over it—but it often causes trouble for members. Eisenhower hated the tree, because it invariably interfered with his slice. At the governors meeting in 1956—after Eisenhower had introduced, at Roberts's request, a resolution in memory of Colonel Jones, who had just died—Eisenhower took the floor to propose cutting it down. Roberts immediately ruled him out of order and adjourned the meeting, and the pine has been known ever since as the Eisenhower Tree. Philip Reed, the chairman of the General Electric Co., was present at the meeting and later told Roberts that he had learned a great deal from his handling of Eisenhower's proposal. "Whenever anyone voices criticism at a General Electric meeting in the future," he said, "I'll just declare it adjourned." The Eisenhower Tree became a more dangerous obstacle for Masters competitors during the summer of 1998, when the tournament tee was moved back twenty-five yards.

Eighteenth Hole—Par Four

ORIGINAL LENGTH		CURRENT LENGTH	
MEMBERS	MASTERS	MEMBERS	MASTERS
395	420	375	405
EARLIEST NAME		CURRENT NAME	
HOLLY		HOLLY	

To Roberts, the eighteenth green was always more than a putting surface; it was also the stage on which the final scene of the Masters was enacted. He wanted the maximum number of spectators to have a clear view of the drama, and over the years he repeatedly reshaped the surrounding terrain in order to accommodate them. To improve sight lines, he had greenside mounds built, moved, and recontoured, and he had both the practice putting green and the tenth tee shifted farther away, to create more standing room. He implemented what he called the Big Circle method of roping greens, in which the ropes were placed not close to the putting surface, as was done elsewhere, but at such a substantial distance that the number of front-row seats was quadrupled. For the same reason, he made sure that the hole was cut in the front part of the eighteenth green on Saturdays and Sundays. "We have followed this practice for many years," he explained in a letter to the television commentator Jim McKay in 1960, "because we know by experience and observation that more people can see the pin location in the front than can see it when it is on the upper level at the back."

In order to determine whether these efforts and others had been successful, Roberts twice asked the Augusta photographer Frank Christian to estimate the number of spectators surrounding the green while the final pair of Masters contestants were putting out on Sunday. Christian did so by taking wide-angle photographs in three directions, combining them into a panoramic picture, placing a grid on top of the composite image, and counting the heads within each square of the grid. Doing that was so time-consuming that when Roberts, in jest, raised the possibility of making a third such census, Christian replied, "The hell you say," and left the room.

The most conspicuous change to the eighteenth hole was the construction in 1966 of a pair of large bunkers in a popular driving area on the left side of the fairway. (Roberts always preferred to think of these bunkers as one bunker with two sections, perhaps because one of Augusta National's distinguishing characteristics had always been its limited reliance on sand: One bunker was only half as many as two.) The eighteenth had had a large fairway bunker from the beginning, but that bunker was positioned more nearly in the center of the fairway and not much more than a hundred or a hundred and twenty yards from the green. It was removed when the new bunkers were built.

It is often said that the addition of the new bunkers was a response to the length of Jack Nicklaus, who treated the eighteenth as a drive-and-pitch hole in the course of winning the Masters in both 1965 and 1966. Nicklaus was certainly a factor in the decision, but other players were nearly as long as he was, and the change had been contemplated for some time. Today, quite a few players are capable of driving past (or over) the bunkers, although the trees that encroach on the right side of the fairway continue to make this a demanding driving hole, especially into the wind. A case could be made that the hole's original fairway bunker, which was some twenty or thirty yards closer to the green, would be a more thought-provoking hazard for modern players.

Nineteenth Hole—Par Three

The course as originally conceived was to have had one more than the regulation number of holes. MacKenzie explained the idea in a letter to Roberts: "Bobby Jones and some of the other directors thought it might be interesting to have a real 19th hole so that the loser could have the opportunity of getting his money back by playing double or quits. This 19th Hole will be an attractive plateau green, narrow at one end where the flag will usually be placed but wide at the other end so as to give a safety route to the player who has not the courage or the skill to pitch to the narrow end of the green."

The hole was to have been ninety yards long. It would have played uphill, toward the clubhouse, between the ninth and eighteenth greens, from a tee near the top of the old practice area. The idea had plenty of supporters (among them Roberts and Grantland Rice) but was dropped partly for the sake of economy and partly because the hole would have impeded the view of anyone in the clubhouse who was trying to watch the action on what was then the eighteenth green—a view that Jones, Roberts, and MacKenzie all wanted to protect.

A local newspaper account of the opening of the course in January 1933 suggested that the hole had actually been built: "Outstanding is the 19th hole—actually—where ties are played off. Some wag has dubbed the locker room of the club house the '20th hole.'" But no other contemporary source or document refers to the hole as anything but an abandoned idea. It seems likely that the reporter's description was based not on firsthand observation but on a printed plan of the course, which still showed the hole, and that "some wag" was himself.

Par Three Course

MacKenzie initially wanted to supplement the main golf course with what he called an "approach and putt" course—a nine-hole short course, which could be played with short irons and a putter. The course was to be four hundred to five hundred yards long. "There is, as far as I know, no interesting approach and putt course in America," MacKenzie wrote in 1932 in a letter to Wendell Miller, the engineer who was then in the process of building the big course. "A really good one requires as much thought and planning as a full course. All those I have seen are terrible. I am just constructing one here [near San Francisco] which I hope will be most fascinating." Roberts shared MacKenzie's enthusiasm for the idea, but Jones was skeptical. After walking the proposed site with an engineer late in 1932, Jones asked that the short course not be included on the site plan but that the area instead be labeled "Reserved for Park." The plan died, not only because of Jones's lack of interest, but also because there was no money to pay for it. Still, in 1933, MacKenzie drew plans for an eighteen-hole, 2,460-yard short course. (The longest hole was to have been one hundred and ninety yards; the shortest was to have been sixty.) It was never built, either.

The club today does have an approach-and-putt course—the par three course, which was built in 1958 and is a little more than twice as long as the nine-hole course MacKenzie originally envisioned. It was designed by George W. Cobb with help from Roberts, who referred to it in his book as "my pet project." A number of members were initially skeptical about the short course—viewing it, Roberts said, as a waste of money and referring to it derisively as a "Tom Thumb course." But it was popular as soon as it was built, and it remains popular today—both among older members, who sometimes play it as a less demanding alternative to the big course, and among those who use it either as a warm-up or as a place to squeeze a few more holes while there's just enough light to play. The course today actually has eleven holes. Two new holes, designed by Tom Fazio, were added during the summer of 1986, so that the original first and second holes could be used for spectator seating during the Par 3 Contest, which takes place the Wednesday before the Masters. The old holes are still maintained and can still be played, though they seldom are.

The Par 3 Contest was first held in 1960 (and won by Sam Snead) after enthusiastic lobbying by Roberts. "I am really rather bullish on the idea of making use of the Par-3 course as a distinctive pre-tournament event," he had written the year before. "If so, it can be quite a feather in the cap of the Masters Tournament. I say this because no other club holding a tournament could duplicate what I am proposing we do at Augusta. So far as I know, no other club has a Par-3 layout and, even if they do, I am sure they don't have anything to compare with ours." The event has always drawn a huge and enthusiastic crowd. It is also popular with the players—even though no winner of the par three event has ever gone on to win the Masters.

The par three course served as a laboratory for the big course in 1978, when its greens were converted to bent grass from a hybrid of Bermuda. The experiment was judged a success, and the greens on the main course were converted two years later. Some players still debate whether the new greens are faster than the old greens—which in 1960 and 1961 had been converted from an older strain of Bermuda—and even whether the original greens might not have been the fastest of all. Jones in 1931 had specifically promised that the putting surfaces at Augusta National would never be kept "saturated." Sam Snead said in 1951 that Augusta was "the only course I ever played where you can hear the ball rolling on the greens," adding, "They're so slick the ball sounds like it's frying." That speed has been a feature of the greens since the earliest years. It is one part of the course that is unlikely ever to change.

CHAPTER SIX

Cattle, Turkeys, and Prisoners of War

FEW PEOPLE REMEMBER today, but for two years in the late thirties Augusta National was the home of a second professional golf tournament. In 1937, at a meeting held in a hotel in Augusta, a committee of aging professionals established a senior division of the P.G.A. and decided to hold a national championship for players aged fifty-five or older. Augusta National offered to host the event. The inaugural P.G.A. Seniors' Championship took place that year on the last day of November and the first two days of December. Alfred Bourne, the vice president of the club, donated $1,500 for a silver trophy and agreed to cover the competitors' bar tab (which amounted to not quite two hundred dollars). "It was a delightful occasion," Allie Berckmans, the club's general manager, wrote shortly afterward in a letter to a member, "and it did one good to see these old fellows enjoy the sport. They didn't give a rap about the prize money, all they wanted was to try to win the cup donated by Mr. Bourne and have a good time." The winner was Jock Hutchison. The tournament returned to Augusta National the following year, when it was shortened to thirty-six holes because of rain. The winner that year was Fred McLeod, who beat Otto Hackbarth in an eighteen-hole playoff. In 1939, the Seniors' Championship found a regular sponsor and moved to Florida.

The club had two main interests in hosting the senior event. The first was that the tournament, though small, brought additional prestige to the club and the course at a time when prestige was deeply coveted. The second was that the tournament gave the club a new opportunity to fulfill what Roberts and Jones increasingly viewed as one of its responsibilities. They had founded the Masters partly out of financial necessity, but they had also had a more idealistic goal of helping to build the game. Hosting the senior event, they believed, was both an opportunity and an obligation. As a result, Augusta National can be viewed as having helped give rise to the earliest ancestor of the Senior P.G.A. Tour.*

A similar sense of purpose was evident in the club's involvement, in the early forties, in a proposal to build a golf hall of fame. In 1941, two new Augusta National members—James Middleton Cox, a newspaper publisher, who years earlier had served three terms as the governor of Ohio, and his son, James Jr.—proposed erecting a large statue of Bobby Jones near the clubhouse, not far from what would later become the site of the Eisenhower Cabin. Jones and Roberts were deeply unenthusiastic about the monument, and both were relieved when the Coxes, at Roberts's suggestion, shifted their attention to the possibility of building a hall of fame on club property. The National Baseball Hall of Fame and Museum had opened in Cooperstown, New York, two years before, and the Professional Golfers' Association had responded by inducting several legendary golfers, among them Jones, into its own hall. But the P.G.A.'s hall as yet had neither a building nor a plan for one.

Roberts embraced the idea and suggested several sites. His favorite, initially, was an elevated six-acre parcel roughly two hundred and fifty yards to the east of the tenth green. This was one of the building lots that the club had been trying to sell for a decade. Among the advantages of the site, Roberts wrote to Jones, was that visitors to the hall "would

---

* Hutchison and McLeod had both competed in the Masters as well, and both continued to do so until 1959. Beginning in 1963, they served as the tournament's "honorary starters" by teeing off first at the beginning of the opening round. Hutchison continued in that role through 1973, McLeod through 1976. There were no honorary starters during the next four years. Gene Sarazen and Byron Nelson resumed the custom in 1981. Ken Venturi took Nelson's place for one year, 1983, when Nelson was ill. Sam Snead joined the group in 1984.

have four good views of the course instead of one." He also liked the idea that "members using the golf course would have a good view of an attractive building"—though from a distance.

Roberts was especially concerned that golf's hall of fame should be more compelling than baseball's. In a lengthy letter to Olmsted Bros., written a few days after the 1941 Masters, he described a number of features that he thought ought to be included. "The more I think about it," he wrote, "the more I feel that a building that houses a few plaques or a few bronze busts and that offers nothing else to the public, would prove to be a dull, worthless type of project, having no excuse for its existence except to attempt to glorify the leaders of golf. And I doubt that very much would be added to their fame." One wing of the building, he continued, could contain "automatic movie machines," which, for a quarter, would show instructional films by the game's great teachers. Another wing could serve as both a comprehensive library and a bookstore. Visitors would be able to buy souvenir booklets, postcards depicting the Augusta National course, and "popular-priced copies" of some of the books in the library. Roberts's boldest suggestion was to construct "a miniature Augusta National course surrounding the Hall of Fame which would be a practical pitch and putt course and could be made a most attractive part of the landscaping scheme." The holes would be scaled-down replicas of the holes on the big course. He proposed a fee of twenty-five cents per round. He also suggested building an "especially attractive" public driving range based on a plan that Jones had come across and thought highly of.

Despite Roberts's enthusiasm, the project never came to anything, and there was no further discussion of building a miniature Augusta National. The Coxes lost interest in the hall of fame, the club was not in a financial position to follow through on its own, and news from Europe and the Pacific soon made other concerns more pressing.

In a letter to the members in 1939, Roberts wrote, emphatically, "I do hope that I can count on *everyone receiving this letter,* keeping in mind as a *live issue the whole year round* the matter of getting desirable candidates to make application for membership." He enclosed several membership blanks, and he expected members to make use of them. The effort paid off. The following year, the club's total membership exceeded one hundred for the first time, and Roberts was able to pay down the club's mortgage. For the first time since 1934, he had solid reasons to believe that the club's most significant financial difficulties might finally be behind it.

There were other good signs as well. In 1939, the club for the first time sold more Masters tickets than it had in 1934, the year of Jones's return. The tournament was still unprofitable, strictly speaking, because Roberts always spent more on course improvements and new tournament facilities than the club netted from ticket sales. But the Masters was beginning to produce operating profits of a few thousand dollars a year, and consequently Roberts's budget for improvements was growing. He felt confident about the future, partly because ticket sales had grown stronger despite six years of bad luck with the weather. (Five times during the first nine tournaments, bad weather forced postponement of a day's play.) In 1939 he wrote, "I think I can see good prospects of eventually building up a gate of $15,000 or more"—a target that represented a fifty percent improvement over that year's results.

Most encouraging of all was the arrival of a new generation of golf stars—chief among them Byron Nelson, Sam Snead, and Ben Hogan. One or another of those three players would dominate the game for the next two decades, until the rise of Arnold Palmer in the late fifties, and the Masters would be a pivotal event for each of them. (Nelson was the first to emerge. He won in 1937, and then finished fifth, seventh, third, second, and first in the next five Masters.) Augusta National, despite its decidedly modest beginnings and continuing financial difficulties, was becoming a leading institution in American golf. "While we may not have expected it originally," Roberts wrote in 1939, "we have created a tournament of such importance that we are bound to see that it continues."

And then came the war. Just as the club and the tournament finally seemed to be taking hold, the world turned upside down. To Roberts, the crisis must have seemed almost inevitable. In the past, every time his life or career had seemed to resolve itself, something devastating had upset it. And now, at what he had thought was the end of a decade-long struggle, he realized that a bigger challenge lay ahead.

Jones, for his part, was eager to continue for as long as possible not only with the Masters but also with the club's normal activities. "My own notion," he wrote to Roberts a little more than two weeks after the Japanese attack on Pearl Harbor, "is that we should keep going until we strike a definite snag." Roberts agreed. Both men soon realized, though, that the inevitable snag was not far in the future. Even if the they could somehow manage to keep the club open for another season, conducting the Masters in the usual manner would be unseemly at a time of growing international crisis. They discussed a number of alternatives: paying Masters prizes in defense bonds, donating tournament proceeds to the Red Cross, encouraging members to make individual contributions to the Red Cross through the club, securing pledges from members to give a certain amount of money to the Red Cross every time a competitor scored a birdie or an eagle. (That last idea had been inspired by the radio program *Information, Please,* in connection with which the American Tobacco Co., the sponsor, gave twenty-five dollars to the Will Rogers Fund every time a contestant missed a question.)

Roberts then had the idea of using a portion of the tournament's proceeds to make golf available to soldiers stationed at Camp Gordon (now known as Fort Gordon), which was the largest military installation in Augusta. Jones thought that was "a swell idea." In a letter to an officer of the club, Jones wrote, "The idea appeals to me as novel and a means of supplying nighttime entertainment as well as giving the boys a taste of something they can fall back on after they get out of the army. It will be a service to the game of golf as well as to the trainees." In a press release the club announced, "A man in an army training camp can't come to a golf course—at least, not often. So golf is coming to him." The club arranged, as a "gift of the 1942 Masters Golf Tournament," to build a practice range and a huge putting green at Camp Gordon. The club donated balls, clubs, tee markers, flags, floodlights, turf from its own property, and maintenance equipment and supplies. Shortly before the tournament, it also sent a group of Masters competitors to the base to conduct an exhibition. Later, the army built (again with the assistance of the club) a small nine-hole course of its own. Roberts and Jones urged other clubs to set up similar programs. A number did, and the United States Golf Association credited the Augusta National with starting the trend.

The 1942 Masters was played in this unsettled environment. Against all expectations, it provided the most exciting finish since Sarazen's miracle win in 1935. Byron Nelson and Ben Hogan tied at eight under par after seventy-two holes; the following day, in an eighteen-hole playoff, Nelson shot 69 (despite beginning with a double-bogey six on the first hole) and beat Hogan by a stroke. It was an outcome that came close to defining the state of the game at that particular moment, and it marked the real arrival of the Masters as a truly significant competition.

Two days later, Roberts sent effusive letters to both men. "I know you will not mind my saying that I will always remember this year's Tournament as being the one won by both Byron and Ben," he wrote to Nelson. "... To my way of thinking, you fellows put on one of the greatest shows that golf has ever known and I wish I could have some more adequate means at my disposal to express our appreciation." Along with each player's letter he enclosed a check for two hundred dollars, "which you may consider as being extra prize money." The bonuses added up to slightly more than the club's net proceeds from additional tickets sold for the playoff.

The celebration following the 1942 tournament was muted, however. Roberts and Jones now realized that the club was going to have to shut down for the duration, and a number of members assumed that it would never open again. More than a few believed that Nelson and Hogan's playoff would turn out to be the last competitive round ever to be played at Augusta National. As Roberts himself wrote ten months later, "the Lord only knows when we will again operate as a golf club."

Roberts announced the club's closing in a letter to the members on October 1, 1942, shortly before what would have been the beginning of the ninth full playing season. By that time, travel had become difficult, Augusta's hotels were about to be taken over by the army, and many of the club's employees and members (among them Jones) were already in uniform. "Some months ago we cut down our staff to just a skeleton maintenance crew," Roberts reported, "but the golf course and the plants are being properly cared for and we can prepare to open just as soon as the war's end is definitely in sight." He suspended dues and appealed to members for voluntary contributions and loans to cover the cost of maintaining the club in a state of suspended animation, a cost that Roberts estimated at $12,000 a year. Toward the end of 1941, the club had taken the precaution of laying in a large supply of golf balls. Now they wouldn't be needed.

In 1942, Jones suggested to Roberts that the club might both contribute to the war effort and improve its financial situation by raising cattle on the golf course during the period when the club was shut down. The idea was that the cattle would keep the Bermuda grass under control while fattening themselves to the point where they could be sold at a profit. One of the club's members had a son who knew about livestock, and he determined that the club had enough grass to support two hundred or two hundred and fifty head. Roberts went ahead with the idea, and suggested that the club might also want to try raising turkeys, geese, fish, "and what-not." (In the end, only cattle and turkeys were tried.)

During the war years, Roberts supervised activities at the club from a distance. He lived in an apartment at the Park Lane Hotel, in New York, and worked at the investment firm Reynolds & Co., where he had become a partner in the spring of 1941. Business was slow. In his book about the club, he wrote that the war years were the second of two significant "lean periods" in his career, the first having been the dark years following the Crash. Charles Yates, who had joined the club in 1940 and was in the navy during the war, remembers seeing Roberts several times in that period. The destroyer on which Yates served had been hit during the invasion of Anzio in 1944, and had come to the Brooklyn Navy Yard for repairs. Roberts invited Yates and his wife, Dorothy—who had come to New York to be with her husband—to stay in his apartment whenever he was traveling on business. He also visited Yates at the shipyard and took him and Dorothy out for meals. "Cliff was so different, if you knew him, from the way he seemed from afar," Yates recalls. "One time, he took us out to lunch, and afterwards we were walking up Broadway, and in front of us was a couple that was moving awful slow. Suddenly, Cliff grabbed Dorothy's hand and started skipping with her. They skipped right by this couple, and as they went past, Cliff turned to them and said, 'Honk-honk! Honk-honk!' " Yates says that Roberts went out of his way to make life easier for him and his wife at a difficult time. "He was a man who kept so much within himself," Yates recalls, "but he was extraordinarily kind."

Toward the end of 1943, Roberts reported to the members that the club's agricultural efforts were going well. The cattle herd was about two hundred strong, and the plan was to purchase another two hundred head as soon as the original animals could be sold. "The Club also purchased 1,423 day-old turkeys and was successful in raising 1,004 of them," Roberts wrote. "These turkeys will soon be ready for market but over 100 are to be retained for Christmas distribution to our members—one to each member." (These Christmas presents were a hit. A member who had received one wrote to Roberts, "It was a peach all right and doubly welcome in these days of tight rationing.") The club also harvested pecans from its own trees. It donated half the crop, through the wife of Grantland Rice, to an army canteen, and it sold the other half in ten-pound bags to members. There was talk of growing corn and peanuts in a field now used as a parking lot for the Masters, but that idea was abandoned as unlikely to succeed.

Despite Roberts's enthusiasm, the livestock experiment didn't turn out as planned. A ceiling had been imposed on the price of turkeys but not on that of feed, and the market for beef was hurt by a sudden cattle glut resulting from drought conditions in the West. By the fall of 1944, the club had lost about $5,000 on the beef operation, not including the cost of damage to the course and its plantings. (The damage had been caused by what Roberts described as "the voracious appetite of the cattle.") The loss was partly offset by a profit on the turkeys. But Roberts concluded, in a letter to the members, that "we have a better chance as a golf club rather than as live-stock feeders."

Restoring the course to playable condition began in late 1944, when the end of the war began to seem imminent. Military use of local hotels had begun to slacken, and Roberts had calculated that the cost of returning the course to playing condition would no longer be significantly greater than the cost of continuing to maintain it as it was. He announced that the club would reopen on December 23, 1944, and that the course would be ready for play sometime later.

Much of the restoration work on the course was done during a six-month period by forty-two German prisoners of war, who were being detained at Camp Gordon, in Augusta, and were available for hire as day laborers by local businesses. The prisoners had been part of an engineering crew in Rommel's Afrika Korps. They had been surprised, upon arriving in America, to find that New York was still standing, because they had been told by Nazi propagandists that German bombers had leveled the city. The club arranged for transportation to pick them up at Camp Gordon each morning and return them at the end of the day. A local member, who used to bring them fruit and visit with them while they worked, says the army had sent them out "mostly just to give them something to do."

In Africa, the German soldiers had built bridges for Rommel's tanks. At the Augusta National, they built a similar bridge over Rae's Creek near the thirteenth tee. It was a truss bridge made of wood, and it was marked by a wooden sign on which the soldiers carved an inscription. The bridge, which is visible in a few old photographs, either washed away in a flood in the early fifties or was taken down in 1958 to make way for a stone bridge dedicated to Byron Nelson. (The Ben Hogan Bridge, which crosses Rae's Creek near the twelfth green, was built and dedicated at the same time.)

The photographer Frank Christian, in his book *Augusta National and the Masters*, recalls spending summer afternoons on the course during this period when he was a young boy. "[M]y older brother, Toni, and I would gather our playmates and walk the few blocks from our house to the inviting shores of Rae's Creek, where we had discovered the ideal swimming hole in front of the twelfth green," Christian writes. "We would take rocks and dam the creek to create several deep holes within the pond, just perfect for running jumps taken from the high side of the creek. . . . After swimming, a great part of our fun was to throw cow biscuits at one another and chase the cows up and down the fairways." Fred Bennett, who would later become a caddie at the club and then caddie master, also came to Rae's Creek to swim and fish. "I remember those cows very well," he recalls. "And when the war was over you could tell they'd been there, because all over the fairways there were circles of bright green grass about a foot across."

In the improving financial climate shortly before the war, a group of club members, led by Bartlett Arkell, had donated $50,000 toward a major renovation of the clubhouse. This was a great stroke of fortune. "If the rebuilding of the clubhouse had not been done prior to World War II," Roberts later wrote, "there is no way of telling when it might ever have been accomplished." He also estimated that the renovation would have cost at least four times as much if it had been postponed.

The final step in the project was the conversion of the building's attic into minimal sleeping quarters for six men, with streams of sunlight provided during the day by the building's cupola. This dormitory, which came to be called the Crow's Nest, was the first overnight lodgings available on the grounds. (For a time, some members also stayed in a house on Washington Road, just east of Magnolia Lane, which had been owned by one of the Berckmanses. The house was later torn down.) The Crow's Nest—which today consists of a comfortable sitting room, four partially enclosed sleeping areas containing a total of five beds, and a bathroom—was completed at around the time the club reopened. It is still sometimes used by members and guests, although the steepness of the staircase limits its popularity among those with unreliable knees. During the Masters, it is offered to any of the tournament's amateur competitors who wish to stay there; at night, they are inevitably drawn downstairs to thumb through the books in the library, look at the photographs on the walls, stand for a while in the champions' locker room, and worry about teeing off the next morning in front of the multitude gathered around the first tee. Among players who slept in the Crow's Nest as amateurs and went on to win the tournament as professionals are Ben Crenshaw, Jack Nicklaus, Mark O'Meara, Craig Stadler, and Tiger Woods.

Construction of the Crow's Nest was followed by what became an ambitious plan to add sleeping facilities. The quality and availability of local hotel rooms was increasingly unpredictable, and Roberts believed that the club needed to become more self-sufficient. In 1945, a member named Edward J. Barber, who ran the Barber Steamship Lines in New York, surprised Roberts by offering to lend the club $100,000 on extremely favorable terms and to leave the club enough money in his will to cancel the debt. (Upon his death in 1953 he actually bequeathed twice as much.) Barber explained that his years as a golfer were running out, and he wanted the club's facilities to improve while he still had time to enjoy them. The end of the war also brought an influx of new members, more than offsetting a decline that had followed the closing of the club in 1942. By the fall of 1945, the club's roster reached approximately one hundred and thirty—an all-time high. The situation was so promising that Roberts for the first time spoke of imposing a membership limit, which he placed at two hundred.

The unexpectedly large treasury provided by gifts, loans, and initiation fees enabled the club to embark immediately on an ambitious building program, which Roberts had previously thought would take many years to complete. The club added residential suites, a golf shop, a kitchen, and a formal dining room, which was called the Trophy Room. (The Trophy Room was originally intended to house "such souvenirs as may have a direct connection with the Augusta National and its members," and so to serve as a modest private version of the abandoned hall of fame; the only souvenirs kept there today are a set of Jones's clubs, some clubs donated by early tournament winners, and the ball with which Gene Sarazen made his double-eagle.) The club also built the first of a series of residential cottages, which are usually called cabins and of which there are now ten.

The first two cottages to be built were named for Burton F. Peek and Bobby Jones. Peek, who joined the club in 1934, was the chairman of Deere & Co. and was once described by Roberts as "our candidate for

top honors as the man who hit the most golf balls in one lifetime." The
Jones Cabin, which is situated to the left of the tenth tee, is still decorated much as it was in Jones's lifetime. The sportswriter Charles Price
used to visit Jones there during the Masters when Jones had grown too
ill even to observe the tournament from a golf cart. "We would sit at a
card table next to a window," Price wrote in *Golf Digest* in 1991. "A curtain prevented spectators from looking in but allowed Bob to peer out."
The cottage has a small front porch that can accommodate just a few
chairs. It has always been an extremely pleasant spot from which to
watch a sunset on a late-spring evening.

Seven additional cottages were built over the years. The best known
are the Eisenhower Cabin, which was built in 1953 (and will be discussed in the next chapter), and the Butler Cabin, which was named for
Thomas B. Butler and was built in 1965. In the basement of the Butler
Cabin is a large, open room that is used as a television studio during
Masters broadcasts. Interviews with the tournament winner and others
are conducted in front of a large stone fireplace at one end of the room.
The space looks intimate on television but is actually cavernous, since it
was designed to accommodate cameras, lights, electronic equipment,
and several miles of cable. Before the Butler Cabin was built, televised
interviews with the winner were conducted in Roberts's bedroom,
sometimes with his extravagantly printed floor-to-ceiling curtains bil-
lowing in the background. At the end of the broadcast in 1960, Roberts
angrily turned around on the couch to correct a CBS correspondent
who had just referred to the tournament's venue as "the Augusta National Country Club." Roberts barked, "Golf club. Not a country club."
It was a distinction that was extremely important to him and one that he
was always careful to maintain.

The last cottage to be built was named for Jackson Stephens and was
built in 1969. Stephens, who served as the club's chairman from 1991
until 1998, recalls that Roberts brought up the subject one evening as
they were walking along a path that connects all the cabins. "Cliff said,
'If you'll underwrite it, I'll get it built this summer,' and I said I would,"
Stephens says. "But I had never won an argument with him, so I said,
'You know, Cliff, I love to swim, and I expect I'll be spending a lot of

time in that house, so I'd like to have a swimming pool underneath it.'
Oh, God, he hated that idea. He felt that a swimming pool had no place
at a golf club. We went back and forth and back and forth, and it kind of
became a thing with me—and Cliff finally acquiesced. Now, I no more
wanted a swimming pool than I wanted a billy goat. I just wanted to win
an argument with Cliff. So I relented as soon as he had agreed, and he
was greatly relieved."

Among the many decisions that had to be made after the war was
whether to revive the Masters. It was not necessarily a foregone conclusion. In October 1945, in a letter to the club's thirty local members,
Roberts pointed out that there were many difficulties, among them the
limited number of hotel rooms. The Bon Air had changed management,
and other accommodations were scarce. "For my part," Roberts wrote,
"I'd like to see the Augusta National do its part to keep Augusta's resort
business alive by continuing the Masters Tournament. I'd also like to see
our Tournament continue to serve the game of golf; but the future of
the Club—as a private organization—is by no means dependent upon
the Tournament. Rather, the Masters is a public event that belongs to
the city of Augusta." Roberts concluded his letter by listing what he believed to be the club's only possible courses of action. There were three:
The first was to put pressure on the Bon Air to make improvements in
its facilities and its services, while also stepping up efforts to sell tickets
locally; the second was to postpone resumption of the tournament until
1947, by which time the hotel situation might have resolved itself; the
third was to "relinquish the Masters name to some other city, and not
bother about the tournaments."

Roberts's letter may have been partly a bluff intended to stir up the
local members, who would have to assume much of the responsibility
for selling tickets and putting the course back into shape. If that was
Roberts's intention, he was successful; within a month, the club was
fully committed to moving ahead.

Roberts's investment business by that time had increased to the
point where he could no longer devote as much attention as he once had

to the Masters or the club. Many tournament preparations became the responsibility of James Searle, who had served as the club's manager since before the war. The list of his chores, which Roberts sent by mail from New York, was lengthy: the underground telephone lines, which linked the scoreboards and crisscrossed the course, had to be tested and repaired; the main scoreboard had to be found, cleaned up, and reinstalled (Roberts couldn't remember where it had been stored); all the old signs had to be found and repainted; the condition of the rest rooms had to be determined and dealt with; a printer had to be found for tickets, badges, and various publications; press releases had to be written; contestants had to be invited. That last task was made difficult by the fact that the U.S.G.A. had held neither the Open nor the Amateur since 1941, and the Royal and Ancient had not held the British Open since 1939. The pool of qualifiers, therefore, was unusually small. Roberts suggested appointing a special committee to make up the difference.

Despite the many challenges, the 1946 Masters went off on schedule and ran smoothly. The winner was Herman Keiser, a relatively unknown professional from Springfield, Missouri, who had once worked as an assistant to Horton Smith. The players called Keiser "the Missouri Mortician," because his long face was usually cast in a darkly gloomy expression.

After two rounds, Keiser, at seven under par, was five strokes clear of the field. He maintained that margin with a 71 on Saturday. On Sunday, he was erratic on the first nine, made eight consecutive pars on the second nine, and bogeyed the final hole, for a 74. Hogan, who had begun five shots behind, came to the eighteenth knowing he needed a birdie to win and a par to tie. He hit his second shot twelve feet from the hole— then three-putted, including a miss from two and a half feet. He finished second by a stroke. (Among those who witnessed Hogan's miss was a fifteen-year-old girl named Pierrine Baker, whose boyfriend had lifted her up so she could see over the heads of the spectators in front of them. Her boyfriend was Hootie Johnson, also fifteen, who is now the chairman of the club. They have been married for nearly fifty years.)

Several times in the last ten years, Keiser, who is now in his eighties, has made accusations concerning what he says was a conspiracy to derail his victory in 1946. In various magazine articles and a book, he has been quoted as saying that two prominent members of the club had each bet $50,000 on Hogan and therefore didn't want Keiser to win; that the club on Saturday paired him with Sam Snead, who was twelve shots behind him, in the hopes that Snead's large gallery would distract him; that for the same reason the club on Sunday paired him with Byron Nelson, who was eight shots behind him; that he and Nelson were sent off in the middle of the pack rather than in the final pairing in the final round in order to place him at a disadvantage; and that Hogan, as the club's favorite, was given the last tee time. Keiser has also said that he had assumed he would be teeing off last on Sunday and that he would have missed his starting time if someone hadn't rushed into the clubhouse while he was eating lunch to warn him that he was about to be called to the tee. "Someone didn't want me to win," he has said—and some sportswriters have taken him at his word.

Keiser's contention that two prominent members had placed gargantuan wagers on Hogan and that the club conspired with them to protect their money is impossible to check directly, but all of his other accusations can be tested against the record—and none of them is supported by the facts. The third-round leader in the Masters today plays in the final pairing on Sunday, but he didn't in the old days. In Keiser's era, the leader played much earlier, in a featured pairing that teed off in the early afternoon. Roberts explained the rationale in 1956 in a letter to Byron Nelson: "The people who drive great distances [to watch the tournament], ranging as high as 200 miles or more, are not going to be willing to make those long trips unless they can arrive at Augusta around noon, get a bite of lunch, and then see the most interesting personalities perform in the afternoon." The tournament had operated that way from the beginning, and it continued to do so for more than twenty years after the war. In the final round in 1934, for example, Horton Smith (the third round leader and eventual winner) teed off at 12:58, ninety-eight minutes before the final group; twelve years later, Herman Keiser (the third-round leader and eventual winner) teed off at 1:12, ninety-six minutes before the final group. The first tournament leader to play in the final pairing on Sunday was Billy Casper, in 1969. (He finished in a three-way tie for second.)

Why did Hogan tee off last in 1946? He didn't. Despite Keiser's recollection, the final pairing that year consisted of Ralph Guldahl (who
was thirty-one shots out of the lead) and Johnny Palmer (who was
twenty shots out). The last few pairings in the early years were typically
assigned to players who were either hopelessly out of the running or
were notoriously slow—a practice that prevented deliberate or struggling golfers from holding up the leaders. Hogan, who was paired with
Jimmy Demaret in 1946, teed off nearly an hour before the final group.

Nor was there anything remotely unusual about Keiser's pairings in
the last two rounds. Pairings in the early years were not based on scores,
and the leader was typically grouped with a player from well back in the
pack. Horton Smith in 1934 played his final round with Denny Shute,
the British Open champion, who stood ten shots behind him. Jimmy
Demaret, who won in 1947, played his final round with Bobby Locke,
the top international player at that time, who was nine shots back. Final-
round pairings with the leaders in those days were essentially cere-
monial. Byron Nelson did the honors four times in the first ten
tournaments after the war, and he brought home the winner all four
times. The only tournaments in which he didn't play with the third-
round leader were ones in which he himself was in contention—and on
one of those occasions, in 1954, his playing companion won anyway.
That was Sam Snead, who beat Ben Hogan (the third-round leader) in
an eighteen-hole playoff. If the club had really wanted Keiser to lose,
they could have greatly improved their odds by pairing him with anyone
but Nelson.

Keiser's accusation about a huge bet by two members—whom he
has never named—is impossible to check. But his contention that the
club tried to alter the outcome of the tournament in order to protect
their wager is easy to dismiss. Beginning in 1934, the club had participated indirectly in the operation of a public Masters auction pool, or
calcutta—a standard feature at golf tournaments in that era—which was
held at the Bon Air Hotel; there were numerous other pools as well, including some at the club itself. (The last Masters calcutta conducted at
Augusta National was held in 1952.) But Roberts always distinguished
those popular activities—in which he himself sometimes participated—
from professional gambling, which he referred to as "banditry" and

fought for years. One of his complaints about the Bon Air after the war concerned his conviction that the hotel had (as he put it in a letter) "made space available to professional gamblers," whose activities he believed were a threat to the game. Any attempt to skew the outcome of the tournament by tinkering with the pairings would have had to be approved by him. The idea that he would have risked the destruction of the Masters and the club in order to preserve the bankrolls of a pair of members, whose alleged wager would have amounted to ten times the purse of the tournament, is preposterous. If their bet was common knowledge at the tournament, as Keiser has suggested, Roberts would have known about it, too, and he would have thrown both of them out of the club.

The 1947 Masters provided another exciting finish. The top players on the leader board included Nelson, Hogan, and Demaret—who won by a stroke. The most thrilling player, though, was a relative unknown: Frank Stranahan, who played the last two rounds in six under par, had the low round on Sunday (68), and finished two strokes out of the lead in a tie with Nelson for second place. The most exciting thing about Stranahan was that he was not a professional. (He would later win the British Amateur twice.) Jones and Roberts had both dreamed since the beginning that an amateur might win the Masters someday, and Stranahan came closer than anyone had.

The following year, Stranahan provided the shock of the tournament when, six days before the first round, the club withdrew his invitation. In a statement issued to the press on Monday of tournament week, Roberts explained the reason: "Mr. Stranahan, last Friday, was advised that his invitation had been withdrawn because of disregard of regulations made for the protection of the golf course and for the benefit of all Players in the Tournament. This was a repetition of similar offenses of which he had been guilty last year and against which he had been warned. In these circumstances, our Tournament Committee felt justified in considering that the violation of its regulations was flagrant and that it had no other choice than to request Mr. Stranahan's withdrawal."

Stranahan had repeatedly violated a club rule limiting players to a

single ball in practice rounds, but his main offense was that he had become belligerent when confronted for doing so by the course superintendent.* The club's statement had been necessitated, Roberts said, by
"continued publicity of the incident, apparently inspired by Mr. Stranahan." In a wire service news story published that day, Stranahan had
been quoted threatening "serious repercussions" against the club's tournament committee, whose members he referred to as "high hats." A
few days later, in a private letter to Joe Williams of the *New York
Telegram,* Roberts wrote, "Needless to say, it was an unpleasant experience—something that's never happened before in this Tournament. We
were sorry to lose a good golfer but you are quite right when you say
there was no other course we could take."

In more recent years, some writers have speculated that there must
have been something sinister behind Stranahan's expulsion—that
Roberts must have been out to get him for some dark personal reason,
perhaps even because he suspected him of having an affair with a secretary of his from New York, as was suggested (without evidence) in a recent book. It has also been suggested that Roberts intimidated Jones and
others into saying nothing in Stranahan's behalf.

But Jones's correspondence from that period as well as other sources
demonstrate persuasively that Stranahan's problem was Stranahan's
alone. He was invited back to the Masters in 1949 and for the next ten
years after that—he remained one of the top amateurs in the world—
but his respect for the rules and his behavior in the tournament continued to be an issue. According to an article in *Collier's* in 1947, Stranahan
had a reputation as "the most egocentric, monomaniacal character who
ever swung a niblick"; that description was undoubtedly an exaggera-
tion, but it was based on well-established fact. Augusta National employees from that era remember him as arrogant and rude. Stranahan

---

*In a two-page letter of apology (handwritten on club stationery), Stranahan ac-
knowledged as much: "I would also like to apologize to Mr. Luke [the superin-
tendent] for talking back as I certainly know better. However, I did not feel he
could have my invitation revoked because of a few heated words or that he could
call me a fresh 'bastard.' "

was (and is) a bodybuilder, and he typically traveled in those days with several hundred pounds of free weights in his luggage. A favorite trick of his was to ask unsuspecting bellboys to bring his luggage, then laugh as they struggled to carry his bags.

Problems with Stranahan, though unpublicized, continued for years. Two months after the Masters in 1956—more than eight years after the notorious practice round expulsion—the situation was severe enough that Jones felt compelled to write a man-to-man letter to Stranahan's father, who was the head of Champion Spark Plug Co., in Toledo, Ohio, and who had financed his son's amateur golf career. "I want very much to have a talk with you about Frank and his relationship with the Augusta National Golf Club," Jones wrote. "Frank is a very fine golfer and I like him personally very much. Quite frankly, though, he needs to be straightened out on a few aspects of his behavior at the Masters Tournament. I would very much hope that a little talk between you and me might have this effect. While it would be possible for us to have this sort of conversation on the telephone, I would very much prefer, and I think you would too, that we might have it person to person." He suggested that they meet in New York.

On August 6, the son responded with a letter to Jones (addressed "Dear Robert"). "As I travel the road of golf," he wrote, "the Masters Tournament—the way it is handled and what it stands for in the game—means more to me than I have been able to display. Please accept my word that there is nothing I would rather do to add to the Masters in any possible way and to help carry out any suggestions or rules that the committees feel are for the good of all."

That response angered Jones. "Your letter of August 6th uses some very pretty words," he wrote, "and I thank you for your kind expressions. It does not, however, give me the satisfactory answer to the problem I discussed with your father. To have you give me your word that there is nothing you would 'rather do' than the things I and others would normally expect of any competitor who accepted an invitation to play in the tournament is not at all what I want you to tell me."

Stranahan sent another letter three weeks later, but again Jones was displeased. "Perhaps I should not expect that you would use words as carefully as is necessary in my profession," he wrote, "but I am sure you will understand that when you say that there is nothing in the world you 'would rather do than to add to the Masters in any possible way and to help carry out any suggestions that the committees feel are for the good of all,' you are not saying that you will do this." Jones sent a copy of his reply to Stranahan's father as well, and he wrote to Roberts to say that he had "made it plain" to both men "that we would not issue an invitation to Frank again this year" unless Jones was satisfied.

Four days later, Stranahan gave Jones what he wanted: a brief, typewritten letter (addressed "Dear Mr. Jones") in which he repeated wording that Jones himself had suggested: "You have my word that I will cooperate and observe all the suggestions, regulations and rules of the committee." And that, finally, was the end of it. Jones wrote back to say that Stranahan's eleventh Masters invitation would be forthcoming, and he urged Stranahan to stop by and see him when he got to Augusta. Stranahan played in the Masters in 1958 and 1959 as well—in 1959 as a professional—and there is no indication in the club's files that his behavior was ever an issue again.

In a letter to Jones in December 1946, Roberts wrote, "I want you to take over as Tournament Chairman in exactly five years," adding, "I'd like you to start saying now, whatever you will, about Tournament policies." In five years, Jones would be fifty years old and beyond competing in the Masters. He and Roberts had both felt that it would be inappropriate for him to have any official involvement in the running of the tournament or the selection of the field for as long as he was a competitor. But Roberts hoped that his friend would take charge of the tournament as soon as his playing days were over, and he reiterated this desire in other letters as well.

Whether that transition would actually have taken place will never be known, because events in the intervening years dramatically altered Jones's life. In a press release issued early in 1949, Roberts explained what had happened: "As the result of an injury to the upper part of the spine which is believed by his doctors to have occurred when he was quite young," Roberts wrote, "Bob has occasionally suffered, for some years, from what he called a 'crick' in his neck and a lame shoulder." Roberts had also noticed at some point that Jones had begun to drag one foot. "The first noticeable discomfort," Roberts continued, "occurred in Scotland in 1926, but the exact cause of the trouble was never accurately determined until 1948." At that time, Jones was diagnosed with syringomyelia, a rare and devastating disease in which a fluid-filled cavity forms inside the spinal cord and, as it grows over a period of months or years, destroys the center of it. Typical symptoms include numbness, difficulty in walking, weakness of the arms and legs, deformation of the hands, and chronic pain. The symptoms are almost always progressive, as they were in Jones's case, and even today for the vast majority of patients there is no cure. Treatments in Jones's day were crude and almost invariably ineffective. He underwent two operations, but they didn't help.

Jones never played golf again. More than fifty of the club's members chipped in to buy him a golf cart, which was among the first to be manufactured, so that he could drive himself around the property and visit friends on the course. The cart became Jones's link to the club and the Masters. He was too ill to take Roberts's place as the chairman of the tournament, but he continued to consult with Roberts on club and tournament matters until shortly before the end of his life. His main public appearances during the tournament were at a dinner for Masters winners held on Tuesday of Masters week, at a dinner for the amateur players held on Wednesday, and at the awards ceremony following the conclusion of the final round.

Today, the guest list for the Amateur Dinner includes not only the amateur competitors—of whom there are now typically four or five—but also five or six dozen others, among them the amateur honorary invitees, various officials of the United States Golf Association and the Royal and Ancient Golf Club of St. Andrews, and numerous members. The first amateur dinner was held in 1948 at the suggestion of Charles Yates, who had played in every Masters through 1947. When he stopped competing, Jones and Roberts asked him if he could help them think of a way to make the amateur players feel more at home. Golf was chang-

ing, and amateurs were no longer stars, as they had been during the hey-
days of Jones and Yates. "I said that we ought to have a pep rally," Yates
recalls, "so that the amateurs wouldn't feel so much in awe of these professionals they'd heard so much about." The dinner was the result.

Jones loved the Amateur Dinner. On the day of the dinner in 1968,
the last year he came to Augusta for the Masters, he was in considerable
pain but was still determined to attend. He told Yates, though, that he
didn't feel well, and he asked not to be called on to speak. Yates complied, and was preparing to dismiss the gathering when he felt a tug on
his jacket. It was Jones. With a great effort, he drew himself to the
podium and said, in a voice that was scarcely audible, "I just want to say
a few words. . . ."

Roberts and Jones had always spoken at the dinners. Roberts would
typically offer advice and inside knowledge about the course. He would
remind the amateurs that they could learn a great deal by keeping their
eyes open as they played—for example, by looking through the trees to
see where the hole had been cut on the third green as they walked down
the second fairway. Jones would usually tell stories.

"There was one story that Bob always used to tell," Yates recalls,
"and it became a tradition to call on him to tell it. It concerned a new
member of the club who was a nervous sort of fellow. He was attending
his first Jamboree, and after dinner he got involved in a bridge game that
deteriorated into poker. To settle his nerves he was drinking pretty
steadily, and when they finally poured him into bed, at three o'clock in
the morning, he was as drunk as a hoot owl.

"Well, at eight o'clock they awakened him and took him out to the
first tee. This fellow had a handicap of eighteen, a stroke a hole, and he
was paired with a fellow who had a handicap that was much lower. On
the first tee, the low-handicap fellow sliced his ball so far that it hasn't
been found yet. Now, our hero, who was about to jump out of his skin,
stepped up on the tee and topped his drive down the hill. The ground
was hard, and it rolled to the bottom. When he got to it, his caddie gave
him a spoon—and he topped it again. But the ball bounced along and
bounced along past that trap on the right side of the fairway, and it
rolled up to where he had about a hundred and twenty-five yards to the

44

The tenth hole, shot from the right side of the fairway at the bottom of the hill.

45

The tenth green in 1935, before it was moved to the rise beyond and above the fairway bunker. Moving the green solved a drainage problem and transformed the tenth from a mediocre drive-and-pitch hole into one of the most demanding par-fours in the world.

46

A member playing his second shot from an area where MacKenzie originally intended to place an enormous fairway bunker. MacKenzie removed the bunker from his plans when he switched the order of the nines, because he felt it would be unfair to make a golfer carry a large hazard with the first shot of the day.

47

48

The eleventh hole today.

49

The eleventh green in 1948, before the club dammed Rae's Creek to create a pond on the left. The twelfth green is visible beyond and to the right. Just visible through the trees behind both greens is one of the fairways at Augusta Country Club, which abuts Augusta National.

The eleventh green in 1935.

The twelfth hole today, viewed from behind the tee. The Hogan Bridge, which was dedicated in 1958, is on the left. The thirteenth tee is on the right.

The twelfth green in 1935. This green was harder to build than any other on the course. During construction, two tractors and eight mules became stuck in the mire and had to be pulled out with long ropes drawn by all the other tractors.

The view from the tee on the thirteenth hole. The green is around the corner to the left.

52

The thirteenth green in 1935. For
a number of years, several of the
bunkers behind the green had good-
sized trees growing in them.

53

The thirteenth green, viewed from
among the pine trees to the right of
the fairway.

54

The fourteenth hole, looking back down the fairway. The bunkers beyond the thirteenth green are just visible in the background. The fourteenth tee is out of sight, beyond the long line of trees on the right.

The fourteenth green in 1935. The mound in front of the green is now mostly gone.

The fifteenth green in 1935. There was no greenside bunker yet. A number of members at the time felt the hole was too short, but Jones vetoed the idea of lengthening it. He believed that par-fives should be reachable in two by better players.

The fifteenth hole, viewed from the left side of the fairway. The preferred landing area for tee shots is to the right.

Arnold Palmer pitching back to the fifteenth green in 1959 after nearly hitting his second shot into the pond on the sixteenth hole.

The sixteenth green in 1935, when the hole ran in a different direction and was considerably shorter and easier. Jones suggested the current design in 1947, and Robert Trent Jones (no relation) executed his plan.

The seventeenth green today.

The sixteenth hole today. The tee is to the left and behind the camera. The old green was at the base of the hill on the far side of what is now the pond; the old tee was to the right.

The seventeenth green in 1935, when it was one of several holes on the course with no bunkers. The fourteenth is the only hole without a bunker today.

64

65

Ben Crenshaw driving from the eighteenth tee at the 1995 Masters, which he won.

The bunkers on the left side of the eighteenth fairway; they were added in 1966. Although there are two distinct bunkers, Roberts for some reason always preferred to think of them as one bunker with two parts.

66

Henry Picard putting on the eighteenth green during an early Masters. The original fairway bunker is just visible as a white sliver beyond the green near the middle of the picture.

The eighteenth green in 1935.

green. He said to his caddie, 'What should I use now?' And the caddie said, 'Oh, just go ahead and use the one you've got—it doesn't make any difference.' Well, he topped the ball a third time. The pin was cut over there on the left, behind that trap. The ball rolled up the front of the green, just missing the trap, and stopped about six feet from the hole.

"So here was our hero with a six-foot putt for par, which would be a net birdie, and his partner was in his pocket. When he stood up to the ball, his hands were shaking on his putter. They kept shaking and he took the putter back. Then, just as he stroked the ball, a great big collie dog came running up from somewhere, and it ran between his legs. Miraculously, though, the ball went into the hole, and the low-handicap fellow rushed up and said, 'Partner, that's the greatest display of coolness and calmness under fire I've ever seen. How in the hell did you make that putt when that collie dog was running right between your legs?' And the fellow said, 'My God—was that a real dog?' "

CHAPTER SEVEN

General Ike

THE SECOND MOST consequential friendship of Roberts's life began on April 13, 1948, when Dwight D. Eisenhower first visited Augusta National. The future president was between jobs. He had completed a two-year stint, at the request of President Truman, as the chief of staff of the United States Army, and he had accepted but not yet begun his first civilian appointment, as the president of Columbia University. His trip to Augusta was arranged by a member named William E. Robinson, who had met Eisenhower during the war and was now the general manager of the *New York Herald Tribune*. Robinson had discussed with Roberts the possibility of bringing the general to the club, and Roberts had been delighted with the idea.

Like many Americans of both major political parties, Robinson and Roberts were disappointed that Eisenhower had not declared himself a candidate for president in 1948. (Eisenhower's party preference at that time, if any, was not known.) But their main motive in bringing the general to Augusta was probably not political. Both men idolized Eisenhower, in much the same way that Roberts and other members had always idolized Bobby Jones. Ike, like Jones, had the easy aplomb of the selfless hero. More than a few members of the club were powerfully drawn to him, apart from any dreams they may have entertained about his political future. They wanted to know him, play golf with him, play bridge with him, have dinner with him, help him, be liked by him.

Roberts found the prospect enormously appealing. On April 18, after Ike had been at the club for five days, Roberts, in a letter to a member from Florida, wrote, "During the past week we have had a distinguished visitor in the person of General Eisenhower and I don't mind telling you in confidence, there's some prospects of him becoming affiliated with this club." Through all the years of their friendship, Roberts saved letters, newspaper clippings, and other memorabilia of their relationship, and for safekeeping he sent them to his sister, Dorothy, who preserved them in scrapbooks.

Ike's first trip to Augusta required a great deal of advance planning. The war had been over for three years and Eisenhower was not yet a candidate for president, but he still attracted huge crowds of well-wishers wherever he went. Roberts hired a crew of Pinkerton guards— the same ones who had provided security during the Masters, which had just ended—and he and Jones decided that that for as long as Eisenhower was on the property there would be a moratorium on other guests. Eisenhower's public mobility was even more restricted than Jones's had been at the peak of his fame. Not long after Eisenhower's first visit to Augusta, he and Roberts decided to attend a play in New York. They made elaborate advance preparations with the theater's manager, arrived by limousine, and were conducted to their seats in the dark just before the curtain was raised. They made it through the first act without attracting attention. "But the minute the intermission arrived and the lights were turned on," Roberts later recalled in a 1968 interview with a researcher at Columbia University,* "he was spotted, and there was the darnedest mass of people that went back into the theater, even though the great majority of them had walked out during this in-

---

* Over a period of four years beginning in the fall of 1968, Roberts gave fifteen tape-recorded interviews about his relationship with Eisenhower in a project conducted by the Oral History Research Office at Columbia University. The interviews, which took place in New York and Augusta, yielded a typed transcript nearly nine hundred pages long. At Roberts's request, the transcript was sealed for twenty years following his death—a period that ended in the fall of 1997. A number of direct quotations in this chapter were drawn from that transcript.

termission." Eisenhower was surrounded by a crush of people seeking autographs or handshakes. He and Roberts were trapped until the manager, the ushers, and two police officers from outside the building succeeded in clearing an escape route through the crowd. "We got out to the car," Roberts recalled, "and it took quite a while and was hard going, but we finally got in the car and got the doors shut, and then people pressed up against this car on all sides, presumably just to get a better look at the man, and the chauffeur blew the horn several times, and the people in front of the car wouldn't move. Finally, he started the car and motioned—just an inch at a time—and they gradually gave way, and we finally were able to go away from there." Roberts found the intensity of the gawkers frightening. Eisenhower said, "Well, that settles that. We're not going to the theater anymore."

For Eisenhower, the club was a sanctuary, as it had been for Jones. He could play golf without a gallery there, and he could always find a bridge game. Despite various security restrictions, Eisenhower was a hit with the members, and vice versa. At the end of his first visit, he posed for pictures in the green jacket of a member who wasn't present, and he later sent a signed copy of one of the photographs to Roberts. It was inscribed, "For Cliff Roberts—who did so much to make our visit to the Augusta National the most delightful vacation of our lives." Roberts later said, "I very quickly discovered that both the General and Mamie were the sort of folks that if they liked you, they liked you a lot, in a hurry." His feelings were shared by the others present, and within a short time—almost certainly before the end of the visit—Ike had been asked to join.

Not least among Augusta National's attractions for Ike was that it was the only golf club that Mamie had ever liked. She didn't play herself. In fact, she got virtually no exercise whatsoever, seldom left her bed before noon, and went outdoors only under protest—often at the insistence of Roberts, who would drive her around the course in a golf cart. But she loved the club and made many friends among the members and their wives. Roberts was one of her favorites; she used to joke about a letter she had received in which she had been accused of setting a bad example for the youth of America by permitting Roberts to greet her at the airport with a kiss.

Historians have often wondered whether there wasn't something calculating about Eisenhower's enthusiastic, wholesale adoption of this new circle of acquaintances. The members of Augusta National included many wealthy executives, more than a few of whom would later provide considerable money and support during both presidential campaigns. Ike flew in their planes, stayed in their homes, and played golf at their clubs. But Eisenhower's letters, diary entries, and other writings from that era give no hint of cynicism. Running for president was close to the last thing in the world that he wanted to do. If anything, he was made nervous by the ardor with which some of his new friends openly yearned for his candidacy. In a diary entry in the fall of 1949 he wrote, "What I dread is the faint possibility that circumstances and people could combine in some way to convince me I have a duty in politics. But I do not believe it, and if I should ever, in the future, decide affirmatively on this point it will be because I've become oversold by friends."

The far more plausible explanation for his ready adoption of a new circle of intimates is that the club had serendipitously offered exactly the sense of belonging that Ike and Mamie were seeking at that point in their lives. They were nearing their sixties and feeling the strains of a hitherto unsettled existence. Ike in 1948 believed that he was well on his way to retiring from public service. That first visit to Augusta National—in which he eagerly grilled Roberts about the workings of the club—probably seemed at the time to offer a glimpse of one of the more tantalizing possibilities of civilian life.

Augusta National provided what may have been the Eisenhowers' first real opportunity as adults to establish ongoing, permanent friendships—much as it had for Roberts more than fifteen years before. Ike and Mamie had been married for a little over thirty years at the time of their first visit, and during those thirty years they had had more than thirty different homes. They had lived in modest military housing or small apartments, and their neighbors and friends had changed as rapidly as Ike's assignments. Their first trip to Augusta National was their first vacation in more than a decade. A number of the people they met then and during subsequent visits would be among their closest friends for the rest of their lives.

Once Eisenhower became president, his Augusta friends played an important role. In *Mandate for Change,* the first volume of his White House memoirs, he wrote, "These were men of discretion, men, who, already successful, made no attempt to profit by our association. It is almost impossible for me to describe how valuable their friendship was to me. Any person enjoys his or her friends; a President needs them, perhaps more intensely at times than anything else." Eisenhower valued his Augusta friends not only because he liked them personally but also because they had the means and the inclination to come when he summoned them, and to seek nothing in return except the flattery of his attention. When the plans called for bridge, the friends usually came four at a time, so that an extra man would be available to keep the game going if Eisenhower should suddenly be called away. Eisenhower viewed his presidency as his patriotic duty; during those eight years, he viewed the loyalty of his Augusta National friends, to some extent, as their patriotic duty—and they would have agreed. Roberts's visits to the White House were so frequent and so important to the Eisenhowers that Ike reserved a bedroom (the Red Room) for his exclusive use, and kept a toothbrush and a pair of pajamas for him in the closet.

The relationship between Eisenhower and Roberts, which was deep and enduring, surprises some people, because the two men's public personas could scarcely have been less similar. Despite appearances, though, Roberts and Eisenhower had a great deal in common. Like Roberts, Eisenhower had been raised in a large family of limited means in small towns in the Midwest and South. (In Eisenhower's case, the towns were Denison, Texas, and Abilene, Kansas.)* Like Roberts, Eisenhower had worked as a child, raised animals, excelled in sports, and found his way into more than a few fistfights. As adults, both men loved golf and bridge above all other recreations. Both were stubborn competitors who played to win. Both were realists. Neither was afraid to

---

* Roberts was so reticent about his past that Eisenhower probably never knew how similar their backgrounds were. In a letter written in 1957, Ike teased Roberts for having been "raised as a city boy"—a misperception that Roberts had clearly done nothing to dispel in nearly a decade of friendship.

make a big decision, and each knew how to delegate responsibility without surrendering control. Roberts was as rootless as a career soldier: He inhabited most of his residences—hotel rooms, apartments, condominiums, his unadorned room at the club—as indifferently as if he had been posted to them. Neither man could tolerate a sycophant. Each was careless of his public reputation. Both were doggedly determined, and both tended to internalize the considerable pressures of their occupations: Each man had trouble with his heart, and each suffered much of his adult life from a variety of gastrointestinal ailments that were either caused or aggravated by stress.

In addition, Roberts had a personality that Eisenhower was probably predisposed to like. In several conspicuous ways, Roberts's character resembled that of Eisenhower's great friend and mentor, George C. Marshall, who had been Eisenhower's predecessor as army chief of staff and was the principal sponsor of Ike's role in the Second World War. Marshall was a forbidding figure who seldom smiled, almost never laughed, had no small talk, and was as hard to imagine out of uniform as Roberts was to imagine in shorts; even Eisenhower, who revered him, described him as "remote and austere." Roberts's outwardly chilly temperament and disregard for public approbation probably struck Eisenhower as engagingly familiar; they certainly would not have put him off.

One of the strongest bonds between Eisenhower and Roberts was golf, about which both were passionate. While at Augusta National, "Ike wanted to play golf, practice golf, or take golf lessons, all day long," Roberts wrote in his book about the club. Of the two, Roberts was by far the more skillful player. (A bumper sticker during Ike's second presidential campaign read, BEN HOGAN FOR PRESIDENT. IF WE'RE GOING TO HAVE A GOLFER, LET'S HAVE A GOOD ONE.) Eisenhower had injured his left knee as a young man while playing football at West Point, and he was forced to swing mostly from the waist up. He was a short hitter and an inveterate slicer. His putting was so poor that sympathetic playing partners would often knock away any ball that was remotely near the leather—a practice that sometimes led to controversy. At the Burning Tree Club, in Bethesda, Maryland, where he often played when he was in Washington, the caddies sometimes made side bets on their players. After Eisen-

hower had jabbed his ball several feet past the hole on one green, his opponent said, "That's good, Mr. President," and a caddie, appalled, said,
"It ain't good by me."

When it was too dark or too wet to play golf, Eisenhower's favorite
activity was bridge. He was a skilled and fiercely competitive player who
was noted in particular for his powers of concentration. "[W]hen Eisenhower was the first candidate for President in memory who indicated
that he was unable to pronounce the word 'injunction' when discussing
the labor problem," Murray Kempton wrote in *Esquire* in 1967, "I suggested to one of his admirers that he seemed extraordinarily dumb. 'If
he's so dumb,' was the reply, 'why is he such a good bridge player?' " At
Augusta and elsewhere, Ike's card games would often begin in the afternoon and continue more or less without interruption until midnight.
"More than once after eighteen holes of golf," Roberts wrote in his
book about the club, "I've wanted badly to stretch out and rest, only to
have Sergeant [John] Moaney [Eisenhower's longtime personal orderly]
come and tell me as I stepped out of the shower, 'The Boss is ready to
play bridge.' "

Roberts also played a great deal of bridge with Eisenhower at Camp
David, the presidential retreat in Maryland. In fact, when the president
wasn't occupied there with official business, they spent almost all their
time at the card table, taking occasional breaks in which they played a
makeshift version of golf. Navy personnel had built Eisenhower a crude
green with three tees arranged around it. The players would hit from
each tee in sequence, keeping score according to a system that Eisenhower had devised. (It was based on hitting greens, avoiding bunkers,
and making putts.) "It was better than nothing," Roberts recalled years
later. "It was better than nothing."

Not long before his first visit to the club, Eisenhower had finished writing *Crusade in Europe*, a book about the war which would be published
later in 1948. William Robinson helped with some of the publishing
arrangements, and Roberts was one of several people who counseled
Eisenhower on how best to structure the financial side of the deal. A

provision of the tax law at that time permitted certain kinds of authors under certain circumstances to treat the proceeds from the sale of a book as a capital gain rather than as ordinary income—an arrangement that led to a substantial savings in taxes—and Roberts recommended that he take advantage of it. Eisenhower did. Doubleday bought all rights to the book for a lump sum of $635,000. After taxes, Ike netted a little less than half a million dollars.

Half a million dollars was a huge sum in 1948, and it seemed especially huge to the Eisenhowers. Ike had been essentially broke when he wrote the book. Upon accepting the job at Columbia, he had been only just able to scrape together enough money to buy an inexpensive automobile, which he and Mamie drove to their new home in New York. Eisenhower later told Roberts that during the drive he had said to Mamie, "I want you to know that this is a car that we must get a lot of enjoyment and use out of, and I hope you like it and you're proud of it, because what we're doing is riding out of Washington on our entire capital."

When Eisenhower received the fee for his book, he went immediately to Roberts. "He knew I was in the investment business," Roberts recalled in 1968, "so he just handed the proceeds of the book over to me, and asked me to put it into income securities for him. For the first few months, I went over with him the things that I thought he ought to own, in the way of stocks and bonds, and I would explain everything to him in detail." Eisenhower was an eager student, Roberts recalled, and he enjoyed his financial education. He later executed a power of attorney that gave Roberts discretionary authority over all the family's investments.

Roberts not only handled Eisenhower's investments but also served as a sort of personal tutor on many financial matters. During Eisenhower's assignment as the supreme commander of Allied forces under the brand-new North Atlantic Treaty Organization—a position he had assumed at Truman's request and for which he took a leave of absence from Columbia—Roberts arranged for Eugene R. Black, who was the president of the World Bank, to visit him in Paris; Black thereafter provided Ike with summaries of confidential financial information concerning countries whose leaders he had to deal with. Later, when

Eisenhower became a candidate for president, Roberts personally gave him a crash course in international finance.

After Eisenhower's election in 1952, Roberts no longer felt comfortable managing his personal investments. He worried that his friendship with Ike created too many possibilities for apparent conflicts of interest, and that on some occasion he might inadvertently invest some of the president's money in a company that stood to gain from some government action of which he was unaware, thus leaving the president (and himself) vulnerable to criticism by what he referred to as "left-wing politicians" or the press. Eisenhower at first saw no need for such a precaution, but Roberts was adamant. The solution he proposed was to place all of Eisenhower's investments in a trust at a bank in Baltimore and to give control of the accounts to two men at an investment firm in which Roberts was not involved. That was done—although Eisenhower insisted that Roberts be consulted before any investment decisions were made. The president received occasional reports on the total value of his holdings, but he never knew any of the specifics during the eight years he was in office, and, in fact, didn't see his tax returns. This was the first blind trust in American politics. Since that time, similar arrangements have become common among political candidates, appointed officials, and other public figures. Eisenhower's only complaint, when he left the White House and for the first time saw his portfolio, was that he owned too many bonds and not enough stocks. After the presidency, Roberts went back to guiding Eisenhower's investments directly. When Ike was offered investment ideas by other people, his standard response was that he would have to "check with Cliff."

During Eisenhower's tour of duty with NATO in France, speculation at home intensified about the possibility of his being a candidate for president in 1952. He was noncommittal, and historians would later wonder whether his refusal to declare himself a candidate was in fact shrewd self-marketing. But Roberts, who was with him often during that period, had no doubt that he was sincere. "Of that I'm just as certain as I am of the fact that I'm alive today," he said in 1968. Roberts very much hoped that Ike would run, but he knew his friend well enough to be certain that no amount of lobbying would ever persuade him, and that Ike would run for president only if he believed the country would suffer if he did not. Eisenhower did once directly ask Roberts if he should run, but Roberts refused to give an opinion, saying (as he later recalled), "I am not going to tell you that you should run, and I certainly am not going to tell you that you shouldn't run." Roberts instead offered to gather information that might help Ike make his own decision, and to quietly assemble a group of Eisenhower's friends, whose opinions Roberts would sound out on Ike's behalf. Ike agreed, and Roberts assembled a small group, mostly consisting of men whom Eisenhower had met at Augusta National, including Jones.

The group formally met just once, in December 1951, in New York at the Park Lane Hotel, where Roberts lived. Its main recommendation—personally delivered the following day to Eisenhower, who was in Paris, by Roberts and Robinson—was that if there was truly no chance that Ike was going to run, then Ike had to immediately issue a statement to that effect. Ike was beginning to receive endorsements from politicians whose future would be harmed if he strung them out for months and then withdrew. "He quickly saw the point," Roberts later recalled, "but I rather doubt that he had understood or weighed that particular problem." When Ike responded that he did not wish to make such a statement, Roberts was privately delighted: that meant that an Eisenhower presidency was not yet out of the question.

Roberts and Robinson got Eisenhower to consider some of the technicalities involved in a (still hypothetical) candidacy. Military regulations prohibited him from actively seeking office—a restriction that suited him entirely, since he didn't want to run—but did not prevent others from making him a candidate by nominating him without his authorization. When Roberts and Robinson told Ike that that was what they intended to do, he said (as Roberts later recalled), "Well, you're talking about something that any American has a right to do, so if that's what he wants to do, let him go and do it." Thus armed with what they believed was Ike's implied consent, Robinson left that night to return to the United States, where he enlisted Henry Cabot Lodge to put Eisenhower on the ballot for the Republican primary in New Hampshire.

Roberts made another trip to Paris just before the New Hampshire primary. He had been asked by the leaders of the proxy Eisenhower campaign in that state to prepare Ike for the strong possibility that he would be defeated. The Republican frontrunner, Senator Robert Taft of Ohio, had made an all-out effort, and a poll commissioned by the Eisenhower team was deeply discouraging. "The somber message I gave Ike did not seem to disturb him," Roberts wrote in his book about the club, "and he went calmly about his business the next day, taking me along to Germany with him." While away, Roberts kept up with the news from New Hampshire. Eisenhower apparently did not, and on the flight back to Paris from Frankfurt, he asked Roberts if he knew how the voting had gone. Roberts said that he did, and that as a matter of fact, Ike had "defeated Senator Taft and defeated him handily, and it doesn't surprise me a damn bit."

"Well, that isn't what you told me to expect," Eisenhower said.

"When we arrived at Orly field," Roberts later recalled, "there was the biggest crowd of newspapermen that I had ever seen in Europe, and they wanted to take his picture. I ducked out of sight. I decided the thing for me to do was to get away from there, because I always felt that the presence of a Wall Street man couldn't possibly be of any help to a potential candidate for political office. So I went around to the General's car and got in and sat down, and these newspaper boys and photographers of course kept him there for quite a little bit before he could get away from them. And after he got in the car, I remember his saying to me, 'My goodness, those folks are certainly excited about this election.'

"I said, 'Well, I'm amazed that you're not more excited about it.'

"If I recall correctly, he said, 'Well, it does make you feel kind of good, [to know] that that many people [who] don't know you at all would express that kind of confidence.'" And they drove back to Eisenhower's house and had dinner.

During the campaign, Roberts and a number of other Augusta National members "became almost full-time campaign workers," Roberts wrote in his book. Roberts was deeply involved in a group called Citizens for

Eisenhower, the purpose of which was to raise money and build support
for Eisenhower's nomination. (The fund-raising effort was so successful
that the group actually returned more than a quarter of a million dollars to its contributors.) At the convention in Chicago, Roberts was part
of the Eisenhower entourage, and on the last night of the convention he
followed the balloting from Eisenhower's suite. As soon as the nomination was secure, Ike left the room in a hurry, took the elevator downstairs, and worked his way through the crowd and across the street to
Taft's hotel. "I tried to follow him," Roberts later recalled. "At that time,
he had a bodyguard consisting of one man, a Chicago policeman, and he
went out of there so fast that this Chicago cop couldn't keep up with
him, and he went through the crowds like a football player, and I
couldn't keep him in sight even. But I knew where he was going."
Roberts found an elevator and asked the operator to take him up to
Taft's headquarters. "And he was in there, shaking hands with Taft, before the cop or I could get there." This prompt and unexpected gesture,
Roberts said, "made a tremendous hit with the Taft crowd." Taft later
campaigned hard for Eisenhower.

Other club members also played big roles in Eisenhower's campaign.
One of the most important was W. Alton Jones, who was known to his
friends as Pete. Jones was the chairman of Cities Service Co. and was a
close friend of both Roberts's and Eisenhower's. He was known at the
club for his generosity. He insisted on picking up almost any restaurant
or bar check that he had anything to do with, and he financed or helped
to finance many improvements at the club. At the same time, he had a
number of miserly eccentricities. The first duty of his caddie was always
to search the grass for usable tees, because he hated to buy them. He
haggled over handicap strokes, attempting, in Roberts's words, "to ensure his being a winner on the golf course, no matter how small the
stakes." And he always traveled with a heavy hand-cranked metal sharp-
ener, which he used to extend the life of his razor blades. He was determined to get at least twenty-five shaves from each blade, and he would
cheerfully spend ten or fifteen minutes honing an edge on one that was
about to expire.

Pete Jones was a fervent believer in Eisenhower. Before Ike officially became a candidate, Jones told Roberts that he would be willing to contribute as much as a million dollars to support him. "I don't want you to ever leave anything undone that money can do," he said, according to Roberts's recollection. Roberts worried that support of that magnitude might backfire—and might, indeed, be illegal. But he did eventually call on Jones for what he calculated was roughly $250,000. "I used to go over to Pete's office or he'd come over to my office and he'd give me $25,000 at a time in currency," Roberts told the interviewer at Columbia. "Then I'd have to figure out how I could get it into the treasury of one of the various committees that were working for General Eisenhower's election. I had a lawyer check into it, and it was very evident that through this operation, Pete and I were skirting around the fringes of the law— and still, despite the laws that were on the books about campaign funds, everybody violated those rules regularly every year, and nobody ever went to jail for violating them, so neither Pete nor I worried too much. I think I may have worried about it a little bit more than Pete did."

Roberts was flabbergasted at the time that anyone would even conceive of making a political donation of that size. He viewed Jones's gesture as an act of patriotism—despite the fact that in order to maintain Jones's anonymity Roberts had to, in effect, launder the money by asking various other contributors to add parts of it to their own donations. "I'd have to go and get a friend of mine that I knew I could trust," Roberts recalled, "and I'd say, 'Here's a thousand dollars that somebody gave me; he wants to contribute but he doesn't want to contribute in his own name. Will you take this thousand and put with it whatever additional amount you want to give, then give me your check—say, for $2,000?' In other words, I'd use Pete's money as seed money. . . ." After Ike became president, Jones bought up the land surrounding the Eisenhowers' farm in Gettysburg, Pennsylvania, in order to provide a buffer between the Eisenhowers and the rest of the world.

In 1962, Jones was among a group of Augusta friends whom Eisenhower summoned to California for a hunting trip. Jones's plane—an American Airlines jet that Roberts would have been on as well if he had not been delayed in returning from a trip to Barbados—crashed shortly after takeoff, killing everyone on board. When the authorities recovered

Jones's body they found $60,000 in cash in his pocket. This discovery, coupled with the fact that he had been traveling to visit Eisenhower, led to speculation that he might have been involved in some sort of illicit political scheme—although Eisenhower had been out of office for more than a year—and a reporter called Roberts to see if he knew anything about it. Roberts's reaction surprised the reporter. "Was that all he was carrying?" Roberts asked. He explained that Jones always carried a lot of cash—and often more than $60,000. In his book about the club, Roberts wrote, "I once undertook to persuade Pete not to carry so much cash (which always included one or more $10,000 bills) unless he had some good reason for doing so. He replied by telling me he was quite poor as a boy, and never had enough in silver pieces to make a jingle in his pocket. He therefore enjoyed the feeling of knowing that, if he saw something in a store window he wanted, he would have enough money in his pocket to pay for it—and he did not propose to allow anyone to deprive him of that very satisfactory feeling."

On election night in 1952, Roberts was with Eisenhower at the Commodore Hotel in New York. Late in the evening, when victory seemed assured but Stevenson, the Democratic candidate, had not yet conceded, the two of them were walking down a hall on their way back to the general's suite. Eisenhower said that he was exhausted but that the suite would be too crowded for napping. "Just then I spied an empty single room with the key in the door," Roberts later recalled. "So I pushed Ike in the door and told him to get into bed, which he did." Roberts locked the door and stood guard outside for half an hour, professing ignorance when asked if he knew where Eisenhower had got to. "Finally, [chief of staff] Sherman Adams, Senator [Everett] Dirksen, and one or two others came along with worried looks on their faces," Roberts said. "They told me Stevenson had conceded and that the General was needed immediately but they had been unable to find him. With that, I unlocked the bedroom door, where we found Ike still sound asleep. In a matter of moments, he was making a brief talk on TV."

The next day, Roberts, the Eisenhowers, a group of Secret Service agents, and half a dozen others took off for Augusta in a plane that Roberts had chartered from Eastern Air Lines several weeks before.

(The plan had been to take Ike to Augusta whether he won or not; Roberts had taken the precaution of chartering a Constellation, an airplane large enough to accommodate the security detail of a president-elect.) Roberts notified the club that they were coming, contacted state and local police, and asked the Atlanta Pinkerton office to send to the club as many guards as it could spare. As will surprise no one who knew him well, Roberts was better organized that day than the president-elect. "Someone had previously handed me a report made by a firm of business consultants which detailed the government posts that were subject to the pleasure of an incoming President," he said later. "Fortunately, I brought it along, and it came in very handy for Ike during the next several weeks."

Eisenhower's intention of going to Augusta after the election—his sixth visit to the club, and his first in two and a half years—had supposedly been kept secret, but the presidential entourage was met by a crowd of as many as 250,000 people. (The population of Augusta at that time was less than 100,000.) "It's close to twenty miles' drive, possibly a little more, from the Augusta Airport to the Augusta National Golf Club," Roberts recalled, "and the road was lined all the way on both sides, from two deep to as many as fifteen in spots." There were so many people, Roberts said, that the cars sometimes were unable to move. "Members of the crowd would call out to open up and let his car pass."

Entertaining a sitting president necessitated a number of changes at the club. Members had to put up with restrictions on guests and with the presence of Secret Service agents, who, when accompanying Ike on the course, often carried golf bags containing Thompson submachine guns. In 1953, at the suggestion of the Secret Service, a substantial chain-link fence was built around the perimeter of the property. The club also extended the west wing of the clubhouse in order to accommodate both a new golf shop and, upstairs, a suite of offices for the president. (Eisenhower's desk and chair are now in the clubhouse library.) That same year, the club added a new cottage, called the Eisenhower Cabin. Like all residential accommodations on the property, it was owned by the club and available for use by all members and guests,

but it was designed around the particular needs of the president's entourage. The dormers on the second floor, for example, provided observation posts for Secret Service marksmen.

Eisenhower suffered a heart attack in late September of 1955 while on
vacation in Colorado. Ann Whitman, the president's secretary, called
Roberts almost immediately with the particulars, and Roberts called
Vice President Richard Nixon and other members of the administration
to urge that at least one civilian heart specialist be brought to Denver, in
addition to the military physicians who ordinarily looked after Ike.
Whitman wrote in her diary that "[Roberts's] reasoning was that while
the army doctors were no doubt competent, we would be criticized for
not bringing in civilian consultants—he wanted three." (Public relations
considerations aside, Roberts placed great stock in medical specialists,
and he visited a number of prominent ones over the years in connection
with ailments of his own.) As a result of Roberts's urging—and despite
initial resistance by Eisenhower's military physicians—Paul Dudley
White, a distinguished cardiologist affiliated with Massachusetts General Hospital, was summoned to Denver. When Roberts himself suffered a heart attack four months later, Eisenhower "returned the
compliment," in Roberts's words, by sending White to look after him.
While Roberts was recuperating, Eisenhower suggested to him in a letter that they exploit their heart attacks by negotiating higher handicaps
at Augusta National. Roberts replied, "Please don't try to out-trade me
on strokes. Let us make the most of our supposed infirmities—and pick
on others."

Eisenhower remained in the hospital—the eighth floor of which had
been turned over to him—for nearly seven weeks. He wore red pajamas
and a cowboy hat, and Mamie, who had been given a room near his, entertained him with selections from the huge volume of mail he received. Roberts traveled to Denver in October at the president's request
and was one of his first visitors, aside from various relatives and a few
members of his administration.

Ike's doctors asked Roberts to keep the conversation away from politics, which Roberts did adroitly. In the course of their conversation, Ike

asked Roberts if he would talk to Mamie about her finances. Ike had given Mamie $30,000 when he sold the publishing rights to *Crusade in Europe,* and she had always kept that money in a savings account, where it earned just one percent a year. (Mamie, when it came to investments, had the "instincts of a squirrel," Roberts said, and had never trusted stocks.) Eisenhower and Roberts had had this conversation several times before; the subject arose again, clearly, because Eisenhower was worried about what would happen to his wife should his heart condition turn out to be fatal.

Roberts then went down the hall to see Mamie. When he mentioned the $30,000, Mamie said that she didn't want to put it at risk because she might need it someday "to buy her way into the widows' home," Roberts later recalled. He suggested, therefore, that if Ike brought up the subject again, they should tell him that they had declared a moratorium on investments as well as politics.

Roberts then did something that Eisenhower had never done: He explained to her how Ike and Mamie's investments were set up and how much their portfolio was now worth, and he assured her that no matter what might happen to Ike she would always have enough money to live comfortably. He described the blind trust and explained why it had been created, and he told her how much its value had grown during the years that Ike had been in office. Mamie was deeply relieved. She said that Ike had never explained anything to her about their finances—in fact, he had given instructions that she was not to be told—and that she was merely issued a check each month out of which she covered their household expenses.

Mamie then unburdened to Roberts about how difficult her own life had been in the aftermath of her husband's heart attack. "She recounted the trip to the hospital after Ike wakened," Roberts later recalled, "and the first four terrible days there, and how she went with almost no sleep during that four-day period, and all she had done since, including the answering and signing of thousands of letters, and how Ike had expressed gratitude to everyone except herself." As Mamie spoke, "her nerves," Roberts noted, "seemed more than raw," and she smoked many cigarettes. He speculated that she was still suffering from "a state of shock."

"I then told Mamie I believed I could explain at least partially why

Ike had never expressed his thanks to her," Roberts continued. "I told her that she knew something about the many services I had tried to render Ike, and asked her if she would be surprised to learn that Ike had never once said thank you to me. She seemed incredulous, saying that only yesterday Ike had said to her, 'Do you know, Mamie, you and I have never had a friend quite so dependable as Cliff.'

"I then went on to explain how I had been able to rationalize the matter. It had finally dawned on me that he regarded our friendship and our readiness to serve each other as something that required no explanation or comment—that he was paying me an extraordinary compliment when he requested me to make up a list of people who required thank-you letters in connection with some project and then failed to inquire why my own name was left off, even though I may have done more work on the project than anyone else. With tears in her eyes, Mamie thanked me for telling her my own experience with Ike and how I figured the thing out in a fashion that had made me a lot happier than the thanks could ever have done." (Later, however—when her tears had dried—Mamie did tell Roberts that, while such a rationalization might satisfy a man, "I'd rather be told that I'm appreciated.")

Roberts's visit with Ike had lasted about half an hour; his visit with Mamie lasted an hour and a half. They had always liked each other before, and the bond between them now deepened. And not long afterward, Mamie surprised Roberts by "meekly" sending him $30,000 to be invested—in stocks.

Chapter Eight

Television

In the fall of 1945, as Augusta National was emerging from its wartime hibernation, Roberts wrote a lengthy memorandum to James Searle, the club's manager, enumerating steps that had to be taken to prepare for the first postwar Masters, in 1946. "I don't suppose anyone will be ready to do anything in the way of television," he wrote in passing, "but if they can by next April, I will naturally want to hear about it." Roberts was surely one of the few people at that time who were even thinking about the possibility of showing golf on TV. Fewer than six thousand television sets were in use in the United States, and they had screens the size of a hand.

Roberts's interest in broadcasting dated back to the first Augusta National Invitation Tournament, in 1934, which had been covered on radio by CBS. That was the first nationwide broadcast of a golf tournament. Roberts felt the radio program was important both because it enabled distant fans to follow the tournament and because it helped stir up interest among potential ticket buyers. In the early forties, CBS declined to renew its radio contract, and the club signed instead with NBC. That agreement also gave NBC the right to televise the tournament—and as late as two months before the 1947 Masters, Roberts believed that it might do so. But NBC declined. Later that year, a local station in Missouri covered the final hole of the 1947 U.S. Open, at St. Louis Country Club. That program—the first television broadcast of a golf tourna-

ment—was not a great success. Golf was poorly suited to the TV technology of the day, since the game was played outdoors in unpredictable
lighting, and the competitors roamed over an area that was hard to
cover with stationary cameras. (Not surprisingly, the most heavily televised sports in the early years of TV were boxing and wrestling, both of
which could be lighted artificially and neither of which required agile
camera work.) Interest among the networks in providing live coverage
of golf essentially vanished. It was revived in 1953 by a broadcast of part
of that year's World Championship of Golf, at Tam O'Shanter Country
Club, near Chicago. The broadcast was crude, the audience was limited,
and the cameras showed only the eighteenth hole—but the tournament
ended with high drama, as Lew Worsham won by holing his final approach shot, on camera, for an eagle. Jimmy Demaret, who was providing the on-air commentary, cried, "The son of a bitch holed it!"

The first live nationwide telecast of a tournament took place the
following year, when NBC provided limited coverage of the 1954 U.S.
Open, at Baltusrol, beginning at the seventeenth green. Roberts wanted
the Masters to be carried on television, too, but NBC wasn't interested;
the network's (understandable) feeling may have been that one major
money-losing golf program was enough. Still, Roberts persisted, and
early in 1956, under pressure from the club, Tom S. Gallery, who was the
director of sports at NBC, wrote to Roberts to say that NBC was declin-
ing to exercise the renewal option in its current contract. That meant,
Gallery wrote, that Augusta National was "free to make such arrangements as it sees fit with respect to the radio and television rights to the
1956 Tournament." The club hastily made an agreement with CBS, and
the first Masters television broadcast took place less than a month later.
Golf fans in most of the country were able to watch live as Jack Burke,
Jr., beat Ken Venturi by a single stroke.

That first Masters broadcast was uneven in the extreme, and it lasted
just a total of two and a half hours over three days, but it was a hit with
golf fans. The number of viewers was estimated at ten million, and
Roberts later learned that in the grill rooms of golf clubs all over the
country, groups of golfers had gathered to catch glimpses of the action
and of the course. Four days after the tournament, William MacPhail,

who was the director of sports at CBS, wrote to Roberts, "Our department has been literally flooded by letters from all parts of the country expressing appreciation that this tournament was brought to the nation. So many commented on the unbelievable beauty of the course, the tremendous crowds in attendance, and the overall fine staging of the event." That viewers were able to acquire even vague impressions of the course is remarkable, given the low resolution of the snowy, black-and-white pictures. But golf fans for years had read about and seen photographs of the fabled tournament at Augusta National, and now for the first time they had had a chance to watch the action for themselves. Roberts was pleased, too. In a letter to William Paley, who was the chief executive of CBS, he wrote that the program had been "the first televised golf tournament broadcast which could be called a credit to a network or a tournament."

That the broadcast had been a success was in no small measure due to the efforts of Roberts himself. CBS had intended to provide only minimal coverage, concentrating on the eighteenth hole. To induce the network to put more cameras on the course, Roberts offered to cut in half the $10,000 fee that CBS had agreed to pay the club—if CBS would invest the extra $5,000 in a second transmission station, to be situated near the fifteenth green. The station enabled CBS to place more cameras on more holes. Roberts confirmed the offer in a telegram a week before the tournament, and CBS agreed to extend its coverage to the fifteenth fairway. Merritt Coleman, a CBS executive, wired Roberts later that the tournament had been "one of the most exciting sports programs I have ever witnessed and your suggestion of a double pick up at the 15th and 18th holes made the telecasts great."

During the Masters that year, Roberts had devoted virtually all of his time to the broadcast, which he called "the most important current Tournament development." He had been struck by the power of television during Eisenhower's presidential campaign—the first in which TV played a significant role—and he believed that the new medium had the potential to transform not only the Masters but all of golf. Television would broaden the popularity of the game, he believed, and the revenues from commercials (assuming that advertisers could be found) would enable Augusta National, the U.S.G.A., and other tournament sponsors to pay bigger prizes. Those benefits were not yet obvious to the players; in the fall of 1956, Byron Nelson wrote to Roberts to say, among other things, that a number of the golfers at that year's Masters had complained that the television equipment and personnel had intruded on the competition. Roberts had to remind him that if televised golf caught on, as he expected it to, the golfers themselves would be the principal beneficiaries. Television, Roberts believed, could turn the poorly paid itinerant players of the early American golf tours into true professional athletes.

Despite his eagerness to build the tournament's purse, Roberts's interest in television was not mercenary. In 1958, shortly after American Express had signed on as the program's first sponsor, Roberts warned Ralph Reed, the company's president (and a member of the club), not to become carried away. "The average golf fan takes his golf pretty seriously," Roberts wrote, adding that "nothing but extreme annoyance could result from untimely, too long or too frequent commercials." He believed that interruptions should be held to a minimum, and that if networks, tournament sponsors, players, or advertisers became greedy they would do themselves and the game more harm than good. In later years, Roberts worried that the U.S.G.A. was in danger of being seduced by television advertising dollars—which he felt the organization didn't need—and he urged its executives to accept lower broadcast fees for the U.S. Open in exchange for guaranteed coverage of tournaments with less commercial appeal.

Paradoxically, perhaps, Roberts's focus on quality rather than money made him a feared negotiator at CBS. He was attentive to financial details, but for him the main issue was always the content of the program. He was willing to accept lower fees in exchange for commitments from CBS to improve the show. He expected the network each year to outdo its previous efforts, and he spelled out exactly how he felt the broadcast could be improved. His approach to television was identical to his approach to the tournament. He believed that every year was a learning experience, and that no matter how good the current year's effort might have been, the next could always be better. Shortly after the tournament each year, Roberts would assemble a group of as many as several dozen club members, local broadcasters, and others to review the television coverage of the tournament that had just ended. The group's observations were distilled into a detailed critique, whose arrival in New York CBS executives came to dread. The critiques would generally begin with praise—"It was our impression that CBS made an all-out effort to do an outstanding job and we are delighted that they did so"—but the club's intention was not to pat the broadcasters on the back. As Roberts explained at the beginning of one of the reviews, "Our purpose, frankly, was to look for things to criticize in order that further improvements may be undertaken in the future."

Roberts was an exacting and often an exasperating partner. Despite the discomfort of the network's executives, though, pressure from the club had a beneficial and quite noticeable impact on the show. The Masters telecast has always served as a sort of advanced-degree program for sports broadcasters. Most of the people who have worked on the show have said that doing so made them better at doing their jobs. The program since the beginning has been viewed by golf fans as the gold standard in televised golf, and it has had a major impact on the way golf is televised all over the world. A significant part of the credit for that achievement belongs to Roberts and other members of the club, who during the early years repeatedly pushed a sometimes reluctant CBS to refine a program that both the network and the club believed to be very good already.

Copies of the earliest Masters broadcasts are hard to find. The networks did not routinely make copies of live programs in the early years. The first commercial videotape recorders weren't introduced until 1956, and they were so balky and expensive that for years they could not be used casually. (In 1953, RCA had built a prototype that needed more than a mile of tape to make a fuzzy four-minute recording. The company's engineers achieved a dramatic improvement in picture quality by removing the first row of seats from an auditorium in which the machine was to be demonstrated, thereby preventing anyone from sitting close enough to see how poorly it worked.) For a long time, the only easy way to record a live television broadcast for later viewing outside of a television studio was to make a film directly from a TV screen; such a recording was called a kinescope. The networks didn't always make kinescopes of live programs, and when they did make them they didn't always keep them, and when they did keep them they didn't always store them carefully. Augusta National today owns videotaped copies of Masters broadcasts from the early sixties. The Museum of Television and Radio, in New York, has a copy of a Masters kinescope from 1958. It also has a recording of the final day's broadcast in 1963. (The programs shown on the Golf Channel's *Masters Classics* series and ESPN Classic's *Masters on Monday* are not copies of early television broadcasts; they are movies that were commissioned by the club and filmed by a separate crew, beginning in 1961.)

The scarcity of recordings of early Masters broadcasts may not be a huge loss. By modern standards, the old shows were dreadful. The announcers, who for the most part had been trained in radio and were accustomed to sports that moved far faster than golf, tended to talk too quickly and too much and to make mistakes that modern golf fans would find laughable. Jim McKay—who was a commentator on Masters broadcasts until he left CBS, shortly after the tournament in 1961, to join *ABC's Wide World of Sports*—was as breathless as if he were providing the play-by-play for a Stanley Cup playoff game. He spoke of "Ben Snead" and "the National Golf Club," and he reported the scoring of the players with ponderous arithmetic: "Fred Hawkins lies, at this time, 69. If he drops this putt, he'll have a 70, and that will bring him in at 284." In 1958, Hawkins and Doug Ford both had longish putts on the final hole to tie the leader, Arnold Palmer, who had finished nearly an hour before; neither putt came close to the hole. The camera cut to Jimmy Demaret, who was standing woodenly on the clubhouse porch. He turned to Claude Harmon, who was standing woodenly beside him, and said, "I don't think I've ever seen a more exciting finish to the Masters." It was not scintillating television.

But the potential was there, and Roberts pushed CBS to try for more. Following the first broadcast in 1956, for example, he urged the network to bury its cables on the course, in order to get them out of the way and out of sight (and to force a wavering CBS to make a commitment to carry the tournament in subsequent years); to extend Sunday's coverage from an hour to an hour and a half, in order to increase the likelihood that the main action at the end of the tournament would not be finished before the broadcast began; and to put more cameras on the course—especially portable cameras, if those were available. CBS resisted all three suggestions. It argued that buried cables might deteriorate, that a longer Sunday telecast wasn't needed, and that seven cameras were plenty for a golf tournament. CBS also reserved the right to preempt the broadcast if, say, a baseball game ran longer than expected.

CBS eventually came around to Roberts's point of view on those and other issues. Burying the cables turned out to save money and to improve transmission quality (although deterioration was indeed a problem); in 1958, CBS lengthened the Sunday broadcast by thirty minutes—although it did so at the expense of the Friday broadcast, which it permanently eliminated; and the network added an eighth camera in 1957, a ninth in 1958, a tenth in 1959, and an eleventh in 1961. (Today, CBS uses twenty-nine cameras in its coverage of the tournament.)

Even with more cameras, though, CBS executives were not interested in showing more than four holes, despite repeated requests from Roberts, Jones, and others that the coverage be extended farther back into the course. The club's television committee, in its report on the 1957 broadcast, wrote, "A most picturesque part of our golf course lies about the twelfth hole and thirteenth green. An attempt should be made through employment of portable cameras to bring this area into live broadcast. If this is impractical, a few films of the area could be shown."

CBS disagreed that there was any need to show more of the course, even on film, despite the fact that the twelfth and thirteenth holes were among the most famous holes on the course—and would become even more famous the following year, when Herbert Warren Wind would give them the name Amen Corner. Seven years later, Roberts—after reading in *Golf World* that CBS was planning to cover six holes at a lesser

tournament, the 1964 Carling World Open, at Oakland Hills—wrote to
Jack Dolph, who was then the network's director of sports, to ask why
the Masters could not be given the same treatment. "It's true that we
are covering six holes of the Carling's rather than four as we do at the
Masters," Dolph replied. "This was a commitment made in acquiring
the rights to the Tournament; one on which Carling's insisted. We have
grave doubts that this extra hole coverage will add to the overall impact
of the tournament, and we are, in fact, giving the extra two holes the
very minimum of coverage." Roberts did not give up, and in 1966 CBS
finally did agree to extend its coverage beyond the fifteenth hole, by
adding a camera near the fourteenth green. Coverage of the thirteenth
green began two years later in 1968 (after Roberts suggested moving a
camera from the far less interesting fourteenth tee). The twelfth hole
wasn't shown live until five years after that, in 1973—sixteen years after
the club's original suggestion.

The twelfth hole might not have received its own camera even in
1973 if Roberts had not effectively tricked CBS into putting one there.
The year before, ABC Sports had asked the club for permission to film
the twelfth hole during that year's Masters for a prime-time sports special that it planned to broadcast on the Monday following the tournament. "As you know," an ABC executive wrote to Roberts, "this hole has
never been shown on the live presentations of the Masters, and our seg-
ment, which would probably be only five or ten minutes in length,
would not only show how some of the top finishers play this hole but
would also capture the many moods and some of the unique happen-
ings that transpire at this locale." Roberts—who knew very well that
ABC for years had yearned to win the Masters contract away from
CBS—agreed. One year later, CBS for the first time placed its own camera on the twelfth hole.

Over the years, Roberts and other club members made many suggestions that CBS resisted but later adopted in whole or in part. In 1956, for
example, Roberts pointed out that a simple way to convey the standing
of the tournament's leaders would be to occasionally focus a camera on

the leaderboard, near the eighteenth hole, thereby circumventing the sometimes faulty reckoning of the announcers. ("According to our calculations . . . ," Jim McKay would begin—making it sound as though scores could be computed only with difficulty and might be subject to later revision.) Scores were a problem for the announcers until 1960, when Augusta National introduced a simple system that has been used at golf tournaments ever since: the over-and-under system, in which the standing of the players is represented by the number of strokes above or below par. After the new method was implemented, Roberts had to point out to CBS in a letter that showing the scoreboards on camera no longer made sense—since red and green numerals were indistinguishable on black-and-white television screens. Roberts also received a letter from a ticket holder who pointed out that the scoreboards were incomprehensible to anyone who was red-green color-blind. In response, Roberts suggested that color-blind patrons seek assistance from club members—who, he noted, could readily be identified by their green jackets. (This story is sometimes offered by older club members as proof that Roberts had a sense of humor—a point not universally conceded.)

During the early years, the club also urged CBS to shoot film footage of holes it did not intend to cover live, to take pictures of the course from the air, and to construct scale models or make accurate illustrations of the holes. CBS at first rejected all those ideas as impractical or too expensive. ("The use of maps or models for visual indication of the distance and lie of balls between tee and green also would overtax our facilities and staff," a network executive wrote.) CBS eventually did make drawings of the holes—and later built models—but the early representations were confusing, undoubtedly because they were prepared at the last minute. Each of the drawings used in the 1958 broadcast, for example, consisted of two pieces of slightly different-colored paper placed side by side. The two halves of each drawing were rendered in different scales, so that the edges of fairways and the banks of ponds did not meet up. The hole location on each green was marked by a white ring that looked like a small frosted donut. The low quality and inaccuracy of the drawings made Roberts furious. It took until the mid-sixties for CBS to produce visual aids that Roberts felt enhanced the show.

Roberts was also concerned with the inventiveness of the camerawork. In 1964, he suggested that CBS attempt to shoot pictures of airborne golf balls from the golfer's perspective, by placing a camera at the back of one of the tees. Camera operators in those days were less successful than they are today at following the flight of a ball, a difficult feat that has been made simpler by the development of better and less cumbersome cameras. Roberts's idea was that a ball would be easier to track from behind, and that a camera placed in back of a tee would clearly show whether a shot was hooking, slicing, or flying straight—information that Roberts felt "would be very meaningful to golfers." The club added a camera platform behind the sixteenth tee and suggested that CBS use it, although the network was skeptical. In later years, of course, camera shots from that angle became a standard feature of all golf broadcasts.

Roberts had a striking intuitive sense of how to structure a compelling television show. Typical of his insights were those contained in a letter he wrote to MacPhail following the broadcast in 1964. Roberts had felt that Sunday's broadcast that year had come close to being the best yet, but that Saturday's had been "the poorest ever." The problem with Saturday's broadcast was that Arnold Palmer, who was running away with the tournament, played faster than anticipated—at one point, his twosome played through the twosome ahead*—and had finished his round by the time CBS came on the air. Roberts felt that Palmer's absence from the broadcast had left those directing the program "upset to a point of not being able to think clearly or act rationally." In particular, he felt, CBS had missed a chance "to present the situation in a much more interesting fashion." He wrote:

> I had spoken on previous occasions to your people about making a contest between the leader and the record book if and when one player should dominate the tournament.
>
> During the entire telecast on Saturday, not one word was said about

---

* Playing through was common in those years. Nicklaus's twosome played through Hogan's the following day.

Palmer having an opportunity to become the first four-time winner of the Masters. Likewise, nothing was said about Palmer having a chance to tie or better the all-time tournament record score established by Ben Hogan in 1953. Not a word was uttered about Palmer's opportunity to tie or better the 7 stroke winning margin established by [Cary] Middlecoff in 1955.

I believe it was approximately 10 minutes from the time the telecast began on Saturday until a scoreboard was shown to the viewers which gave them an accurate picture as to how matters stood and this of course is something we have discussed in the past as being of paramount importance at an early period in each show. . . .

I was informed after the show ended on Saturday that CBS had taken the precaution to tape Palmer's play of the last four holes.* That being the case, it seems a pity that the producer or director failed to run off early on Saturday his playing of the last three or four holes. It would have been necessary, of course, to first explain Palmer's domination of the tournament and the records he had an opportunity to match or to break. It was approximately 38 minutes after the start of the program that [Chris] Schenkel said something about a tape of Palmer in action. Palmer was then shown at Hole No. 16 only, but the viewers must have been confused because Palmer's action at No. 16 was interrupted after he had hit his tee shot in order to show something live on another green. About four minutes afterward, the camera went back to the 16th Green to show Palmer holing his putt.

Roberts's ideas about how to put together an interesting broadcast in the absence of a leader seem self-evident to a modern viewer of televised golf tournaments. At the time, though, they made CBS executives grind their teeth. A few years earlier, CBS had even declined Roberts's offer to supply the network's announcers with historical lore about past tournaments so that they might have something interesting to talk about during just such situations.

---

* This precaution had first been suggested, several years before, by Roberts himself.

Despite various disagreements with CBS over the years, Roberts had reasons for wanting to maintain the club's broadcast agreement with that network. One was that, despite his reputation for being hard to work with, he believed in continuing relationships. He liked to use the same lawyers, bankers, photographers, doctors, suppliers, and contractors year after year, and he usually made changes only with reluctance. (The club has used the same bank since the thirties. Roberts felt that clever lawyers could always find ways to wiggle out of contracts, and that business relationships therefore needed to be founded on more than pieces of paper.) The main reason for his commitment to CBS, though, was that CBS had more affiliates, more viewers, and higher ratings than either of the other two networks. Roberts was skeptical of television ratings, which he felt were close to fictional, but he studied them and brooded about them, and he was determined that the Masters should earn higher ratings than any other tournament.

Roberts also felt that remaining with CBS helped to maintain a balance of power among golf broadcasters. He explained his thinking in a letter to one of the club's lawyers in 1972. "I like ever so much the people who run the Sports Department of ABC," he wrote, "but I do not see how we can move over in that direction. They have all of the top tournaments excepting the Masters and to my way of thinking we would not be rendering any service to the game of golf if we also joined ABC." NBC, too, had made offers, but Roberts felt that "the talent they employ does not seem to be capable of staging a good telecast of a golf tournament."

The closest Roberts came to being tempted away from CBS came in the early sixties, and it involved the issue of broadcasting in color. Augusta National wanted the Masters to be shown in color, and CBS did not want to make the change. The club had begun pushing for color in the early sixties without success, and in a letter in 1964 Roberts called color the club's "most difficult problem" with the network. Jones suggested, the same year, that the club might be able to circumvent CBS by showing the tournament on closed-circuit television in movie theaters, as was sometimes done with boxing matches. Roberts looked into the idea, but eventually rejected it. "I cannot visualize golf fans buying a five dollar ticket in order to spend an afternoon in a theater to watch the Masters Tournament or any other tournament," he wrote to Jones. "They do it in connection with a world championship fight, about which there is always great excitement, but I question if golf fans will ever get excited to that extent about a golf tournament."

In resisting color, CBS argued (among other things) that the number of cameras it used on the course would have to be cut back, and that the number of holes shown on the broadcast would therefore have to be reduced. As the club discovered, that claim was disingenuous. While it was true that CBS could handle only a limited number of color cameras with the two remote broadcast units that it used at that time, the problem could be solved by adding a third unit, a change that would have a cost but would be relatively easy. The club also felt that CBS had overstated the probable expense of switching to color.

That CBS put up a fight over color was in many ways surprising, because in 1939 the network had developed the world's first color television system. That system was based on a camera in which a wheel containing red, blue, and green filters was spun at high speed before the lens. In 1950, the Federal Communications Commission, after lengthy hearings, chose CBS's system as the national color television standard. In doing so it rejected a competing system that had been developed by RCA, which owned NBC. The RCA system—which used three separate tubes—had the advantage of producing images that looked good on black-and-white sets, while CBS's system did not. But the FCC believed that the RCA system was unreliable, and CBS carried the day.

The victory was short-lived. CBS made a few attempts to broadcast in color, but its system didn't catch on. Then RCA found ways to improve and simplify its own system. Late in 1953, the FCC reversed itself and approved the new RCA standard—which is in use to this day—and real color broadcasting began. NBC moved aggressively, investing in new equipment and marketing itself as the color network. (Hence the origin of the network's use of a peacock as its logo.) It had an extra incentive to do so, since the rise of color programming increased demand for color TV sets manufactured by the network's corporate parent, RCA. Still, the transition was slow. The number of color sets in use in the United States did not reach a million until 1962.

CBS, which had been stung by its early foray into color, held back. The network's hesitancy did not immediately appear shortsighted, because for a time color seemed as though it might not catch on at all. By the early sixties, however, the club believed that CBS was lagging. The program's sponsors encouraged Roberts to push for color, and one of them warned him that the broadcast would come to be viewed as "second rate" if the change were not made soon. In January of 1964, William Kerr, who was the chairman of Augusta National's television committee, wrote to MacPhail, "I am deeply concerned that if we continue to stand still on this score it will be detrimental to the best interests of the Tournament, the sponsors, and CBS." Roberts asked the director of the club's tournament films to send copies to CBS, to show the network "what this place looks like in color during the Tournament." (CBS had been offered the opportunity to produce the films but had turned it down.)

At around the same time, CBS was coming under similar pressure from another major event on its schedule, the Miss America Pageant. The pageant's owners wanted a color broadcast, and they asked CBS, which had carried the program for years, to submit a proposal. CBS's cost estimate was so high that pageant officials decided the network was trying to make the pageant's sponsors bear most of the cost of upgrading the entire CBS system. Largely as a result, they moved the program to NBC—a great blow to CBS, since the pageant broadcast had become the top-rated special program in history, with ratings nearly as high as those of the two episodes of the *Ed Sullivan Show* on which the Beatles appeared in 1964.

Unhappiness over the color issue contributed to a decision by the club to demand a renegotiation of its current contract with CBS. Roberts felt that the network had been unresponsive to the club's requests on that and other matters, and he was bothered by the fact that the existing contract gave CBS the right of first negotiation and first refusal on any new agreement. The club's side of the bargaining was handled by a young New York attorney named J. Richard Ryan, who had represented the Miss America Pageant in its own fight with the network (and who still represents the club in its television dealings). Ryan told Roberts that the club could turn the first-negotiation clause to its own advantage, by presenting CBS with a "wish list" of demands and making it clear that the club was willing to change networks if CBS didn't accede. The most important provision of the new agreement was probably one that limited the network to just two minutes of commercials per half hour and prohibited "chain breaks," which were brief commercials sold by local stations.

CBS executives were appalled by the advertising provisions, which they viewed as naive. But Roberts believed that commercials were not only less intrusive but also more effective if they were used sparingly. (Roberts also felt that sixty-second commercials, the standard at the time, were too long—a view that advertisers and television networks later came to believe themselves.) He wasn't opposed to advertising; indeed, the club and not CBS had been the source of all the broadcast's sponsors. Augusta National's earliest television contracts had called for CBS to pay the club a fee of $10,000 if it carried the broadcast on a "sustaining" basis—that is, without a commercial sponsor—and $40,000 if an acceptable advertiser could be found. CBS had failed to find a sponsor for either of the first two broadcasts—a fact that may seem astonishing to a modern viewer but was not necessarily unusual at the time. In 1958, the club stepped in and provided a sponsor of its own: American Express, which remained with the broadcast until 1962. Travelers became a sponsor in 1959. Cluett, Peabody & Co., the manufacturer of Arrow shirts, replaced American Express in 1962, and was in turn replaced by Cadillac in 1969. (Not coincidentally, American Express, Travelers, Cluett, Peabody, and General Motors—as well as Young & Rubicam, the advertising agency that represented the early sponsors—were all run by club members.) Roberts had first suggested Cadillac as a sponsor in 1958, but CBS had rejected the idea. "Television is a mass medium," a network executive responded dismissively, "and Cadillacs are not merchandised to the masses—even though it appears that way in some parts of the country." Today, of course, Cadillac is one of the leading sponsors of televised golf—and has been a sponsor of the Masters broadcast for more than thirty years.

Roberts felt that the best commercials were ones that fit in with the tournament as seamlessly as possible. He especially liked ones that had golf themes, if not Masters themes, and he encouraged advertisers to take advantage of the club as a shooting location. The Arrow commercials, for example, were shot on the course itself shortly before the tournament began. One—a laughably sexist tableau featuring two attractive young models wearing Arrow's "Mr. Golf" and "Miss Golf" shirts, which cost five dollars and were made of a cotton-and-Dacron blend called Decton—was filmed on the practice putting green; another featured two couples enjoying a friendly match at Amen Corner. In 1964, one Arrow commercial showed a Decton-clad young man enjoying a beverage behind the clubhouse and then hitting a ball with a Masters logo on it.

Despite CBS's objections, the club refused to back down on the commercial issue. Roberts knew that the Miss America Pageant had won a similar concession, and he made it clear that he, too, was prepared to change networks in order to get what he wanted. CBS had to give in. The restriction became a part of the signed agreement, and it has been a part of every one of the club's television contracts since that time. The minimal number of commercials during a Masters broadcast is even more striking today than it was then. In the early sixties, the standard allocation for advertisements in a two-and-a-half-hour program was eighteen minutes; today, programs sometimes cram nearly that much advertising into a single hour.

Although the terms of the proposed contract were tough, Roberts's aim was not to harm or humiliate CBS but rather to guarantee that the Masters would receive the sort of television treatment he felt it deserved. Most of the key provisions actually worked to the ultimate benefit of the network. With fewer commercials to work into the broadcast, for example, the program's directors had a broader canvas on which to work and were in far less danger of cutting away from important action—a major peril in the days before instant replays. Even the insistence on color probably helped CBS, by forcing the network to take a necessary step somewhat earlier than it would have done on its own.

The principal announcer on the first Masters broadcasts was Jim McKay. He was joined several years later by Chris Schenkel, who was probably Roberts's favorite Masters announcer ever. McKay left CBS for ABC shortly after the tournament in 1961, and Schenkel followed him three years later. In 1965, Jack Whitaker, who had first worked on the broadcast in 1963, took Schenkel's place, and served as the head commentator for two years.

Whitaker is the subject of one of the most frequently repeated (and embroidered) stories about Roberts. Peter Dobereiner wrote one version: "One well-known broadcaster once referred to a group of excited spectators as 'that mob,' and he was banished from Augusta for 15 years." Melvin Durslag, writing in *TV Guide* in 1971, presented a slightly different version: "The committee chairman of the Masters, it seemed, was most distressed that Whitaker would be so indiscreet as to call the Masters gallery a 'mob.' He demanded that Jack be given the foot. Grudgingly, CBS acceded." Henry Longhurst's version, published in 1976, was more elaborate—and contained dialogue: "[Roberts] once sent off the field, so to speak, a most distinguished and respected television commentator for exclaiming in the excitement of the moment: 'There goes the mob, running after Palmer!' Unfortunately, Mr. Roberts was tuned in. 'We do not have mobs at the Masters,' he said. 'And they do not run. Kindly leave the grounds.'" Many other versions of the same story exist.

In whatever version, the story is usually presented as evidence that Roberts possessed a hair-trigger temper and that no announcer—or, for that matter, anyone else—was ever safe in his presence. But the facts were different. The conversation recounted by Longhurst never took place. Whitaker was never told to "leave the grounds." The replacement of Whitaker on the broadcast, by Pat Summerall in 1968, was not the result of anyone's use of the word "mob." And Whitaker's absence from the Masters broadcast did not last fifteen years; in fact, when Longhurst wrote his story, in 1976, Whitaker had been back on camera at the Masters for four years.

It is true that Roberts did not like the word "mob." During the 1960 broadcast, Jim McKay and Jim McArthur used it four or five times between them on Sunday alone. Roberts noticed, and in a letter written a few weeks later he let McKay know that he disapproved—but he was far from apoplectic. Roberts began his letter by calling the 1960 broadcast "the best ever." He wrote, "The speed and the timing of the switches from one scene of action to another on Saturday was easily the best work that has ever been done in connection with a golf tournament. In the main, the comments [by the announcers] were quite good and, from my point of view, they were especially good because they were not overdone. I think too much chatty conversation by a commentator as a part of a golf tournament show is about the worst thing of all. The main thing the golfing fan wants is understandable and accurate information and you and the others come closer to doing a perfect job in this connection at the Masters Tournament than I have observed in any other television golf show. There are a few minor things, however, that I would like to bring to your attention and I have no hesitancy in doing so because I know you are always wide open to an opportunity to make improvements. . . ."

One of the "few minor things" Roberts wished to address was the use of the word "mob." He wrote, "I think this is an uncomplimentary way to describe the large groups at the Masters. Aside from being in bad taste, it tends to discourage television viewers from ever attending the Masters. I think a more complimentary way to describe the sizable concentrations of spectators would be to refer to them as the 'large crowds' or the 'great numbers in attendance' or the 'wonderful tournament crowds at Augusta.' In other words, most anything would be better than the word 'mob' which denotes uncontrolled numbers or disorderly, unlawful groups." Roberts concluded his critique by inviting McKay to lunch.

When Whitaker joined the broadcast in 1963, his role was minor. In the request for credentials that CBS submitted to the club that year, he was listed not with the broadcast team but on a separate page devoted to sponsors, advertising agency representatives, actors, and commercial announcers. His contribution to the broadcast that year was limited to doing prerecorded introductions for Travelers commercials. The following year, 1964, he was stationed on the seventeenth hole, although he was given virtually no airtime on Sunday.

When Chris Schenkel left CBS for ABC in 1964, Whitaker was tapped by CBS to take his place as the lead announcer for 1965. Roberts liked the 1965 broadcast a great deal—in a memorandum to CBS he said that the program on Sunday had been "quite a substantial improvement over anything done in the past"—but he was disappointed by Whitaker. He felt that Whitaker was insufficiently conversant with the game, the course, the history of the tournament, and the eighteenth hole, coverage of which was his principal responsibility. (He also noted that Whitaker might have once used the word "mob" to describe the crowd at the eighteenth, but he said he wasn't sure, and his observation was listed as a "minor criticism.") Roberts concluded, "There is room, and in fact, a great need for an outstanding individual who can sense the highlights that need to be emphasized and to bring them out in a clear-cut fashion at the proper time."

Roberts did not believe that Whitaker had no place on the broadcast; he simply felt that Whitaker was not knowledgeable enough to be the centerpiece of the program. When CBS submitted its list of announcers for the following year's broadcast, Whitaker's name was on the list— and Roberts approved the lineup. The club's television committee (with Roberts's consent) suggested that Henry Longhurst, who was also on the list, might be used as the broadcast's "command hand" at the eighteenth green, a move that would have made it possible to place Whitaker at a different hole. Frank Chirkinian, who produced and directed the broadcast, rejected that idea on the grounds that Longhurst was "not prolific in the ways of a professional broadcaster upon whom we rely for duties other than just golf announcing," and said that Whitaker would again have that role. Chirkinian indicated, though, that Whitaker would be made part of "a broader dramatic structure"—a change that was meant at least in part to address the club's criticisms of his performance.

The 1966 Masters was the first to be broadcast in color, and the club was delighted with the results. Roberts's critique of the broadcast began, "We have heard and read more complimentary remarks than in any previous year. Some have said it was the best outdoor color show of a sports event ever done and we do not quarrel with that sort of appraisal. . . . We also wish to recognize the ability and willingness of CBS to make available an extra 63 minutes of time on Monday for the [eighteen-hole] play-off. The pictures were as usual exceptionally clear, the coverage extensive and the shifting from one scene to another was expertly handled." He felt that the Saturday broadcast had been ragged, but that the program on Sunday had been "splendid." As had been true the previous year, his only lengthy and sustained criticisms were of Whitaker, who he said had done "a poor job" as head announcer and to whom he devoted a full page in his critique. In particular, he chastised Whitaker for repeatedly referring to the club as the "Augusta National Golf Course," for grossly exaggerating (at fifteen thousand) the size of the crowd around the eighteenth green, for discussing prize money (a forbidden subject in the view of both Roberts and Jones, and an issue that was covered explicitly in the contract with CBS), and for misleading viewers about how soon the players would reach the fourteenth hole— the first hole with a camera—during coverage of the eighteen-hole play-off on Monday. (The players didn't reach that hole until nearly an hour into the broadcast; Roberts felt that Whitaker had suggested they would be along almost immediately—as he had, although his intention was undoubtedly to keep viewers from tuning out.)* Roberts concluded, "We

---

* Jack Nicklaus, Tommy Jacobs, and Gay Brewer, Jr., had tied after seventy-two holes. During the playoff—which Nicklaus won, making him the first player to win the Masters two years in a row—they played excruciatingly slowly. The entire round took more than five hours, an unheard-of pace at a time when the average Masters round lasted three or three and a half hours. Roberts and other members of the club had been upset because they felt that CBS, despite having had ample warning that the players were crawling over the course, not only hadn't prepared material to fill the first part of the broadcast but also didn't seem to have a coherent approach to covering the final holes. There were many gaps and odd juxtapositions, and for almost twenty minutes the picture on the screen

question whether Whitaker has any important interest in golf. We do not doubt his ability in other fields and he is an agreeable person. We continue to believe however that he does not possess the ability to do the kind of job as head announcer that the event requires."

In *Preferred Lies and Other Tales,* a memoir published in 1998, Whitaker wrote that in March 1967 he was told by Jack Dolph, the network's director of sports, that Whitaker would not be part of the broadcast crew at that year's Masters. "You called the gallery a mob and didn't mention there would be a green coat ceremony on the putting green after the players checked their cards," Whitaker says Dolph told him. Whitaker's failure to mention the ceremony had indeed been cited in Roberts's 1966 critique; the word "mob" had not. It is not clear now whether Roberts had directly asked that Whitaker be removed from the broadcast team or whether MacPhail or someone else at CBS had decided to reassign him in the expectation that doing so would make Roberts happy. The latter possibility seems more likely. William Paley had made it clear to MacPhail that keeping the Masters broadcast at CBS was absolutely essential, and MacPhail was consequently terrified of doing anything that might make Roberts angry.

It is entirely possible to argue that Roberts's low opinion of Whitaker in the mid-sixties was mistaken, unreasonable, or both. But Whitaker's removal from the broadcast was not the result of a moment of anger on Roberts's part, and it did not occur because Whitaker had called the tournament's gallery a "mob." As it turned out, when the tournament took place a few weeks later, Whitaker wasn't the only broadcaster who was missing from the program: The American Federation of Television and Radio Artists had gone on strike, and that meant that CBS's usual commentators, who were members of that union, could not participate. Roberts conducted auditions among the club's membership and settled on two distinguished amateur players, Charles Coe and Billy Joe Patton,

---

was mainly of the backs of spectators near the thirteenth and fourteenth holes. Gerry Achenbach, who was one of a group of about forty members who reviewed that year's broadcast, wrote in a memo to Roberts, "I had the distinct feeling that there were moments when those directing the show were near the panic stage in groping for something to do."

to fill two of the vacant spots. Coe had won the U.S. Amateur twice and been the runner-up to Jack Nicklaus in 1959, and in the 1961 Masters he had finished tied for second with Palmer. Patton had led the Masters after two rounds in 1954, then ended up in third place behind Snead and Hogan. Both men had played the course for years.

Coe and Patton did creditable jobs as commentators, and their minimal dialogue confirmed Roberts's belief that less is more in golf broadcasting. CBS was pleased as well, and MacPhail passed along a sampling of the large volume of complimentary mail the network had received. One viewer wrote, "[T]he quiet, sincere comments of your members, which were entirely adequate, were a refreshing change from the glib, and sometimes overly talkative, 'pros' we usually hear." Another wrote, "What an absolute pleasure it was to watch a player, under severe pressure, walk up to a putt *in silence*—the silence any gallery always accords a player, but which the announcers feel impelled to fill with chatter. In this case, one truly felt present, with a real sense of actual participation." The broadcast turned out so well, in fact, that CBS executives credited it with breaking the strike.

Whitaker returned to the program in 1973. He happened to be attending the tournament as a guest of CBS, and was drafted at the last minute by Chirkinian to fill in at the sixteenth hole in place of Henry Longhurst, who had suddenly become ill. Chirkinian took Whitaker to Roberts's office to seek official approval for the change. Whitaker recalls that Roberts greeted him warmly and said, "Young man, we are very fortunate that you are here." Whitaker remained a part of the Masters broadcast team until he left CBS for ABC in 1981. But he never again served as the head announcer.

The man who ran CBS's Masters broadcasts from 1959 until 1996 was Frank Chirkinian, a profanity-spewing, chain-smoking, self-promoting vortex of ego, anxiety, and nervous energy who is widely and fairly credited with being one of the pioneering geniuses of televised sports. Roberts and Chirkinian were like matter and antimatter. Roberts affected to be unable to pronounce Chirkinian's name—"It's spelled

T-A-L-E-N-T," the producer once explained to someone else—and Chirkinian cursed Roberts with unquotable ferocity. One of the low points in their relationship came in 1966, when *Sports Illustrated* published a behind-the-scenes account, written by Dan Jenkins, of that year's Masters broadcast (the first one in color). Roberts felt that Jenkins had portrayed Chirkinian as the virtual inventor of the Masters, and that he himself had been depicted as an interfering fool. Chirkinian, for his part, had clearly used Jenkins's story as a means of getting back at Roberts, who had annoyed him for years.

The incompatibility of the two men's characters probably prevented either from fully appreciating the merits of the other—although Roberts consistently praised the program, and Chirkinian adopted what he perceived to be Roberts's management style. (His colleagues at CBS later called him the Ayatollah—a nickname that he says he was given by Pat Summerall.) Both were extraordinarily driven individuals for whom the Masters was a personal obsession. The friction between them led to tense moments, but it also contributed to the sustained strength of the broadcast. Each man kept the other on his toes.

It is probable that Roberts never truly grasped the difficulty of Chirkinian's job—or the degree to which the director's blustering ego was a tool he used to get it done. Chirkinian had to create a narrative from the jumble of images on a bank of television monitors, while supervising a sometimes unruly and unreliable crew of commentators. The plot of the narrative could change from moment to moment, as one leader displaced another, stars dawdled over putts, caddies stepped between cameras and players, and shots that seemed crucial turned out to mean nothing. Roberts sometimes held up the club's tournament films as examples of what he felt the broadcast ought to be, but covering a golf tournament live and making a movie about one after the fact are different disciplines. The director of the films had the huge advantage of being able to work backward from the ending. Chirkinian could only react.

It is equally likely that Chirkinian undervalued Roberts's contributions to the broadcast and his frequently astute and even visionary sense of what worked and did not work on television. Chirkinian and his colleagues dismissed Roberts and other club members as meddlesome old men who didn't have enough sense to stay out of the way. When a "green jacket" appeared in the doorway of the CBS broadcast trailer, Chirkinian's blood pressure spiked. But many of the innovations for which Chirkinian's career is celebrated were in fact suggested by Roberts or other members of the club. Roberts was focused on the tournament twelve months a year, and he knew it inside out; it is not surprising that he was able to make valuable suggestions, no matter how much Chirkinian disliked the feeling that he himself was not completely in control. Moments of animosity between the club and the network sometimes obscured the fact that both partners gained much from the relationship.

Chirkinian was especially annoyed by numerous restrictions—some of them contractual—that the club expected the commentators to adhere to. There was to be no promotion of other CBS programs, no estimate of the size of the crowd, no reference to "sand traps" (the preferred term was "bunkers"). The most important restrictions, from the point of view of Roberts and Jones, were the ones that had to do with anything that might be perceived as an attempt to commercialize the tournament. There was to be no mention of prize money, for example. Roberts wanted the Masters purse to be one of the most generous in golf—and he pioneered the practice of paying players who missed the cut—but he believed that publicly focusing on money cheapened the competition. Most Masters fans don't even know how much the winner earns; that's exactly how Roberts and Jones would have wanted it.*

Not all of the Masters broadcast rules were handed down by Roberts. In fact, most of the ones that had to do with word choice originated with Jones. It was he, for example, who insisted that sand-filled hazards be referred to as bunkers rather than traps. He explained his preference in *Golf Is My Game*: "Throughout this and all my other writings on the game, I have used the word 'bunker' in what I have understood to be the traditional golfing sense, meaning a pit in which the soil has been exposed and the area covered with sand. I regard the term

---

* In 1998, first prize was $576,000, and the total purse was $3,199,480. Each player who missed the cut received exactly as much as the total purse during the first nine tournaments: $5,000.

'sand trap' as an unacceptable Americanization. Its use annoys me almost as much as hearing a golf club called a 'stick.' " Jones was equally particular about references to the two halves of the course. He wanted them to be called "the first nine" and "the second nine." He disapproved of "front" and "back," partly because the terms were not, strictly speaking, accurate, and partly because they created the possibility of referring to the second nine as the "back side"—a phrase he viewed as a vulgarism and a synonym for "rear end." Jones also originated the club's now well-established practice of not releasing attendance figures for the tournament; he believed that allowing reporters and others to overestimate the size of crowds, as they inevitably did, was a shrewd marketing tactic at a time when the tournament's fiscal health depended almost entirely on ticket sales. (Shortly after the Masters in 1952, Roberts wrote to Jones, "If you count the employees, caddies, etc., there were more than 14,000 people on the grounds the last day of the Tournament. I am still sticking to the policy you prescribed of never giving out figures in connection with the Masters Tournament and I have asked everyone else to refrain from doing so. Sometimes I wonder if we will continuously be able to get away with this policy because the curiosity and interest become more intense each year. The pressure on me, particularly, is sometimes rather severe but I am still willing to keep mum on the subject so long as you think, from a public relations point of view, that it is wise for us to do so.")

The club's strictness regarding terminology had a positive effect on broadcasters. Clichés are unavoidable in live television—no one has the poise to be continually original for hours on the air—but precision is a worthy goal. Roberts was right to suggest, as he did in 1960, that Jim McKay should speak of "mounds" instead of "humps" in describing the terrain on certain holes, because "mounds" was the word more commonly used by knowledgeable players. The announcers undercut their authority, Roberts believed, when they used odd terms, misidentified holes, made absurdly precise estimates of the length of long putts ("Palmer is one hundred and twelve feet from the hole"), described pin positions from their own perspective rather than that of the players (as both Whitaker and Longhurst were prone to do), mispronounced the names of contestants, garbled the name of the club, gave the wrong

number for the par of the course, or in other ways suggested to discern-
ing viewers that they did not know what they were talking about. "On
Sunday the announcer first said Palmer's drive was 260, then it was
changed to 280 and a moment later it was described as being 300 yards,"
Roberts wrote to CBS in 1962. "If you want to announce the length of
drives, we can readily put [in] some distance markers for you." Roberts
also encouraged the announcers to putt balls on the greens before the
broadcasts began, so that they could comment more accurately on the
direction in which contestants' putts were likely to break. Chirkinian
hated to receive those memos, but their overall effect on the program
was decidedly positive.

Roberts was feared at CBS not because he made unreasonable demands but because the currency of his deal-making was not money. He
wanted results, not fees. Under the 1965 contract, CBS paid Augusta National just $125,000 for the right to broadcast the tournament—perhaps
a third of what the club would have received in an auction with all three
networks. "It's our feeling that the practice of a little moderation at this
time is desirable," Roberts wrote that year in a letter to Hord Hardin,
who was an official of the U.S.G.A. (and who in 1980 would become Augusta National's third chairman, a position he would hold until 1991).
Roberts told Hardin that the U.S.G.A. should use its considerable bargaining power not to bring in more cash but to put more of its tournaments on TV. "I am completely certain in my own mind that a great
many people might prefer for a change to see the amateurs in action on
TV," Roberts wrote. "Moreover, the Women's Open would be appealing
to a considerable number of people. There is no reason on earth why
the [male] professionals alone should be permitted to monopolize the
television screen." If Augusta National, the U.S.G.A., and other tournament sponsors insisted on extracting every dollar they could, Roberts
argued, the time devoted to commercials would have to increase to
cover the networks' inflated costs. With less of every broadcast hour devoted to golf, viewers would lose interest in all but the biggest tournaments, and events with smaller audiences would disappear. The proper
way to think of television, Roberts believed, was as a long-term investment rather than a short-term bonanza.

CHAPTER NINE

Roberts's Rules

THE FIRST PROFESSIONAL at Augusta National was Ed Dudley, who was Bobby Jones's first choice for the job. (His second and third choices had been Macdonald Smith and Willie MacFarlane.) Jones explained his criteria to Roberts before the two of them approached Dudley: "First of all I want a gentleman. Next, I feel we should select a pro who likes to teach. And, finally, I believe we want someone who is a good player." A fourth requirement was that the new pro be willing to work without a salary, since there was no money to pay him. Dudley at first had to scrape by on what he could earn from his minimally stocked golf shop—a tough proposition, considering how few golfers wandered through in the early years. Beginning in 1934, he supplemented his income with earnings from the Masters, in which he competed fourteen times. He finished in the top ten seven times during the first eight tournaments, and he came close to winning in 1937, when he finished in third place behind Byron Nelson, who was the winner, and Ralph Guldahl. (He also twice set course records at Pine Valley.) Dudley was widely admired by other professionals, and was elected to seven consecutive one-year terms as the president of the P.G.A. of America—a position through which he advanced Roberts's and Jones's vision of the club as a sort of independent service organization for the game of golf.*

---

* In 1948, Roberts and Jones quietly brought about a rapprochement between the U.S.G.A. and the P.G.A.—which for some time had been at odds over tourna-

Dudley retired from Augusta National in 1957 and was succeeded by his assistant, Gene Stout, who had also been his assistant at the Broadmoor, in Colorado Springs, where he worked during the summers. Stout was replaced in August 1966 by his assistant, Robert Kletcke. A young pro named David Spencer was hired as the new assistant.

In the spring of 1967, at the end of Kletcke's first season as the club's head pro, he and Spencer were called to Roberts's room for a meeting with Roberts, another officer of the club, and Phil Wahl, the club's manager. Kletcke and Spencer were both nervous about the meeting, because they figured they must have done something to displease the chairman. When they arrived, though, they found Roberts in a good mood, and he told them they had done a good job. He said further that he and the other members were tired of getting to know and like the club's assistant professionals only to have them move on to other jobs after just a few years. He said that he would like for both Kletcke and Spencer to remain at the club, and that if they continued to do a good job they could stay for as long as they liked.

"But I don't want Bob eating steak and Dave eating hamburger," Roberts went on. He said that he had arrived at a solution, which was for the club to have two head professionals, or co-professionals. He had had Phil Wahl draw up a partnership agreement, and if they would sign it the jobs would be theirs. He said he realized that such an arrangement could lead to tensions, and that he did not want the two men to think of themselves as rivals. As a result, he said, if a situation ever arose in which he felt compelled to fire one of them, he would fire them both.

Kletcke and Spencer were surprised by Roberts's offer, and they asked if they could take the proposed agreement back to the golf shop to talk it over. On their way past the clubhouse, Spencer said, "Gee, Bob,

---

ment rules, among other issues—by holding a joint testimonial dinner at the Bon Air Hotel in honor of Dudley and Fielding Wallace, who was a member of the club and the president of the U.S.G.A. The dinner was held during Masters week, and the guest list included virtually every official of both organizations. The dinner was a success, and the dispute essentially ended that night. In a letter to O. B. Keeler later that year, Roberts wrote, "To me, this was one of the really important contributions that the Augusta National made to the game."

I don't know about this." He had planned to stay at Augusta National for a few years, as was customary for assistants, and then use the job as a springboard to a head professional's position at another club, probably in the Midwest.

"I don't know either," Kletcke said. "I'm not sure it's a good idea." Kletcke had been thinking he would like to try to play on the professional tour. (He later did so briefly, with Roberts's encouragement and with financial backing from several members of the club.) Neither man was enthusiastic about sharing a job. They weren't sure they would be compatible partners, and they weren't excited by the thought that a misstep by either one of them, in Roberts's eyes, could put both of them out of work. The two men talked about the proposal for some time, and came to the conclusion that it didn't make sense for them. It had been considerate of Roberts to make the offer, but the arrangement was clearly unworkable. The only matter left to decide was which of them would tell Roberts.

"I've been here longer," Kletcke said. "Why don't you go back and tell him?"

"You know him better than I do," Spencer said. "I think you ought to go."

There was a long silence. Each man imagined knocking on Roberts's door and explaining that neither of them liked his plan. They looked at the ground.

"Maybe we could both go."

There was another long silence.

At last, Spencer held out his hand and said, "Well, how do you do, partner?" And the two men have been business partners, golf partners, and good friends ever since. They sit side by side at identical desks in the office in the golf shop, and they live within a short distance of each other in the same neighborhood in Augusta. If either of them had had the nerve to return to Roberts's room after their meeting in 1967, they would both, in all likelihood, be working somewhere else.

For a number of years, a popular feature of the club's Jamboree was a humorous film, which was made by Frank Christian and was shown at

the awards dinner on Saturday night. The first film consisted mostly of
footage of the members on the golf course. "Mr. Roberts asked us to
produce another the following year, only better," Christian has written,
"which was typical of his instructions." The next year's film showed a
gorilla (not a bear, as reported in some accounts) running over the golf
course, stealing clubs, and standing in a buffet line in the clubhouse. In
the final scene the gorilla removed a mask, revealing himself to be Clifford Roberts. (In all scenes but the final one, the man wearing the gorilla
suit had been Fred Bennett, the caddie master.) The film was a hit, not
only with the members but also with Roberts, who had enjoyed both
the performing and the laughter at the Jamboree.

One of the most popular Jamboree films showed Roberts pacing
rapidly back and forth while holding a rubber duck and apparently
singing the children's song "Rubber Ducky." To make Roberts's motions
look rapid and jerky, Christian had filmed him at slow speed and played
the film back at regular speed. To make him appear to be singing, Christian had asked him to explain for the camera why there were no ducks
or geese in the ponds on the club's property; the song was dubbed in
later. At the Jamboree dinner on Saturday night, the film was received at
first in silence. Roberts had not been expecting the song, and he glow-
ered at the screen. The members watched him, afraid to laugh. "Finally,
they couldn't hold it in any longer," Christian recalls. "They started
laughing, and then they started laughing harder, and then they started
falling on the floor. Finally, Mr. Roberts laughed, too, and I thought,
Thank God—my ass is saved."

Except during the parties like the Jamboree, the principal form of
competition among local members at Augusta National has always been
a best-ball competition known as the Games. In it, every foursome competes against every other foursome, with complex adjustments for pars
and birdies. The team assignments and score tabulations are handled by
the golf shop. Roberts, not surprisingly, usually ended up with a good
team. (He would often choose his playing partners himself, by placing
small, precise check marks on a list in the golf shop beside the names of
the men he wanted to play with.) To ensure that his team would remain
attentive to the task at hand, he prohibited wagering within the four-

some. "I don't want you out here fiddling around because of some other bet," he would say. "I want you to pay attention, because I want to get going." When a teammate was out of a hole, Roberts expected him to pick up his ball.

When the number of golfers available for the Games was not divisible by four, the golf shop would supply reinforcements. Kletcke and Spencer's first assistant was a young man named Robert Barrett, who had been raised in Augusta (but was not related to Thomas Barrett, the former mayor and early member of the club). Shortly after Barrett came to work at the club, he was drafted to fill a vacancy in Roberts's foursome. Barrett played well, shooting nine consecutive pars on the first nine. When the group had putted out on the ninth green, though, Roberts said, "Bob, we don't need any more pars. Why don't you go back to the golf shop and have them send out someone who can make some birdies?" Barrett thought at first that Roberts was joking, but a member in the group indicated that he was not. A pro's job on Roberts's team was to contribute birdies; pars without handicap strokes were irrelevant. Barrett and his caddie took the long walk back to the shop, and Spencer came out to take his place. (Barrett was nevertheless one of Roberts's favorite assistants, and Roberts later helped him get the head professional's job at another club.)

Roberts believed that golf was an afternoon game and that teeing off before lunch was uncivilized. His rounds invariably began within a few minutes of one o'clock. He and the other members of his foursome would walk from the clubhouse to the first tee, and Roberts would ask, "Who's up?" The response was always, "You are, Mr. Roberts," no matter how crowded the course might be or how many golfers might be waiting. A member named Edward L. Emerson once recalled that shortly after joining the club in 1964, he had been asked to join Roberts for a round on the par-three course during the October opening party. In those days, members reserved tee times on the par three course by placing balls behind one of the markers on the first tee. Roberts asked Emerson if he would mind going over early and leaving a ball in the queue in such a way that they would be assured of teeing off at one. "I lurked in the bushes," Emerson later recalled, "and at what I thought was an appropriate time placed a ball on the tee." He felt pleased at having accomplished the chairman's assignment. But when Roberts arrived at the appointed time and asked, "Who's up?," Emerson realized that his efforts had been unnecessary.

For many years, the only golf balls Roberts used were Spalding Dots. The golf shop would order six dozen before each season—all with Roberts's name printed on them—and he would send his caddie to the shop whenever he needed a new sleeve. When the first balls with Surlyn covers were introduced in the sixties, Roberts played a round with a member who was using one of them. "They're longer than the old balls," the member said, "and you can't cut them." Roberts told his caddie to go back to the shop and return immediately with one of the pros. "These balls I've got are no goddamned good," he said when the pro had hurried over to see what was the matter. Roberts switched to the new balls, and liked them—a change that left the golf shop with six dozen Spalding Dots that had CLIFFORD ROBERTS printed on them. "There was nothing else to do with them," Kletcke recalls, "so I put them in my shag bag." A short time later, Roberts borrowed Kletcke's shag balls to practice with. (He always said that using striped range balls made him dizzy.) "Well, I'll be goddamned," he said as he teed one up. "These balls have my name on them." And he loaded them all into his golf bag.

Roberts's handicap ranged between six and nine during his best playing years. He had a reputation as an excellent putter, especially under pressure, and he expected his playing partners to putt well, too. Val Hastings, a member and a close friend of Roberts's, says, "If you were playing with Cliff, he would tell you exactly where to putt your ball, and if you didn't putt it there, he would raise hell. He would say, 'Damn it, that isn't what I told you to do.' " Although Roberts was a focused competitor, he also paid close attention to his surroundings as he played. If he noticed a tree branch, an azalea, a bunker, a green, or some other feature of the course that needed attention, he made a note of it, and he later made certain that the problem was taken care of. While playing the ninth hole once, he decided that the frame of a dormer that was then under construction on the west wing of the clubhouse was not plumb.

He asked his caddie, "Is that dormer crooked?" The caddie put down Roberts's golf bag, stooped, cupped his hands around the bill of his cap, pretended to study the roof of the building, and gave the only possible answer: "Why, yes, sir, I believe it is." Roberts told the other members of his foursome, "I'll meet you gentlemen on the tenth tee." By the time the group had finished the round, there were carpenters on the roof banging hammers against two-by-fours.

Roberts's influence as a competitor lasted long after his death. In 1983, Ronald Reagan visited Augusta National as the guest of George Shultz, who was then the secretary of state. (Reagan and Shultz had come to the club not only for golf but also to plan the invasion of Grenada, which would take place the following week.) A local resident named Charles Harris, after hearing that Reagan was at the club, crashed a truck through a gate on the property. He took hostages in the golf shop and demanded a meeting with the president, who at the time was playing the sixteenth hole.

Secret Service agents immediately surrounded the shop, and sharp-shooters set up on the putting green. (One of the sharpshooters told a club member that the scope on his rifle was so precise that he would be able to hit a half-dollar coin on the first green, more than four hundred and fifty yards away.) Harris eventually released all his hostages except David Spencer, the co-professional. Harris held a pistol to Spencer's head, and he threatened to shoot off Spencer's fingers one at a time if the president wasn't brought to see him. At one point, to prove that he was serious, he fired a bullet through a window in the front of the shop. Spencer was held at gunpoint for two tense hours. He finally managed to escape during a moment of confusion when some food was sent in for Harris. The first person he ran into was Dr. Stephen W. Brown, a member. Spencer said, "Dr. Brown, I was just as nervous as if I was standing over a three-foot putt and Mr. Roberts told me to make it."

After a frustrating early period that lasted roughly until the end of the Second World War, Roberts built a successful Wall Street investment ca-

reer that eventually made him a millionaire.* Like many well-to-do people of his generation and upbringing, though, he distrusted his prosperity and seldom spent money on anything that today would look
remotely like an extravagance. His one consistent indulgence was his
wardrobe, which contained a number of expensive items, although
most of them were so subdued in style that they didn't look as costly as
they were.

Roberts was a sharp but somber dresser on the golf course. At one
point, he devoted considerable study to finding a way to wear a necktie
with a golf shirt, although he was never satisfied with the results. He ex-

---

* Curt Sampson, in *The Masters*, stated that Roberts was worth a little over $100
million at the time of his death—an absurdly inflated guess apparently based on
speculation by Kenneth Roberts, who is a son of one of Roberts's brothers. No
inventory of Roberts's estate was filed with his will in Probate Court in New
York City—state law did not require one at the time—but several members of
the club who knew him well and were indirectly familiar with his finances say
that his maximum possible net worth at the time of his death would have been
$3 million to $5 million. A fortune of $100 million in 1977 would have made
Roberts one of the two hundred or so richest people in America—quite a feat for
a part-time stockbroker. Kenneth Roberts guessed in an interview that Roberts's
partnership in Reynolds & Co. was worth $25 million at the time of his death, a
figure that Sampson also used. That is an impossibility, since Reynolds had
ceased to be a partnership in 1971, when it went public as Reynolds Securities,
Inc. (At that time, the market capitalization of the entire company was smaller
than the figure Sampson claimed as the value of Roberts's supposed share.)
Roberts, Jones, and a number of other Augusta National members for many
years had a partnership called Joroberts, which operated Coca-Cola bottling
plants in South America. The value of Roberts's stake in that enterprise is unknown, but Roberts and Jones were equal partners and Jones's total net worth at
the time of his death, in 1971, was less than a million dollars, according to Sidney
L. Matthew, the author of *The Life and Times of Bobby Jones*. Roberts's single most
valuable piece of tangible property was probably his apartment in the Bahamas;
a few months before his death, he put it on the market, fully furnished, for
$165,000.

pected others at Augusta National to dress with similar restraint. When Charles Yates entered the clubhouse one day in shorts, Roberts studied him grimly for a long time, then asked, "Charlie, what do you have planned for today?" Yates said that he was planning to play golf. Roberts stared at him in silence again, then asked, "Where?" Yates quickly returned to the locker room and changed into long pants. Roberts was skinny as a young man and was trim and sometimes gaunt-looking when he was older. In the last years of his life, he had trouble finding golf shirts that fit. Small shirts were too small, he said, and medium shirts were too large. "God damn it," he used to say, "I need a small-medium." But there was no such thing. A member named Blake Clark knew a man who owned a shirt company in North Carolina. One day, Clark persuaded him to make a small number of "small-medium" golf shirts for Roberts in a variety of colors, and he wore them for the rest of his life. To make the shirts, the factory had to shut down all other production.

Roberts's two largest personal expenditures came toward the end of his life, and both were for residences. Since the nineteen thirties, he had lived in comfortable but by no means luxurious apartments in New York. (One of them was in the Park Lane Hotel; its successor was in an apartment building on Park Avenue near Sixty-second Street.) When he was in his seventies, he bought a large apartment in Freeport, Bahamas, and spent much of each winter there. His principal interest in the Bahamas was probably tax avoidance—he actually became a citizen—but he was attracted to Freeport in particular by the compactness of the sand on its beaches, a subject he had researched. (He walked for exercise and disliked doing so on soft sand.) During the same period, he built a condominium on a lot that he had purchased at Grandfather Golf & Country Club, in Linville, North Carolina. When Roberts first visited Grandfather, he said the area was the most beautiful he had ever seen, and he bought his lot that day.

After building at Grandfather, Roberts decided he needed a car to get himself back and forth between Augusta and Linville. That decision was viewed as ominous by people who knew him well, because he was an extremely poor driver. Jerome Franklin used to tell a story about an inci-

dent in East Hampton, New York, one summer when Roberts had borrowed a car and then, having mistakenly shifted into first gear instead of
reverse, drove it through the rear wall of a garage. Roberts was such an
inept driver that many of his friends assumed he had never learned to
handle a car as a young man. His mother's diary reveals, however, that
as a teenager he had driven his father's car, sometimes over long distances, and had even had some aptitude as a mechanic. But any ease he
felt behind the wheel had long since disappeared. "He could drive," a
friend says, "but it didn't look right."

When Roberts decided he needed a car, a member who owned a
Chevrolet dealership in Augusta sold him a green 1972 Caprice Classic.
(The first car was the wrong shade of green and had to be replaced.)
Roberts then asked Fred Bennett, the club's caddie master, to tell him
how to get to Grandfather. Bennett began to describe the most direct
route, which followed a succession of state highways, but Roberts interrupted him. "That's too damn much trouble," he said. So Bennett suggested a route that had fewer turns but would take him some eighty
miles out of the way. Roberts happily took that.

At Grandfather, Roberts's car was easy to identify, because it was always poorly parked. It was also easy to hear. When Roberts started it, he
kept the key turned in the ignition long after the engine had kicked over,
as though he were trying, with his usual meticulousness, to make sure
the vehicle was quite thoroughly started. The sound did not inspire confidence in passengers. When Bennett came to Grandfather once on an
errand, Roberts asked him if he would like to have a tour of the course
in a golf cart. The course is laid out in a valley that is flanked by steep
mountains, and Roberts liked to show off the breathtaking views. Bennett looked at the precipitous cart path they would have to follow with
Roberts at the wheel and declined, saying that he had seen the course
before and remembered it well. When Roberts died in 1977 his car had
less than a thousand miles on its odometer.

Roberts's condominiums in North Carolina and the Bahamas, both of
which were purchased late in his life, were the first residences he owned

that really looked like homes. He didn't spend much of the year in either place—in fact, he seldom lived anywhere for more than a few months at a stretch—but both of those dwellings seemed settled and substantial in a way that most of his others did not. That was probably at least partly the result of the influence of his third wife, Betty, whom he married in 1972.

During many periods of Roberts's life, it was entirely possible to be a friend of his and not realize he had been married at all. His wives didn't spend much time at the club, and he seldom talked about them, even with people he knew well. Friends who knew his last two wives often did not realize there had been a first. Marriage, in Roberts's mind, had nothing to do with the club or the tournament and was therefore unlikely to arise as a topic of conversation.

Roberts married for the first time in 1937, when he was forty-three. His bride was Mary Agnes Bishop, who was ten years younger. She was from Fort Fairfield, Maine, and she had spent Augusta's just-concluded resort season working as a telephone operator at the Forest Hills Hotel. The wedding took place the week after the tournament, and was conducted in the living room of Dr. Roger Fry, a Presbyterian minister. Roberts had known Fry for several years because the minister and his family, after moving to Augusta in 1933, had lived briefly in a house belonging to the Berckmanses just east of Magnolia Lane. (The house was later torn down.) Louise Fry Scudder, the younger of the minister's two daughters, said in 1998, "My father was quite a golfer, and all the golfers from Augusta National would come over and chat with him instead of taking my sister out on dates, which wasn't very much fun for her. Balls from the old practice range would come bouncing into our dining room windows and break them every week. I was thirteen when we moved in, and I used to come through the hedge to the tournaments. I had my first golf lesson with Ed Dudley."

Scudder, who has since died, said that Roberts called her father on a Friday and said that he wanted to be married that night. Jerome Franklin was the best man; his wife also attended the wedding, as did two other club members and their wives. Scudder's sister, Betsey, was the maid of honor. "She knew Cliff and went around with all those older people,"

Scudder said, "because she married a man as old as our mother. His name was Tom Silver, and he was a member of the club, and he was even older than Cliff. Those were very interesting days, and Cliff was quite a character. He was kind of tall and hawk-eyed and hawk-nosed. He wasn't handsome, but he had a lot of charm when you got to it, which took a bit of doing. He was an old crotchet, but he had a heart of gold. When I was seventeen, I went on a date with him and my sister and Tom Silver, and Cliff taught me how to drink a Scotch Mist. I'm not sure how you make one of those; I think you pour a lot of Scotch over a lot of rocks. Agnes, his wife, was lovely. She was petite, and brunette, and very attractive. But, let's face it, I don't think Cliff was cut out for marriage." Agnes made the same discovery not long afterward, and she and Roberts divorced.

There may have been at least one earlier romance in Roberts's life. For many years, he corresponded with a Frenchwoman named Suzanne Verdet. The two may have met during Roberts's brief tour of duty in the First World War, and he may have visited her on subsequent trips to France. It's also possible that they met after the war, possibly in New York. According to family lore, he credited her with having saved his life by once persuading him to remain with her an extra day, thus preventing him from traveling on an airplane that crashed. Roberts corresponded with her for the rest of his life, and the tone of his letters was always affectionate. "The only thing I can think of to do at the moment is to express my love for you and to hope that I may soon receive more favorable news about your injury," he wrote in 1977, not long before his own death, after learning from a friend of Verdet's that she had been hospitalized. "I am enclosing a few small bills with the thought that you can use them as a means of expressing your thanks to the nurses who are looking after you." Roberts had been sending her money for many years, and she was one of a small group of individuals to whom he left money in his will.

Roberts waited more than twenty years after his first wedding before trying marriage again. In a Christmas letter to his sister, Dorothy, in 1958, he wrote, "I am, for the second time, undertaking matrimony. My wife has been married before, and she is not so young that it will appear to be a foolish undertaking for one of my age." Roberts's new wife was named Letitia. According to the recollection of one friend, they had met in the waiting room of an ear, nose, and throat specialist, whom Roberts may have been seeing as a result of trouble with his tonsils. (He had them removed in 1956.) Roberts was in his early sixties at the time of the wedding; Letitia was ten or fifteen years younger and had a grown son. The honeymoon was not romantic in any conventional sense: Roberts invited another couple to go along so that he would have someone to play golf with and Letitia would have someone to talk to while he was playing golf. The other couple were Freeman Gosden—who was a close friend, a member of the club, and the voice of Amos on the *Amos & Andy* radio program—and his wife, Jane. "I have no idea how we were invited," Jane Gosden says today. (Her husband died in 1983.) "Cliff must have called Freeman in California and said, 'We're going to Puerto Rico—do you want to play golf?' We all stayed in a suite at the resort, and at six o'clock sharp each evening Cliff would come into the living room dressed for Wall Street, in a dark suit and tie. He would sit on the couch and read a book and wait for Letitia to get dressed. I would go sit with him while he waited, and probably just disturb his reading. You had to know Cliff to know how amusing it was to see him in this new setting as a bridegroom."

The hotel where the two couples stayed was the Dorado Beach Resort, which had just opened. The pro at Dorado's brand-new golf course (which had been designed by Robert Trent Jones) was Ed Dudley, who had retired from Augusta National in order to take the job. Roberts and Freeman Gosden would play golf with Dudley during the day, while Jane commiserated with Letitia. "There was an alligator bag that she wanted," she recalls, "and I had to tell Cliff. She would just dissolve in tears, and Cliff wouldn't understand, so I had to explain to him that he needed to buy her things, and I showed him which bag she wanted. He really didn't understand women, and I don't think women understood him, either. But he had a mush heart, I hate to say." Roberts's marriage with Letitia was not a success. There were probably strains between them from the beginning, and they almost certainly would have divorced sooner than they did had Letitia not been diagnosed with cancer.

Roberts continued to support her financially and to pay her medical bills long after the marriage ended. She died in the late seventies.

Roberts's third wife, an Irishwoman named Betty Lister, was probably the love of his life. They met in the early fifties on a blind date at a baseball game, and by the time they married, in 1972, Roberts deeply regretted that they had not done so sooner. Roberts once told a relative that he had initially been afraid of Betty's "Irish temper." For her part, Betty at first seems to have worried—undoubtedly with justification—that she would never be more than a peripheral interest in Roberts's life. In a letter to Roberts written in 1955, shortly after a visit during which they had apparently argued, she concluded, "Don't laugh (for I never can at this) but as I flew back [to California], all my poor little brain kept repeating was, 'He only wanted to see me between whistle stops.'" By all accounts, though, the marriage was a happy one. They spent a great deal of time apart—Betty didn't like the club, and Roberts didn't like Beverly Hills, where Betty had a house (which she kept and often returned to after they were married). But they were loving and affectionate together, and were even seen, on at least a few occasions, holding hands. Acquaintances who were accustomed to Roberts's frosty public persona were surprised at the vulnerability he revealed when he was with his wife, who often called him Cliffie. Not long after they were married, he hired two of the club's employees to come to New York to pick up a carload of his possessions and transport them to the condominium at Grandfather. When he asked one of the men to go around the corner to pick up some packing boxes at a neighborhood store, Betty intervened and told him to go himself. He said, "Don't you think he's got enough sense to go around the damn corner?" She said, "Yes, but he doesn't know the city. You go instead, Cliffie." Roberts smiled meekly but contentedly, put on his vest, coat, and hat (garments without which he would not venture outside), and not only got the boxes but also packed them, wrapped them, and made handles for them—skills that dated back to his years as a clerk in his father's store.

Roberts surely inspired few romantic fantasies, and being married to him must have been a challenge. He probably felt most comfortable with women who didn't expect him to treat them all that differently from the way he treated men. But he had reasonably close relationships with a number of women over the course of his life, among them not only his mother, his sister, his wives, and various secretaries, but also, notably, Mamie Eisenhower and the wives of a number of his best friends at the club. They almost invariably found him to be, as Louise Scudder and Jane Gosden did, a man whose gruff demeanor didn't extend very far below the surface.

Socially, Roberts usually preferred the company of men; hence his decision to bring a golf partner on his honeymoon. But he was not afraid of women or scornful of them. One of the members of Eisenhower's cabinet of whom he thought most highly was the secretary of health, education, and welfare, Oveta Culp Hobby. She was also one of the few Democrats whose political judgment he respected. Roberts had first encountered her during the campaign, and he, like Eisenhower, admired her not only as a person but also as an executive and a strategist. The two of them were closely involved in raising money for Ike, and they took part in deliberations about, among other things, the consequences for the administration of the president's first heart attack. On the subject of working women, Roberts had views that were, for his age and era, practically enlightened. He was also close to Ann Whitman, Eisenhower's principal White House secretary. On an official trip through Asia once, Whitman had been left by local authorities in one country to take a taxi instead of an official car, and in India she had been forced to sleep in a doorless passageway that was used early in the mornings by waiters and other service personnel. Roberts was outraged, not because he felt this was no way to treat a lady but because he believed that Whitman's ordeal was the result of a wrongheaded societal prejudice against "women who work"—and he used those terms. Women, in general, may have baffled him, but work was a subject he could understand.

If Roberts really did meet his second wife in a doctor's waiting room, the setting would not have seemed ridiculous to him. He was not a hypochondriac, but he was an attentive student of his health and of the health of other people. In later years, he made certain that the local membership of Augusta National included physicians in a variety of specialties, and he took a genuine interest in the ailments of members and employees. He disliked ever being asked how he was, because he believed, no doubt correctly, that the asker wasn't interested in the response. (When Phil Wahl asked him that question one day, Roberts replied, "Goddamn it, I feel terrible, and don't you *ever* ask me how I feel again.") But with someone who genuinely cared about medical matters, he was capable of holding what for him were animated discussions.

One of Roberts's favorite medical institutions was St. Luke's Episcopal Hospital in Houston, Texas. That was the hospital he visited in the fall of 1977 immediately before taking his life. In 1973, at the Texas Heart Institute, which was associated with that hospital, Roberts had an operation to repair a large aortic aneurysm. The operation was performed by Denton A. Cooley, the renowned surgeon who in 1968 had performed the first successful heart transplant in the United States.

In 1948, when Jones was first diagnosed with the agonizing spinal malady that eventually killed him, Roberts urged him to seek treatment from another of his favorite medical institutions, the distinguished Lahey Clinic in Boston. Jones went instead to a surgeon in Atlanta who had had experience in treating problems similar to his. His condition steadily worsened after the operation, though, and in 1950 he took Roberts's advice. "I was not in the Boston hospital during the second operation," Roberts wrote in his book about the club, "but I saw the head surgeon who performed it shortly afterward. He informed me everything that could have been done had been accomplished in Atlanta; and that, aside from removing some proud flesh which might make Bob more comfortable, nothing more could be done. The surgeon went on to explain that, as the central nervous system had been permanently damaged, there would occur a gradual deterioration of his system of nerves below the point of damage. He finished by asking me to help convince my friend that no mistake was made in the first instance." Roberts himself was treated at Lahey for a variety of ailments, among them gastrointestinal complaints that he believed were aggravated by the stresses of his occupation. He also sent Bowman Milligan, the club's steward, to Lahey to be examined and treated when Milligan's health began to fail in the early seventies.

Several members of the club worked at the local hospital in Augusta. Shortly after the Masters in 1970, two of them told Roberts that Barbara Spencer—the wife of David Spencer, one of the club's co-professionals —was gravely ill. She had given birth in the hospital several weeks before, and the birth had contributed to a major flare-up of ulcerative colitis. Neither of the club members was in charge of her treatment, but both were involved in the case and were alarmed by her condition. "She was going to die," one of them says today. Roberts immediately called David Spencer and said that he thought they ought to get Barbara to Boston right away to see his own doctor at Lahey. David thanked him but declined the offer, believing that his wife was in capable hands and that she was, at any rate, too ill to move. A few days later, Roberts talked to the doctors again and called back. This time, David agreed.

It was a Saturday night. Roberts made arrangements in Boston, then set out to find transportation. There were several members at the club that night who had their own airplanes, but only one of the planes had a bench seat, which could be made into a bed. It belonged to Carl Scott, who was the head of the Canadian division of Ford Motor Co. Roberts told Scott, "Carl, we need your plane." Barbara had suffered congestive heart failure that evening. As soon as she could be moved, she was taken to the plane by ambulance. A nurse went along on the flight and flew back with the pilots, and Barbara was taken by ambulance from Logan Airport to New England Baptist Hospital. She was so ill when she arrived that the doctors at Lahey had to postpone surgery for two days. They told David privately that the prognosis was not good and that if there were any family members who wanted to see her, they should be sent for immediately.

The operation was harrowing but successful. Barbara was kept in intensive care for a week and wasn't able to leave the hospital for two months after that. "My daughter was three weeks old when I went to Boston," she says today, "and she was almost three months old when I got home. And our son was just a year and a half old. I had these two babies at home, and David had to spend a lot of time in Boston with me.

We didn't have any money at all. When we first got to Augusta, I earned more as a teacher than David did as a golf professional. We would never have been able to manage any of it if it hadn't been for Mr. Roberts."

Two members offered to pay the Spencers' uncovered medical bills, child care, and travel expenses, which amounted to roughly $10,000. Roberts told them they couldn't do that, because the Spencers would then be saddled with gift taxes they couldn't afford. Instead, Roberts sent letters to a hundred members, asking each for a gift of a hundred dollars—since checks of that size would be well below the gift tax threshold. He also made sure that the Spencers' expenses were covered again in the fall, when Barbara had to return to Boston for a second operation.

"Mr. Roberts was responsible for getting me out of Augusta and making sure I got to the right doctors," Barbara says today. "People have this idea that he was cold and heartless, but he wasn't like that at all. It would have been so easy for him not to get involved. David was new, and the season was ending, and I was in a hospital and presumably being taken care of. But he stayed with it, and he kept calling David, and he made it possible for me to go. He basically saved my life."

Gene Sarazen putting for a photographer with a movie camera before the Masters in 1947.

Byron Nelson and Ben Hogan in 1942.

Clockwise from bottom left: Lawson Little, Charlie Bartlett, Billy Burke, Tommy Armour, Ben Hogan, and Olin Dutra.

Bobby Jones's father, Colonel Robert P. Jones. According to Roberts, members were disappointed when the Colonel played well, because he swore so colorfully when he played poorly.

Local servicemen, with WAC caddies, putting at Augusta National in 1942, before the club closed for the duration.

Sam Snead, after winning the Masters in 1949, being helped into a green jacket by runner-up Lloyd Mangrum. (Johnny Bulla, who tied with Mangrum, is at Snead's feet.) This was the first time a green jacket was presented to the winner of the tournament.

Wounded soldiers watching the Masters from litters placed beside the eighteenth green in 1947; the club gave them free tickets and preferred seating.

Jones practicing at the next to last Masters in which he competed, in 1947. His badge identifies him as player No. 1. This picture was printed from one of a number of forgotten color negatives that were found in an old file cabinet several years ago.

Roberts with Arnold Palmer and Dwight Eisenhower—the two men whose ties to Augusta National and the Masters most defined the club to the public in the fifties and sixties.

One of three oil portraits that Dwight Eisenhower painted of Roberts. This one on loan from the Herkelrath family, hangs in the clubhouse library.

A bumper sticker during Eisenhower's second presidential campaign read: BEN HOGAN FOR PRESIDENT. IF WE'RE GOING TO HAVE A GOLFER, LET'S HAVE A GOOD ONE. Ike was a short hitter and an inveterate slicer, but he loved golf above all other sports. Watching him swing are Bill Zimmerman, Billy Joe Patton, and Roberts.

Roberts was seldom given credit for being funny, but his close friends knew he had a sense of humor. At Ascot in 1958, he clowned around with Freeman Gosden and Barry Leithead.

Roberts holds the "rubber ducky" to whom he appeared to be singing in one of the humorous films shown at the Jamboree, the club's main annual gathering for members.

80

Roberts was a favorite of Mamie Eisenhower's. She used to joke about a letter she received in which she was accused of setting a bad example for the youth of America by permitting Roberts to greet her at Augusta's airport with a kiss.

82

The club gave Roberts an eightieth birthday party in 1974. In his speech, he honored four men who had worked at Augusta National since the beginning: Robert Reynolds, who was ninety-one years old and had helped to build the course before going to work at the club; Ben Smalley, who was one of the club's first caddies; John Milton, who was the head chauffeur; and Bowman Milligan, who had recently retired as the club's steward.

Sidney Walker, aka Beau Jack, who became the lightweight champion of the world under the tutelage of Bowman Milligan. This picture is from a 1942 issue of *Collier's*. Milligan is on the left.

Frank Carpenter, the club's wine steward. Carpenter was a waiter when Roberts urged him to educate himself about wine by tasting every bottle he opened. He went on to assemble a wine cellar that today is viewed as one of the most distinguished in the world.

The fairways at Augusta National are mowed in one direction only, and by a squadron of mowers driving in formation. An entire fairway can be cut in less time than it takes for the members of a foursome to walk to their drives.

The Crow's Nest—a dormitory under the cupola of the clubhouse—as it appeared in the early forties. Today it's more comfortable and offers a bit more privacy; during the Masters, it is offered to any of the tournament's amateur competitors who wish to stay there.

Seve Ballesteros waist-deep in azaleas above the twelfth hole, after pulling his tee shot and overshooting the green. Tournament week finds the course at its most beautiful, with its greatest concentration of trees and shrubs in flower.

Clifford Roberts (in glasses) and Bobby Jones in the Butler Cabin following the 1965 Masters, with Downing Gray (the low amateur), Gary Player, Arnold Palmer, and Jack Nicklaus.

Clifford Roberts's favorite photograph of himself. A few months before he took his life, in 1977, he sent signed copies to close friends. "You're never going to see him again," the wife of a member told her husband. "He's saying good-bye."

CHAPTER TEN

Inside, Outside

MORE THAN A few readers of Roberts's book about Augusta National have been alarmed by several passages in which he discusses various black employees of the club. It requires generosity to describe his tone even as condescending. The most unsettling anecdote is one regarding Claude Tillman, who before working at the club had been employed by Thomas Barrett, Jr., the mayor of Augusta and one of the earliest members of the club. When Barrett died in 1934, Tillman was hired to run the club's kitchen, in circumstances that Roberts described:

> Tom Barrett's war injuries were credited with bringing on a fatal illness, and during that time he told me that he wanted me to have Claude. He apparently made a stipulation to that effect, because Tom's widow, Louise, placed a Christmas wreath around Claude's neck, tied a card to it bearing my name, and sent Claude to me. After conferring with Bowman [Milligan, the club's steward], I passed along my gift to the club by placing Claude in charge of the kitchen. After my arrival in Augusta from New York some six weeks later, the following conversation took place between Claude and me:
>
> "Claude, how are you doing in the kitchen?"
> "We is doin' jus' fine."
> "Are we doing a good volume of business?"
> "We is doin' lots of business."

"Are we making any money?"

"Yes, suh!"

"But how do you know? Give me an example."

After scratching his head for a bit, Claude said, "You takes my milk.
I measures it out very careful and I serves five glasses from a bottle at
fifteen cents a glass, and a bottle only costs us fifteen cents. And on that
basis, Mr. Cliff, we is 'bliged to show a profit."

The image of the wreath around Tillman's neck—with its overt suggestion of human bondage—might have appalled a thoughtful observer
even in 1934, when the "gift" took place. Nearly as shocking today is the
fact that Roberts elected to preserve the episode in print when he wrote
his book more than forty years later. Sandy Richardson, who was
Roberts's editor at Doubleday, and a group of club members who had
read the manuscript before publication tried futilely to persuade him to
leave it out. Ken Bowden—a writer and a former editorial director of
Golf Digest who was hired by Roberts to help him prepare the book for
publication—says that arguing with Roberts, who was then in his eighties, was hopeless. "He felt that the story was part of the club's history,"
Bowden recalls, "and that it was fun, and that there was no reason not
to include it."

Nevertheless, Bowden says, Roberts's point of view regarding matters of race is not so easy to characterize as it may seem. "It would be
hard to put the word racism to it," he continues. "I think the explanation is that he was a man of a generation and a background that simply
didn't perceive the problems. He was actually kind and generous to the
club's employees, and I never had any sense that he was hated or disliked. But he was sort of oblivious. He came from a time and a world
where black people served white people. I think it was as simple as
that."

With Roberts, though, nothing is ever simple. His views on race are
worth exploring, not only because they were part of his character but
also because perceptions of them have figured in the history of the club
and the tournament and therefore in the history of the game. Partly as a
result of Roberts's writings and public pronouncements, the Masters

and Augusta National have routinely been portrayed as bulwarks of prejudice in a sport still haunted by a legacy of exclusion. As is usually the case with Roberts, the full story is more complicated than it may at first appear.

When Roberts was born, in the final decade of the nineteenth century, slavery and the Civil War were still very much a part of the living memory of the United States—no further removed in history than the Vietnam War is today. In 1904, when Roberts was ten, his father, Charles, wrote to his mother, Rebecca, that he had traded the contents of a store he owned for a one-hundred-and-sixty-acre farm, forty-five acres of cotton, "& a family of Negroes," according to an entry in Rebecca's diary. She added, in quotation marks, a caveat from her husband's letter: "Not a good title to the Negroes though." Rebecca's entry, like a number of other entries about her husband's business adventures, was almost certainly sardonic. As for Charles's comment, that's impossible to say.

Whatever Charles may have felt about the notion of holding "title" to human beings, there is no doubt that Clifford grew up at a time in which relations between black and white Americans were primitive, to say the least. In 1906, Rebecca reported that Clifford and his brother had attended a "darkey picnic" and been "greatly amused by the darkeys dress & dancing." Beyond such glimpses, Clifford and his siblings would have had virtually no experience, direct or indirect, of what it was to be nonwhite in the United States in the early twentieth century. Nor would that have been an issue to which they gave much thought, if any. To say that black Americans were not a part of the world in which Roberts and his white contemporaries grew up does not come close to describing the division. And neither the army nor Wall Street would have enlarged his conception of society.

Roberts's first close interaction with men and women of color was almost certainly at Augusta National. He was undoubtedly a man of his time, as Bowden suggests, but he had not grown up in the South and his point of view was never that of the average white southerner of his generation. In September 1957, Orval E. Faubus, the governor of Arkansas,

sent National Guard troops to prevent black students from entering
Central High School in Little Rock, in defiance of a Supreme Court ruling on the integration of public schools. President Eisenhower responded by dispatching a thousand army paratroopers to protect the
black students and end violent rioting by whites. Six weeks later, Eisenhower visited the club and, Roberts later recalled, met a chilly reception
from white residents of Augusta. "I remember clearly as though it were
yesterday," Roberts said in a 1970 interview with a researcher from Columbia University, "that I was dumbfounded and chagrined to find supposedly sensible people who had become so bitterly critical of the
President because he sent the troops into Arkansas." Roberts said that
the view of the vast majority of white southerners at that time was that
sending troops "was just like resuming the Civil War. And it was so bad
that there was no possible way of discussing the matter in a sane fashion
with the Southern white people at that point, because those who were
ordinarily quite broadminded and reasonable just couldn't be reasoned
with at all on the subject of integration."

Roberts clearly included himself in the category of the "broadminded and reasonable"—although he admitted in the Columbia interview that in later years he came to believe that those same irrational
southern whites "were a lot more right about it than I thought they
were at the time," and that he had come to believe that marriage between members of different races was a mistake. He said that he based
that opinion partly on his business dealings in Brazil, where he felt that
workers of mixed race were "the most worthless of all in every respect." Those two points of view—that opposition to the idea of racial
equality was irrational, and that the mixing of races was disastrous—
probably came close to defining the boundaries of Roberts's personal
views about race in the last years of his life.

When Roberts turned eighty in 1974, several friends of his among the
membership proposed to give him a birthday party at the club. Roberts
consented to the plan, although, characteristically, he took charge of the
program himself. He stipulated that there was to be no gift, and that the

event could not be frivolous but had to "serve some useful purpose." Roberts found two such purposes. The first was to boost the turnout at the final members' gathering of the year, a theretofore thinly attended outing called the Closing Party, which was held each May before the club shut down for the summer. The second was to honor some of Augusta National's earliest employees. Roberts devoted the bulk of his speech that night to four black men who had been associated with the club for more than forty years. He had reached the end of what he knew would be one of his last seasons as chairman, and he wanted to underscore his belief that the strength of the club lay in the commitment of those who served—a category in which he included himself. As he said that night, "I'm only a part of an organization that has made this club a little more important than the average."

The men whom Roberts honored were Robert Reynolds, who was ninety-one years old and had helped to build the course before going to work at the club; Ben Smalley, who had been one of the club's first caddies; John Milton, who was the head chauffeur; and Bowman Milligan, who had recently retired as the club's steward, a position in which he had managed the staff and many of the internal operations of the club. Of the four, Milligan was the closest to Roberts and the one who had played the most significant role in Augusta National's history.

Milligan was the first employee Roberts hired. He arrived one day as the club was forming and asked for a job. At that time, he worked in the locker room at the Forest Hills Hotel, which was struggling to stay in business. His father had worked for the Berckmanses when the Augusta National property was a nursery, and he knew Claude Tillman, whom Roberts liked immensely and whose opinion he trusted—despite the very different impression he would later convey with his story about Tillman and the Christmas wreath. Roberts hired Milligan on the spot. "It was one of the quickest and best decisions I ever made in my life," he said during his birthday speech. Milligan's first job was running the club's locker room, but Roberts rapidly broadened his responsibilities. The two men's working relationship lasted for more than forty years. Even after ill health forced Milligan to retire, he remained a presence at Augusta National and at the Masters.

Milligan and Roberts were exactly suited in temperament, and they had very similar views of what the club ought to be and how it ought to be run. Both were perfectionists, and both had seemingly limitless capacities for work. Milligan would often arrive at the club before dawn and not leave until after midnight. He ran the service side of the operation—purchasing, housekeeping, meals and beverages, the locker room, the chauffeurs—and he did all the hiring and firing of service employees. His power over the club's staff was absolute. Tips constituted a large part of the compensation of employees in those days, and Milligan controlled the flow. Members would often leave cash with him for distribution among the staff, and he would pass it around—or not, as he saw fit. "My main memory of Bowman is of him having lots and lots and lots of money in his pockets," an employee who knew him says. *"Thick money. Lump here, lump here, lump here, lump here. He used to pat his wallets and say, 'I got it. I got the first count. Run into me. I got all of y'all in my pocket.'"* In the later years of his career at the club, the lumps added up to tens of thousands of dollars. (Shortly before his retirement, when he had grown increasingly ill, he collapsed one day in front of the caddie house, and one worried employee told another on the phone, "Quick! Get to him before the caddies do!") Much of the money in his wallets had been there so long that some of the bills had stuck together and could not easily be peeled apart.

Milligan was widely believed to be well connected in the world of horse racing. Members and employees would sometimes travel to Triple Crown races to place bets on horses he had recommended, and he himself was said to win (and occasionally lose) huge sums. In Augusta itself, Milligan had an extensive network of relationships and connections which he cultivated for the benefit of the club and the tournament. Roberts, in a letter in 1947, wrote that the club was under no pressure to find an overall manager because Milligan, as steward, "does a better job than anyone I know." Milligan's role in the operation of Augusta National was so far-reaching that when he retired he could not be replaced by a single person; his departure necessitated a full-scale reorganization of the club's service department.

Roberts's favorite story about Milligan concerned a visit to the club by Albert Bradley, who was the chairman of the board of General Motors (and who later became a member). "He was my guest," Roberts recalled at his birthday party, "and he hadn't been here more than fifteen minutes when he spotted Bowman. He leapt over and shook hands with him and patted him on the back and in many ways indicated that one of the great moments of his life was renewing an acquaintance with Bowman." The explanation, it turned out, was that during Prohibition Milligan had worked at a golf club in Michigan to which Bradley belonged. Part of his job had been maintaining a supply of liquor for the members. One night, the club was raided by the local sheriff and half a dozen deputies. Roberts said, "The sheriff announced, 'We're looking for a man by the name of Bowman Milligan.' And Bowman said, 'I know just where he is. I'll go get him for you.' And he went right on out the back door, and he has never been seen in Michigan since."

One of Milligan's duties during Augusta National's earliest years was to provide evening entertainment for the members, who in those days stayed not at the club—which as yet had no overnight accommodations—but at the Bon Air–Vanderbilt and other local hotels. He arranged for performances by local dancers, gospel singers, and others, and he put on boxing free-for-alls in which half a dozen or more young black men from Augusta would slug it out, sometimes while blindfolded, in a ring in the Bon Air's ballroom until all but one had been knocked down or had given up. The members of the audience then passed the hat, and Milligan distributed the proceeds among the boxers, each of whom made about ten dollars a fight.

Among the participants in at least one of the free-for-alls was a slightly built, illiterate teenager named Sidney Walker, whom Milligan decided had the makings of a professional boxer. Milligan gave Walker a job in the locker room at Augusta National, called him Beau Jack, and helped him build a fighting career that eventually led to the lightweight championship of the world. Sportswriters since that time have sometimes portrayed Beau Jack as a victim of Milligan, Roberts, or other men connected with the club. But such allegations are unfounded, as a factual accounting of Beau Jack's career reveals.

When Beau Jack's first season as an Augusta National employee ended, Milligan took him with him to his summer job, at Long Meadow Country Club in Massachusetts. Over the next two seasons, Milligan spent roughly $4,000 on Beau Jack's training and expenses, and entered him in a succession of fights in western Massachusetts. Beau Jack's career might have ended there had it not been for the intervention of William E. Robinson, who was a member of the club and the general manager of the *New York Herald Tribune*. (A few years later, Robinson would introduce Dwight Eisenhower to Augusta National.) Robinson pitched Beau Jack's story to one of his own sportswriters, Richards Vidmer, and found a veteran sports publicist named Chick "Hercules" Wergeles, who was willing to help Milligan manage him and arrange for a fight in New York. Vidmer "improved the story he was writing" (in the words of an article about Beau Jack that appeared in the September 1955 issue of *Sport*) by approaching twenty-three prominent men, most of whom were Augusta National members, and asking each to contribute twenty-five dollars to the fighter's expense fund. They did, and in 1941 Vidmer wrote in the *Herald Tribune* that Beau Jack had the backing of a "syndicate" of "twenty millionaires"—among them Roberts, Grantland Rice, and Bobby Jones. The article gave Beau Jack marquee value in New York and brought him his shot at the big time. Milligan returned the group's contribution—a total of about five hundred dollars—as soon as Beau Jack had won his first significant purse.

Wergeles pushed the Augusta National angle as well. "There's always a bunch of the millionaires at all The Jack's fights," he wrote (untruthfully) in 1942. "And after he belts some lug out in a couple of heats they all stop in the dressin' room to shake his hand and congratulate 'em. So, if and when The Jack meets up with that guy, [lightweight champion Sammy] Angott, I got a strong hunch me and the millionaires will be celebratin' the crowning of the new champ. Where? Oh! Probably the Stork Club."

Beau Jack lived up to his hype, and in 1942 he was declared the lightweight champion. According to his tax returns, his total net income for the next five years, including income from investments, amounted to a little less than $125,000—big money at the time, although the wartime federal income tax rate reduced it by more than a third. The beginning of the end of his fighting career came in late 1946, when he broke a kneecap during training. He severely reinjured the same knee in a fight a few months later, and Milligan urged him to retire. Beau Jack parted with Milligan over that issue and, once his knee had improved, continued to fight what were essentially exhibition matches. He never again won a significant bout, and he retired for good in 1951.

Beau Jack lived the high life during his five years as a star and for a short time after. He bought a farm, lost or settled at least two paternity lawsuits, bought an expensive car, shared Milligan's taste for the racetrack, and raised a family that eventually included nine children. He sought and received investment advice from Roberts during those years. (Another club member, Ellis Slater, helped draw up his fight contracts.) Roberts persuaded Beau Jack to preserve at least part of his assets by purchasing a $10,000 annuity. When the fighter injured his knee, Roberts persuaded him to convert the remainder of his savings—roughly $12,000—into government bonds and to place them in an irrevocable trust. He did so. He was paid just the interest from the trust, although he was able to draw down the principal in emergencies, as he did when he withdrew $6,000 to start a drive-in barbecue restaurant on his farm.

Beau Jack is still alive. He runs the shoeshine concession at the Fontainebleau Hotel in Miami Beach, and he still receives income from either the annuity or the trust. Sportswriters have sometimes accused Roberts, Milligan, and various club members of having exploited him for their own gain. But Beau Jack's career was his own, and the financial role of the "twenty millionaires" began and ended in the *Herald Tribune*'s publicity stunt. The main financial advice that Roberts gave to Beau Jack and Milligan was the same financial advice he gave to anyone who would listen: Put at least some of your wealth in a place where you can't easily get at it. (Roberts created Eisenhower's blind trust as a political expediency, but the innovation perfectly suited his cautious view of money management, which had been formed during five decades of hardship and loss.) Beau Jack is far from wealthy today, but he is surely one of the few prizefighters of his era who still has money that he earned in the ring.

Some of the wilder tales about Milligan obscure the true significance of
his position at the club during the bulk of his career. Roberts—who was
not reluctant to tell people how to perform their jobs—usually deferred
to Milligan's judgment in the areas under Milligan's control. With
Roberts's approval, Milligan ran what was essentially an employment
agency for black Augustans. Many of the workers he hired remained at
the club for decades, and it was those workers whom Roberts credited
with having built the club from nothing.

The extraordinary level of hospitality enjoyed by Augusta National's
members and their guests was in many ways Milligan's invention. Frank
Carpenter, who is Augusta National's wine steward, first worked at the
club as a bartender during the 1953 Masters. Milligan eventually persuaded him to accept a job during the regular season, even though at
that time Carpenter also worked as a clerk at the Post Office. "Bowman
became my mentor," Carpenter recalls. "I learned everything from him
about service. He was a service-oriented person, and he always believed
in satisfying the members. He taught me how to deal with that, and
how to handle people—how to handle employees. He used to say that
you can't do it collectively—you have to do it individually. You have to
take each individual and learn how to get the most out of that person.
Then you assign your employees to the jobs that they are best suited for
and that they will be most productive with. You can't group everyone
together and give orders and think that everyone will give you the same
performance. And the same is true with the way you treat the members."

"Service," in the context of a social club, is a notion that today carries heavy emotional freight; it is equated with servility. But Milligan
and Carpenter didn't feel that way about what they did for a living, and
neither did Roberts. Indeed, all three men had strikingly similar notions
of their duties at Augusta National. Service was the guiding principal
behind Roberts's perfectionism and his conception of almost every as-
pect of the club and the tournament. His practice of calling ticket buyers "patrons" was a reflection of his belief that the purpose of the club

during Masters week was to serve the people whose support had made the tournament possible in the first place. He had a similarly solicitous attitude toward the players who competed in the Masters and the sportswriters who covered it. His relentless quest for improvement was close to the essence of his character. The club was a cherished retreat for its members in large measure because Roberts was pleased to treat his own membership as a job.

Perhaps surprisingly, given his reputation among sportswriters, Roberts was viewed by the club's employees as a good man to work for. He was particular about what he wanted, but he was not fickle. "He believed in consistency," Carpenter says. "He used to say, 'Continuity in everything'—in the food, in the service, in everything we did. He believed that if you could do something one time, you could do it again." Roberts's standards were high, but the working atmosphere he helped to create was congenial. Carpenter became the club's wine steward because Roberts urged him to build a knowledge of wine by tasting every bottle he opened. Today, Augusta National's wine cellar, which Carpenter assembled, is regarded as one of the finest in the world.

Roberts was also loyal to the club's employees. Fred Bennett says, "If he liked you, there was nothing that anyone could say that would turn him against you. The only person who could do that was you yourself." When a favorite employee was arrested once, Roberts dispatched a lawyer to try to get him out of jail, without first asking what he had been accused of. (Homicide, it turned out.) Roberts chastised members who arrived for dinner after eight o'clock, because he felt that their tardiness was an imposition on workers who might also have to be on hand to serve breakfast in the morning. In the forties, he installed a system that centrally controlled many of the electric lights on the property. The purpose of the system was to prevent members from keeping nighttime bartenders and waiters on duty past the hour at which they were supposed to be able to go home. The lights would go off briefly a few minutes before midnight, then shut off for good at the stroke of twelve. The system was later removed, but while it was in place Roberts was adamant that the curfew be observed. In 1946, Jim Searle, the club's manager, wrote to Roberts, "I am going to have to cut in one or two

more lights to the circuit as last night one party moved to the shower
room to finish a backgammon game. I had gone home sometime earlier
believing everyone intended to retire about 11:00 o'clock. Rest assured
that this matter will be under control and the 12:00 o'clock closing
strictly enforced."

To the surprise of some, Roberts is invariably spoken of with affection in Augusta National's caddie house. More than a dozen of the club's
current caddies knew Roberts well, beginning when some of them were
teenagers. "He was the caddie's best friend," one says—a sentiment that
among the caddies is close to universal. Mark Eubanks, who has worked
at the club for more than thirty years and is one of the six co-authors of
a manual that used to be used to train new caddies, says, "He was a fair
man, and he was a good man." Eubanks and other caddies say that
Roberts went out of his way to protect their interests. Roberts created a
charitable foundation at Augusta National and on several occasions made
disbursements from it to support former caddies who had fallen on hard
times. A Masters winner who now plays on the Senior P.G.A. Tour has
called Roberts a racist in conversations with sportswriters; the caddies
say the same player grossly underpaid his caddie the year he won, and
that Roberts intervened at the caddie's request and forced the player to
significantly increase the fee, leaving the player bitter about Roberts to
this day. Such interventions by Roberts were not uncommon. When the
caddies felt they had been mistreated, they knew they could turn to him.
Roberts himself was known as a generous if not a flamboyant tipper. He
typically invited new members to play with him during one of their first
rounds as members, and often at some point during such a round, the
new member would ask Roberts how much he should pay his caddie.
"Pay him what you think he's worth," Roberts would answer. When the
member persisted, Roberts would say, "If you think he's worth a hundred
dollars, pay him a hundred dollars. If you think he's worth a dollar, pay
him a dollar." This formulation usually worked to the benefit of the caddie—as the caddies and, presumably, Roberts were aware.

With Roberts's encouragement and support, Augusta National's caddies became legends in the game. For many years, the standard practice
at tournaments everywhere had been for players to use caddies supplied

by the clubs where the tournaments were held. Both the P.G.A. and the U.S.G.A. originally forbade the use of outside caddies at their tournaments. "The reason for this regulation," the U.S.G.A. explained in the thirties in a set of confidential guidelines that was supplied to clubs conducting Open or Amateur championships, "was to prevent the use of so-called journeyman caddies, or caddies who make a profession of travelling from one Championship to another. Many of them are totally irresponsible and their presence tends to disrupt a Club's caddie force." The P.G.A. had a similar ban, which it justified with the contention that a pro's use of a traveling caddie was "merely another form of taking advantage of the field." Those rules were later dropped or ignored as players began to prefer working with the same caddies from one tournament to the next. But Roberts maintained Augusta National's commitment to the old idea. Even when most of the top players on tour retained their own regular caddies, Roberts insisted that Masters competitors hire the club's.

The club dropped its caddie requirement for the tournament in 1983, five and a half years after Roberts's death. Pressure from tour players had been building for years. But the Augusta caddies themselves were responsible as well. At the Masters in 1982, a number of them had been late to report for work on Saturday morning for the completion of the second round, which had been halted by rain the day before. Some players had also complained that their equipment was poorly cared for during the rain. Given the level of discontent among the tour players, the club could no longer maintain its old position.

Some of Augusta National's caddies believe they would still be working the Masters if Roberts were alive today. That almost certainly isn't true. Even though Roberts was committed to protecting the caddies' franchise, the evolution of professional golf by the early eighties had made the change inevitable. If it hadn't happened in 1983, it would have happened within the next few years. Caddies had become so important to the touring pros that the pros could no longer be required to compete without their regular partners. But the issue is still a bitter one in the caddie house, and Roberts's name is still spoken there with deep respect.

It is a standard allegation among sportswriters that Augusta National for many years prohibited black golfers from playing in the Masters, until relenting in 1975 by issuing an invitation to Lee Elder. That view is incorrect. No black player qualified for the tournament before Elder did. He did so by winning the 1974 Monsanto Open, and he received his invitation automatically, as has every other player who has ever qualified.

It is often said that Charles Sifford was denied an invitation to the Masters in 1967, when his victory at the Greater Hartford Open gave him the historic distinction of being the first black player to win a P.G.A. Tour event. In 1998, for example, a reporter for the Associated Press wrote, "Sifford never got to play in the Masters because when he won a tour event qualifying rules were manipulated to exclude him." That accusation is false. Golf fans later came to think of the Masters as a tournament of tournament winners, but a tour victory did not become a Masters qualification until 1972, and it had never been one before that time. Indeed, there were numerous pros in that period who won tour events but did not qualify for the following Masters, among them Dave Hill (who won both the Tucson Open and the Denver Open in 1961), Ted Kroll (who won the 1962 Canadian Open), Miller Barber (who won the 1962 Metropolitan Open), Charles Coody (who won the 1964 Dallas Open), George Archer (who won the 1965 Lucky International), Homero Blancas (who won the 1966 Seattle Open), Richard H. Sikes (who won the 1966 Cleveland Open and finished second in two other events), Joe Campbell (who won the 1966 Tucson Open in a playoff with Gene Littler), Dave Stockton (who won the 1967 Colonial Invitational), Dudley Wysong (who won the 1967 Hawaiian Open), Lou Graham (who won the 1967 Minnesota Classic), Chi Chi Rodriguez (who won the 1967 Texas Open), Bob Lunn, (who won the Memphis Open Invitational and the Atlanta Classic in consecutive weeks in 1968), Jim Colbert (who won the 1969 Monsanto Open), Tom Shaw (who won the 1969 Doral Open), and Hugh Royer (who won the 1970 Western Open). Tournament winners tended to be the tour's best players, and the tour's best players usually managed to meet the qualification requirements—but they didn't always, and when they didn't they weren't invited.

There is no denying that golf, among the major professional sports, has an especially shameful history with regard to race. A black player named John Shippen competed in five U.S. Opens between 1896 and 1913—and earned the distinction of being the first American golf professional to have been born in the United States—but the U.S.G.A. in later years directly and indirectly prevented black players from playing in tournaments that it controlled. On the P.G.A. Tour, black golfers who did manage to make their way into formerly segregated events were at first forced to endure unspeakable indignities from organizers, fans, and white pros. Calvin H. Sinnette, in a recent book called *Forbidden Fairways: African Americans and the Game of Golf,* writes of an attempt by Sifford, the legendary black pro Ted Rhodes, the boxer Joe Louis (who had become an accomplished golfer), and a black amateur named Eural Clark to qualify for the 1952 Phoenix Open: "After being denied use of the locker-room facilities, Louis, Rhodes, Sifford, and Clark were sent out as the first group of the morning in the qualifying round. At the first green, they were greeted by the revolting sight and smell of human excrement that someone had surreptitiously placed in the cup." Until May 1961, the constitution of the P.G.A. of America explicitly limited that organization's membership to "Professional Golfers of the Caucasian Race." The P.G.A. went out of its way to enforce the clause, which was broadly supported by white touring professionals, and it dropped the restriction only after the attorney general of California threatened to prohibit the organization from conducting tour events in that state and to share his decision with attorneys general from other states.

Augusta National Golf Club was certainly a part of the culture that for decades made golf virtually unapproachable for black players. If Roberts ever even conceived of the possibility that his club might one day have black members, he almost certainly didn't do so until the last years of his life. But to say that Augusta National Golf Club was staunchly white is both indisputable and unilluminating; in that way, it was no different from other private golf clubs (and many supposedly public ones) all over the United States. The more significant accusation has to do with the tournament: Did the club devise qualifications for the purpose of keeping black players out of the Masters? Records of the tournament's qualification requirements show decisively that it did not.

The first qualification requirements for the Masters were announced before the second tournament, in 1935. Those qualifications were essentially the ones the club had used informally the year before, and they were the basis from which all subsequent qualifications evolved. In 1935, there were seven automatic categories:

1. Past and present U.S. Open champions
2. Past and present U.S. Amateur champions
3. Past and present British Open champions
4. Past and present British Amateur champions
5. Present members of the Walker Cup team
6. Present members of the Ryder Cup team
7. The first twenty-four players in the first Augusta National Invitation Tournament (which had been held the year before)

That added up to a very small group of golfers in 1935. To fill the rest of the field, the club invited players who had noteworthy competitive records, with "particular consideration being given to scoring averages established in the various leading tournaments in 1934." It also invited the five professionals who had achieved the lowest scoring averages on the current winter tour. The P.G.A. in those days was not remotely comparable to the organization it is today. The fall and winter tours were mismatched collections of uneven events, most of them poorly funded and poorly run. Even the P.G.A. Championship—which today is considered one of the four major tournaments—was so little regarded that its reigning winner did not receive an automatic invitation until the third Masters; past champions didn't make the list until two years after that.

As the years went by, more categories were added, and they became both broader and more clearly defined. The club had needed some flexibility in the earliest years simply to be assured of rounding up a reasonable number of players. As golf became established as a professional sport, tournament results provided a better measure of the quality of the players, and the list of requirements reflected that change. By the

time of the 1940 Masters, for example, the number of automatic qualifications had grown to fifteen:

1. Past and present Masters Tournament champions

2. Past and present U.S. Open champions

3. Past and present U.S. Amateur champions

4. Past and present British Open champions

5. Past and present British Amateur champions

6. Past and present P.G.A. champions

7. Members of the current Walker Cup team

8. Members of the current Ryder Cup team

9. The first thirty players in the 1939 Masters Tournament

10. The first thirty players in the 1939 U.S. Open Championship

11. The last eight players in the 1938 U.S. Amateur championship

12. The last eight players in the 1939 P.G.A. championship

13. The two professionals not on the above list who established the best
    scoring records during the current winter circuit

14. One amateur not on the above list selected by ballot by the U.S. Ama-
    teur champions

15. One professional not on the above list selected by ballot of the U.S.
    Open champions

The club by then no longer made any selections of its own among
American players. Only two players were selected according to partially
subjective criteria (categories 14 and 15), and both of those were chosen
by outsiders.

After the Second World War, the popularity of the tournament grew
dramatically, and players who qualified were far less likely to turn down
invitations. Mainly to keep the field from becoming too large—a goal
that was extremely important to Roberts, who felt that spectators would
lose interest if they could not conveniently follow the main action in an
afternoon—the club scaled back the number of players included in
many of the categories. In 1947, for example, the number of Masters
and Open finishers who were extended invitations was reduced by six,

to the top twenty-four; in 1958, the number of qualifying Open finishers was further reduced, to sixteen. Those changes were also made partly to maintain the tournament's uniqueness in the eyes of the public and of the players. In a letter to Jones late in 1946, Roberts wrote, "Aside from the prestige you contributed, I think our tournament has enjoyed an upward trend in attendance and general interest because of unique regulations, the name of the tournament, the 4 days schedule and various other new tournament methods introduced here. But many players and press men emphasize 'class,' 'champions only' and 'quality' as being our sustaining features. Now that so many tournament managers have adopted our regulations which begin with 'the first 30 in the US Open' my commercial sense tells me to undercut them by 6 even though we are not actually reducing our field [because virtually all those dropped would qualify anyway]." Similar reductions were made in most other categories. Winning the U.S. Open entitled a player to a lifetime exemption until 1963, when invitations began to be issued only to champions from the last ten years; in 1968, that category was further reduced, to include just champions from the previous five Opens—although all living Open champions continued to receive honorary invitations to attend as noncompetitors.

Meanwhile, the club was gradually increasing the number of automatic invitations reserved for tour players—a change that reflected the growing stature and stability of the tour. Between 1936 and 1961, just the top two pros who had not otherwise qualified were entitled to invitations; the club increased that number to four in 1962, to six in 1968, and to eight in 1971. In 1972, the club adopted its best-known qualification: any winner of a P.G.A. Tour co-sponsored tournament considered by the tour to be a major event would automatically receive an invitation to the following Masters.*

---

*Late in 1998, Augusta National announced that beginning with the 2000 Masters, winners of P.G.A. Tour events would no longer automatically qualify. That change was one of several made in an effort to "ensure that the best players worldwide are invited to the Masters each year," according to Hootie Johnson, the club's chairman. Among other changes, the club also increased the number of spots for Tour players (from the top thirty on the money list to the top forty)

Those changes in the sixties and seventies, which coincided with the establishment of black players' right to compete on the tour, had the effect of increasing rather than decreasing the likelihood that black players would qualify—as Roberts and other members of the club were aware. Fewer slots were being allocated to the past winners and top finishers of major tournaments—groups that at that time included no black players—and more slots were being allocated to players on the regular tour, where black golfers had begun to build careers. Had Roberts and Augusta National wished to keep black golfers out of the Masters, they could have gone a long way toward doing so by keeping the tournament's qualification requirements exactly as they were in 1967, the year of Charles Sifford's breakthrough victory at the Greater Hartford Open. But they did not. Changes that the club made in 1968, 1971, and 1972 essentially guaranteed that a black player would soon qualify. Beginning in the early sixties, Roberts and Jones had both said repeatedly and publicly that they looked forward to that day, and that no player who qualified for an invitation would fail to receive one. In 1961, in a letter responding to an accusation that black players were banned from the Masters, Jones wrote, "You will note that [the tournament's] qualifications do not include any limitation based on race or color. I can assure you that no such limitation is contemplated for the future." Jones personally assured Sifford in a letter in 1968 that Sifford (like any other golfer) would be invited if he qualified, adding that "I for one would be particularly happy to see you realize this ambition." (A year later, Sifford was quoted in a newspaper interview as having said that Jones had "threatened" him in that letter—an accusation that was not true.) At a press conference at the tournament in 1971, Roberts said that "the Masters is the loser by never having had a black golfer." That was certainly true, and there is no reason to doubt that Roberts meant it.

Of course, the fact that the Masters was a southern tournament and that Augusta National was laid out on a former plantation made both institutions potent symbols of exclusion at a time when racial issues deeply and sometimes violently divided the nation. It could be argued

and extended invitations to the top fifty players in the Official World Golf Ranking.

(and has been argued) that those symbols—as well as the historical barriers to black players within the sport beyond the Masters—were so overwhelming as to make the tournament's qualification rules irrelevant or even despicable. A few weeks before the Masters in 1973, a group of eighteen members of the United States House of Representatives made just such a case in a telegram and letter sent to Roberts. "We are writing to express our very deep concern over the fact that a black touring professional will not be competing in the Masters golf tournament this year," they began, "and that after 37 years the color barrier will still not be broken." They urged Augusta National to "take affirmative action" and waive its regulations in order to invite Lee Elder, who at that time ranked thirty-first in earnings on the P.G.A. Tour.

In response Roberts wrote, "We have much respect for Lee Elder as an American representative of the game of golf both in the United States and abroad. He tied last year with Lee Trevino for 1st place in the Greater Hartford Open Championship and he would have earned a player invitation to the Masters had he not lost in the sudden-death playoff. If we were to make an exception in favor of Mr. Elder or any other golfer who had failed to qualify, we might quite properly be condemned by all other golfers including the growing number of black players who are making a career of tournament golf."

Of course, the most significant reason why no black player had yet qualified for the Masters was that opportunities to do so, by building distinguished professional or amateur careers beyond the circumscribed world of black competitive golf, had been limited or nonexistent until very recently. The columnist Jim Murray had made the same case in 1969, shortly after Sifford had won the Los Angeles Open. "It is a feeling of this 22-handicapper," Murray wrote, "that the Masters ought to send a car for Charlie and, considering he's the only guy in the field who couldn't get started on his golf career 'til he was 33 years old or his tournament career 'til he was almost 40 because it took democracy so long to catch on in this country, maybe they ought to give him two [strokes] a side." But Roberts and Jones believed that the Masters requirements were clear and fair and that the achievements of black golfers would be diminished if they were judged by a separate set of standards. Lee Elder apparently agreed; at the time of the publication of the congressmen's telegram, which had been sent without his knowledge, he announced that he would turn down any invitation that he had not earned in the ordinary way.

A little more than a year after the telegram was sent, Elder made the questions moot. On April 21, 1974, one week after the 1974 Masters, he beat Peter Oosterhuis in a sudden-death playoff at the Monsanto Open, in Pensacola, Florida. The victory marked the end of one form of intense pressure for Elder ("Every time I had a chance to win a tournament, I'd always be asked about the Masters," he told a writer from *Golf* in 1975) and marked the beginning of another, since the next Masters was nearly a year away. His picture appeared on the cover of *Sports Illustrated* and he had to withstand barrages of questions from sportswriters at nearly every tournament he played in for a year. But he held up under the pressure and qualified for the Masters in a second category as well, by finishing the year among the top players on the tour.

After Elder's victory, Roberts said, "The only quarrel I have with Lee is we're sorry he didn't do it sooner." The two men met for the first time in June, on the dais at the annual awards dinner of the Metropolitan Golf Writers in New York. They were introduced by the master of ceremonies, and, according to an account in the *New York Post*, "There was a stunned silence for a moment, then as Roberts waved to Elder and began walking to the center of the dais while Elder came toward him, the crowd of 1,000 responded with a standing ovation." The *Post* called their meeting, which had not been planned, "the unexpected highlight" of the evening. The *Post*'s hyperbolic account—had the reporter expected the two men to exchange blows?—reflects the huge emotional import that Elder's invitation had acquired.

Officially, Roberts had said that Elder would be accorded no special treatment for the Masters. Unofficially, he and the club made numerous efforts behind the scenes to make Elder's experience easier—for example, by issuing him twice the number of tournament guest tickets that were normally allocated to competitors. A month before the Metropolitan Golf Writers dinner, J. Paul Austin, who was a member of the club and the chairman of the board of the Coca-Cola Company, had written to Roberts to ask if Austin might bring Elder to Augusta National to play the course as his guest well in advance of the tournament—a public gesture that had been suggested by Deane Beman, who had just succeeded Joe Dey as the commissioner of the P.G.A. Tour. Roberts, in response, said he thought such a visit would be a good idea. He also reminded Austin that as a member he was entitled to bring anyone he liked to the club, so long as his guest played with him, and that he didn't need Roberts's permission to do so. Furthermore, Roberts said, Elder, like any other player who had qualified for the Masters, could come to the club on his own to practice at any time except during the handful of parties that were limited to members. But Roberts agreed that making a special invitation would both be good for the public image of the club and possibly help Elder withstand the media attention he was bound to receive during the tournament itself. "At best," Roberts wrote, "he is going to be under all sorts of pressure that will make it difficult for him to produce his best brand of golf when he first plays in the Masters." Roberts was encouraged that Elder had retained Roberts's old friend Lincoln Werden, a sportswriter who had recently retired from the *New York Times*, to handle his public relations.

Austin and Elder made their trip to Augusta National in the fall, when the course reopened. The club held a small luncheon for Elder, and afterward he and Austin played with Beman and an Atlanta amateur named Jimmy Gabrielsen. Elder was assigned a veteran caddie named Henry Brown, who was himself an accomplished player and had once shot 68 on the course. At the tournament itself, Elder attracted large galleries. In an account in a black golf magazine called *On the Ball*, Arthur Goodson, the editor, wrote, "For the 1975 Masters, Lee said he just wanted to hit that ball straight down the fairway on his first tee. Well, he did just that, and for the 36 holes he did play, I had to marvel at his blow-by-blow cool. In fact, maybe he was too cool, smiling even while bogeying. But Lee rose to the occasion like the great golfer and gentleman that he is. Elder was paired with Gene Littler on April 10th and shot a 74. He was paired with Miller Barber on April 11th and shot a 78 for a 152 total, missing the cut by four strokes. Beyond it all, in the gallery, both Black and White could be seen wearing buttons that bore the legend, 'Good

Luck, Lee.' " Although he missed the cut that year, he played again in five of the next six Masters Tournaments. His best finish, seventeenth, came in 1979.

An argument often made by sportswriters before Elder qualified for the Masters was that the club ought to treat invitations for black American players with something like the flexibility that it had long used in inviting players from other countries. It is true that Masters invitation guidelines for foreign players have always been more flexible than those for Americans. Jones and Roberts had always yearned for the Masters to become an international tournament, and from the beginning they practiced something akin to affirmative action where players from other countries were concerned. In 1969, Jones wrote, "We allow ourselves a bit more latitude with foreign players because, in most cases, they do not have the opportunity to prove themselves against U.S.A. players." In the early years particularly, the acceptance rate among international players was so dismally low that Roberts and Jones had had to cast a wide net to be assured of securing even one or two entrants from abroad. Judging and comparing foreign players also involved guesswork, since tours in other countries were uneven in the extreme, and there were virtually no international events.

Had the club applied a similar standard to, for example, the all-black United Golfers Association—where Elder, Sifford, and other black pros first built their reputations—a black player would have been invited to the Masters much earlier than 1975. Roberts and Jones probably would have argued that no similar accommodation had ever been made for any other American players after the first few tournaments, back in the thirties—although it is doubtful that either man had more than a passing awareness of any black professional golfers until at least the mid-fifties. Perhaps the best that can be said for both men is that they applied the club's invitation requirements equally to black and white Americans— an evenhandedness that may have been a dubious virtue at that time, given the state of relations between the races. And it is certainly true that neither Roberts nor Jones ever used his huge influence in the major golf organizations to correct inequities that, in the minds of many, Augusta National itself came to symbolize. Nor, incidentally, did the leading white players of that era use their influence. For many years, one Masters invitation was controlled by past winners of the U.S. Open, who each year selected one top professional who had not qualified otherwise. The Open winners could have chosen Sifford, Elder, or another black pro, but never did. U.S. Amateur winners and Masters winners conducted similar ballots and also could have chosen a black player, but did not. (In 1969, when Sifford won the Los Angeles Open, he received one vote—from Art Wall, Jr.—in the balloting of Masters winners, a plurality of whom selected Bob Murphy. The club had included both Sifford and Elder on a list of twenty likely candidates which it sent to the Masters winners along with their ballots that year. Deane Beman, Chi Chi Rodriguez, and Lanny Wadkins were also on the list. Rodriguez received one vote, from Bob Goalby; Beman and Wadkins received none.)

On the international side, Roberts and Jones were ahead of their time. Most foreign invitees were British, but competitors came from many countries, among them Mexico, the Netherlands, Taiwan, Australia, New Zealand, Thailand, Spain, Japan, the Philippines, South Africa, France, and a number of countries in South America. Invitations to Japanese and Chinese players were extended from the beginning and continued throughout the extended period when the P.G.A. did not permit non-Caucasian members. In a letter to the president of the Japan Golf Association in 1958, Roberts noted with pride that the club had had a Japanese member in the thirties. His name was Reisuke Ishida, and he was an acquaintance of Roberts's from New York, where he worked for Mitsui & Co. He joined the club in January 1934, and his photograph appeared among those of other prominent members of the club in the program for the second tournament. Ishida resigned from the club in 1937 upon receiving word that his company was transferring him back to Japan. "I am very sorry to do this," he wrote to Roberts, "as I have enjoyed my membership in the Club very much." Roberts asked him if he would consider retaining his membership on the chance that he might one day return to the United States, or possibly pass it along to a Japanese associate at his firm. Ishida replied that he had attempted to interest several of his associates in joining, but that for various reasons all had declined.

Sportswriters have often suggested that Augusta National altered its invitation requirements in 1962 in order to thwart Sifford, who that year came close to winning the Canadian Open. Curt Sampson, in *The Masters*, wrote,

> Sifford shot 67 to lead the Canadian Open in '62. Shortly thereafter, according to Charlie, someone from Augusta called the clubhouse at Royal Montreal Golf Club. A sign was immediately posted on a bulletin board: "The Masters golf tournament has announced that it will not offer an automatic invitation to the winner of this year's Canadian Open," which it had in the past. The Royal Canadian Golf Association could not confirm Sifford's charges.

The Royal Canadian Golf Association could not confirm the charges because the charges aren't true. (For one thing, the Canadian Open that year was played not at Royal Montreal Golf Club but at Laval sur le lac.) Augusta National in those years had a policy of inviting *Canadian* winners of the Canadian Open, Canadian Amateur, and Canadian P.G.A. Each summer, Helen Harris, Augusta National's office manager, would write to the Royal Canadian Golf Association to request the names and addresses of the winners of those events. If the winners were Canadian natives who resided in Canada, they were invited; if they weren't, they weren't. (For Canadian players, the Open qualification has always been essentially hypothetical. In the eighty-five years since 1914, only one Canadian has won the tournament: Pat Fletcher, in 1954.) Nothing about that policy changed before, during, or after Sifford's second-place finish in 1962. For American players, the Canadian Open was treated as just another event on the American tour, and a victory on the American tour didn't guarantee an invitation until a decade later.

One of the strongest international contingents at the Masters during Roberts's lifetime consisted of players from Argentina, Brazil, Chile, Colombia, and Mexico. Roberts and Jones made regular trips together to look after the business of Joroberts, their South American

Coca-Cola partnership, and they took those opportunities to scout for likely Masters competitors whose reputations had not yet reached the United States. The best player in that group was Roberto de Vicenzo of Argentina, who competed in the Masters fifteen times between 1950 and 1975.

De Vicenzo is best known today for his second-place finish in 1968, an outcome that has long been viewed as one of the most heartbreaking in tournament golf. It has also been one of the most grotesquely misunderstood. De Vicenzo that year signed a scorecard for his final round which added up to one stroke more than he had actually shot. (The original error was made by Tommy Aaron, who had been keeping de Vicenzo's card and marked him for a four on the seventeenth hole rather than the three he had in fact made. De Vicenzo hadn't noticed the mistake at the time or when checking his card before signing it immediately following his round.) The rules of golf dictated unequivocally that the higher score had to stand. That kept de Vicenzo out of a tie for first place with Bob Goalby, who became the winner. "What a stupid I am," de Vicenzo said. The Masters film that year showed Goalby finding and correcting an error on his own scorecard—a scene that made de Vicenzo's moment of inattention seem all the more poignant.

To be kept out of a Masters playoff by a clerical error concerning a score that no one disputed has always seemed so regrettable that, more than three decades later, sportswriters and others still brood about the ruling. A columnist in *Golf World* suggested in 1997 that Augusta National should have ignored the rules and thereby created a tie, or that Goalby should have refused his green jacket and insisted on a playoff, whether official or not. Others have disparaged Roberts and the club for not writing a rule of their own. Charles Sifford has even suggested that de Vicenzo's second-place finish might have been the result of prejudice on Roberts's part against a foreign player.

The notion that the club should have imposed a rule of its own has a certain emotional appeal but is hard to understand. Roberts and Jones cherished the club's independence from golf's major governing bodies, but both believed in the rule book—as they had demonstrated twenty years before, when they had helped to settle rules differences between the P.G.A. and the U.S.G.A. The Masters rules committee has always been headed by leading officials of the Royal and Ancient Golf Club of St. Andrews and the U.S.G.A., the two organizations responsible for governing the game. The ruling on de Vicenzo's score was made not by Roberts or Jones but by the tournament's chief rules official, Isaac Grainger, who had been the president of the U.S.G.A in 1954 and 1955. Grainger—who was born in 1895 and is the oldest living member of Augusta National—still recalls the incident vividly, calling it "the most difficult but also the easiest decision I ever had to make." He says, "I took the precaution—although I knew the answer—of talking to Bob Jones and Cliff Roberts about it, down in the Jones Cottage. I knew what the answer was, but I wanted to be able to tell Roberto that it wasn't my answer alone. It was really a very sad thing, because it eliminated the possibility of his winning the Masters in a playoff. But he was quite a gentleman. I remember I had dinner with him, and when we left the dining room and separated, he said to me, 'I am sorry I caused you so much trouble.' That shows you what a sportsman he was. It was a very sad thing for him. And I remember when he finished on the eighteenth hole, his wife was so nervous she took hold of my hand, and she held my hand until he had putted out."

The scorecard rule is no less important and no more arbitrary than, say, the rules governing the accidental moving of a ball, the grounding of a club in a hazard, the carrying of more than fourteen clubs, or the soliciting of advice from another golfer. It is true that television cameras had shown de Vicenzo birdieing the seventeenth hole. But the foundation of golf's rule book is that it places responsibility for enforcement on golfers themselves—a responsibility borne by athletes in no other sport. De Vicenzo, like every other player in the tournament, was accountable for the accuracy of his own card because only he was in a position to be certain of his true score. The rule book is unambiguous on that point. De Vicenzo felt stupid about his oversight, but he agreed with the ruling—as did the Argentine Golf Association, which wrote to Roberts to say that it not only supported Grainger's decision but also had made the same ruling itself with other players in tournaments of its own.

The accusation that Roberts was out to get de Vicenzo is even more absurd. The two men were close friends, and, in fact, during Masters week, de Vicenzo and his wife often stayed in the home of Wilda Gwin, who was one of Roberts's secretaries at the club. De Vicenzo's birthday fell on Masters Sunday in 1968, and the tournament staff, with Roberts's assistance, had planned a surprise party for him. Kathryn Murphy, Roberts's tournament secretary, remembers sadly throwing away the birthday cake when it became clear that holding the party was now out of the question.

Roberts always held a dinner for the tournament winner at the end of each Masters, and that night he broke convention by inviting de Vicenzo to attend as well. He worried that the outcome had harmed both men—by depriving de Vicenzo of a shot at the financial bonanza that followed a Masters win, and by overshadowing the spectacular charge that Goalby had made in his own final round. Like all Masters winners, Goalby received a silver cigarette case on which had been engraved the signatures of all the players in the field. Roberts quietly had an identical box made for de Vicenzo as a private acknowledgment of his ordeal. Roberts also asked J. Richard Ryan, the attorney who handled the club's television and movie contracts, to offer his services to both men as an agent—an occupation that had just begun to have an impact among the better players on tour. He especially hoped that Ryan could help de Vicenzo make up for opportunities he had forgone.

All these gestures—none of which were public—were entirely characteristic of Roberts. The somber face he wore on television as he explained the scorecard ruling belied the personal devastation he felt for both men. The tragedy, in his view, was that two exceptional performances had been overshadowed by a single careless mistake. He never doubted the correctness of the ruling, and he never regretted that it had been made. But he quietly worked behind the scenes to make things right for both men.

Tiger Woods, after a brilliant amateur career that culminated in a record-setting third consecutive victory in the U.S. Amateur, turned professional in the fall of 1996 and almost immediately began to dominate the world of professional golf. As the spring approached, he was picked by many as the favorite to win the Masters. A number of sportswriters savored what they believed to be the irony that the Masters might thus become the first major golf tournament to be won by a black player. In the Augusta National press building before the tournament that year, more than one sportswriter speculated that Clifford Roberts must be "turning in his grave" over the possibility that a black player might be poised to win his beloved tournament.

All such gleeful speculation amounted to a gross misreading of Roberts's views about race insofar as they applied to the tournament. When confronted by a reporter with similar sentiments in 1971, Roberts had responded, incredulously, "Think how much it would help our TV rating if we had a Willie Mays at the Masters." That comment can be viewed as crude or insensitive, but it was a true reflection of Roberts's invariably pragmatic analysis of the tournament and its results. Woods in 1997 was establishing himself as the most important player in at least a generation; Roberts, far from being appalled by the notion that he might win the Masters, would have welcomed his victory. He wanted the tournament to be dominated by the players who dominated the game. He would have been delighted that a new champion was rising to take the mantle that had been handed from Nelson to Hogan to Palmer to Nicklaus and beyond. He would have been sad only that Woods had elected to turn professional before making one more attempt to win the Masters as an amateur.

For sportswriters who expected the walls of the Augusta National clubhouse to crumble, Woods's great victory must have been a disappointment. But it was not viewed that way anywhere else at the club. The mood was just as joyful in tournament headquarters as it was on the course, in the clubhouse, in the cabins, in the kitchen, and in the bag room, where half a dozen employees crowded around a television set to watch the final, record-breaking putt. "I've never seen as much excitement as we had in the clubhouse," Jack Stephens, the chairman at the time, said at a press conference the following year. "When he made that putt on eighteen, that clubhouse exploded. There was pent-up excitement pulling for him to break the record." Clifford Roberts would have been happy, too.

CHAPTER ELEVEN

Monuments

"I SPRAINED MY ankle just before the Jamboree one year," Dr. Stephen Brown, a member, recalls, "and I had a cast on my leg, so I couldn't play. But I came over here anyway, just to visit. Bob Jones asked me if I would chauffeur him around, so I got in his cart and took him onto the course so he could watch some of his friends. Then he said, 'Steve, I want to get a haircut.' We had a barber shop back of the pro shop at that time, and I drove him over there in the cart. There was a little step in front of the shop, and he couldn't raise his foot high enough to get over it. He said, 'Steve, how about putting my foot up there?' So I reached down and picked up the foot of this great athlete and lifted it six inches onto the step, and tears came into my eyes."

Jones bore his illness heroically, but his long and painful decline was hard for his friends to watch. The sportswriter Charles Price, who was close to Jones during the last years of his life, wrote about some of their final visits in a column in *Golf Digest* in 1991. "By 1968 Bobby Jones' health had slipped from the terrible to the abysmal," Price recalled. "His eyes were bloodshot from the spinal disease he had endured for 20 years, his arms atrophied to the size of a schoolgirl's, his ankles so swollen by body fluids that they spilled over the edges of his shoes." His hands were gnarled and misshapen. To sign his name, he used a ballpoint pen inserted in a rubber ball and a spring device that helped to support his hand and wrist. His script was large, shaky, and round; it looked like the scrawl of a third grader. He sometimes drank more than he should, undoubtedly to dull the unremitting pain that is one of the distinguishing symptoms of syringomyelia.

"Bob smoked more than two packs of cigarettes a day, sometimes in chain fashion," Price continued, "and they were lined up on the card table in neat rows for him, each in a holder so he would not accidentally burn himself. An elegant lighter, covered in leather, sat ready. All he had to do was push down a lever that any child could. But even that was becoming an effort. So, with as much nonchalance as I could devise, I'd pull out a cigarette of my own, thereby giving me the excuse to light his." Shortly before he died, Jones sent the leather-covered lighter to Price with a note, typed by his secretary: "You weren't fooling me a bit."

Jones was so ill in the spring of 1969 that he was unable to make the trip from Atlanta to Augusta for the Masters, a development that worried and depressed Roberts. Then, two weeks before the tournament, Eisenhower died. "This is an unhappy period for me," he wrote in a gloomy letter to his sister. One of the two most important men in his life was dead and the other was dying, and he had begun to feel his own age as well. At dinner during Jones's last visits to the club, Roberts always included him at his table in the Trophy Room. Jones was confined to a wheelchair, and he had great difficulty eating, but he liked to be part of the conversation. During the last tournament Jones attended, in 1968, Roberts went to confer with him in his cabin. Jones was suffering from an intestinal virus in addition to his steadily worsening spinal condition, and he was nearly helpless. Roberts was visibly shaken when he returned to his room. "I will never let that happen to me," he said to J. Richard Ryan, the attorney who handled the club's television contracts, who had been waiting for him. Jones died in December 1971; a few days beforehand, according to Price, he told his secretary, "If I'd known it was going to be this easy, I'd have gone a long time ago."

In recent years, a few writers have suggested that there was a falling out between Roberts and Jones in the last years of Jones's life. But according to people who were in a position to know, the two men remained good friends to the end. Charles Yates, who knew both men well, says they were always close. Kathryn Murphy, Roberts's tournament secretary, says she never noticed any tension between them and that they remained in regular contact even after Jones was no longer well enough to travel to Augusta.

Correspondence between the two men shows the same thing and proves, in addition, that Jones continued to play a role in the direction of the tournament and of the club until shortly before his death. Roberts regularly consulted him by mail and by telephone on a broad range of issues concerning the Masters; before and during each tournament, large packages containing schedules, bulletins, pairing sheets, and other documents were sent to Jones from tournament headquarters virtually every day. Jones wanted to be kept informed, and Roberts often sought his advice. In 1970, when Jones's illness was approaching its final stages, they engaged in an extensive correspondence over arrangements for an award ceremony at the club honoring Fred McLeod and Jock Hutchison. Jones himself had arranged for the club to hold the ceremony, which he had scheduled for just before the tournament. In Jones's absence, Roberts handled the details according to directions that Jones provided by mail.

Roberts also regularly sought Jones's advice concerning potential new members of the club. Augusta National had accepted applications until 1946, after which time membership was offered by invitation only. The club then had a nominal membership committee, although most decisions were made by the executive committee, and especially by Roberts, Jones, and local member Jerome Franklin. (A member from Charlotte, who had been trying for several years to get an acquaintance into the club, once asked a friend on the membership committee what he might do to expedite the process. "I don't know," he said. "I've been on the committee for seven years, and we haven't had a meeting yet.") Jones had the final say on potential members from the Atlanta area, and he continued to exercise it until shortly before he died.

In recent years, a few writers have suggested that Roberts betrayed Jones in 1968, the last year he attended the tournament, by telling CBS not to include Jones in the televised award ceremony. Steve Eubanks, in *Augusta*, wrote,

Roberts thought it unseemly to have Jones's withered physical condition broadcast to the entire country. Therefore he told his old friend that CBS (specifically MacPhail) had decided Bob should not continue to be part of the presentation. Hurt to the point of tears, Jones confronted MacPhail. As he had done every year with Roberts, Bill listened, only this time he didn't smile. Instead, he turned away. MacPhail let Jones go to his grave thinking CBS was responsible for his ousting. The truth, MacPhail knew, would have been far too painful.

Eubanks presented the story without attribution. MacPhail died in 1996—like Roberts, he was a suicide—so no one who is mentioned is still alive. Judged on its own, though, the story doesn't ring true. The least plausible element, given the history of the relationship between the network and the club, is the notion of Jones accepting an explanation from Roberts that CBS had dictated to Roberts how the televised presentation would be run. Nor would it have been characteristic of Jones to "confront" MacPhail during the tournament, even if he had had an opportunity to do so—which was not likely, since Jones that week was virtually confined to his cottage. And even if there was a confrontation, Jones would have known that CBS had no involvement in the *main* award ceremony, which was held on the putting green for the benefit of the tournament patrons and was not televised. Yet Jones did not appear at that event, either—undoubtedly because of his health. Shortly after the tournament, he wrote to Herbert Warren Wind that he had been too sick to attend the ceremony but that he would have made an effort to be there if he had realized how the decision about Roberto de Vicenzo's scorecard was going to be received.

This dark period in Roberts's life was lightened somewhat by the success of the tournament, which now more than ever defined the state of the game at the highest level. The Masters in the sixties had been dominated by Palmer and Nicklaus, who between them had won six times in the period from 1960 to 1966. In 1966, the Masters became the first golf tournament ever to be sold out months in advance. Nicklaus won again in 1972, in the first tournament following Jones's death, and again three years after that. Gary Player won his second green jacket in 1974. Ray Floyd, in 1976, tied Nicklaus's scoring record of 271, which he had set in 1965. In 1977, Tom Watson beat Nicklaus by two strokes in a victory that marked the beginning of the first convincing challenge to Nicklaus's domination of the sport.

Roberts, meanwhile, was feeling the effects of age. He was nearly eighty years old, his health was tenuous, and the pressures of running both the club and the Masters had begun to weigh on him. In the early seventies, he settled on a successor—an Oklahoma banker named Frank G. McClintock, who had been a member since 1965. But then McClintock suffered a stroke and couldn't take the job. "I'm going to get out as soon as I can," Roberts told a writer from *Golf Digest* in 1974. But he was determined to find the right man to take his place.

Roberts finally found him in William Lane, a businessman from Houston, Texas, and announced his retirement at a press conference the day before the beginning of the Masters in 1976. He stressed, though, that he wasn't stepping down quite yet. "I am still chairman of the tournament," he said. "I want no interference from [Lane] until he's installed in office." When a reporter later asked Lane about his background, Roberts interrupted: "Mr. Lane is to remain silent." Roberts's brusque comment provoked chuckles, although it was not widely perceived by reporters as a joke. The comment was entirely characteristic, though. Roberts did not intend to be treated as a lame duck at his fortieth Masters; more important, he wanted to spare Lane an interrogation for which he had not prepared. Sportswriters tended to note the harshness but miss both the humor and the kindness, as they often had before.

Roberts's retirement as the chairman of the tournament did not dramatically simplify his life. He was still the chairman of the club, he had just published a book, and he was about to become deeply involved in a legal issue that some of his friends would later blame for initiating the final stage of his physical decline.

The legal issue had to do with the name of the tournament. Some months before, the club had discovered that the Northwestern Mutual Life Insurance Co. intended to sponsor an official event of the Ladies

Professional Golf Association, to be known as the Ladies Masters. The tournament was to be held on a course at a new real estate development in Hilton Head, South Carolina, called Moss Creek Plantation, in which Northwestern Mutual had a large financial stake. Francis E. Ferguson, who was the president of the insurance company, had visited Augusta National as a guest a few years before. He had been deeply impressed, and he believed that the Masters name would help to sell building lots adjacent to the Moss Creek course. Ray Volpe, who had recently been named the commissioner of the L.P.G.A., believed that using the Masters name would add distinction to the women's tour, which had been struggling for years.

When Augusta National learned of the L.P.G.A.'s plans, the club objected. Roberts said that use of the name implied a nonexistent connection with the tournament in Augusta, and that Northwestern Mutual's main interest appeared to be not golf but real estate. Roberts said the Masters name had been adopted by tournaments in half a dozen foreign countries—a fact that didn't bother him, since there was no question of a connection between the copies and the original. However, he said, "When it comes to the United States, we would greatly prefer that this is the only tournament which is called Masters."* The club asked the company and the L.P.G.A. to find a different name.

The L.P.G.A. complied, and the first tournament, in 1976, was formally known as the Women's International. Still, the tournament's organizers, various L.P.G.A. personnel, some sportswriters, and some players used the Masters name unofficially. And while NBC had been very interested in broadcasting a Masters Tournament for women, it was considerably less interested in broadcasting an anonymous L.P.G.A. event in a real estate subdivision. Northwestern Mutual approached Augusta National about possibly licensing the Masters name, or perhaps devising a version of the name that the club could live with. (The company suggested "Moss Creek Ladies Masters.") The company sought to

---

* Roberts had no quarrel with an American junior tournament called the Future Masters, because he felt that there was no possibility of confusion and that the name was "a compliment."

register "Ladies Masters" as a trademark, then withdrew the application. When it became clear that Northwestern Mutual and the L.P.G.A. were going to proceed regardless—and intended to hold their tournament one week after the Masters—Augusta National sued.

On trial, in effect, was the work of Clifford Roberts's life. A number of sportswriters interpreted the lawsuit as an attempt by a rich and powerful organization to crush a poor and vulnerable one, but Roberts didn't see it that way. NBC and the sponsors of the Women's International coveted the Masters name precisely because they knew that golf fans would mistakenly assume the new tournament had some relationship with Augusta National. Northwestern's president even acknowledged that his intention was to "ride the coattails" of the celebrated tournament.

Most of the club's case consisted simply of recounting the long and unlikely history of the championship that Roberts and Jones had created in 1934. The Masters name was magical in the world of golf, the club argued, only because the tournament's architects had worked for decades to make it that way. Building the Masters had required more than forty years of pain, debt, good luck, hard work, focus, and obsession. To allow that accomplishment to be usurped for the sake of a brazenly commercial enterprise, the club said, would be a desecration.

One of the most effective witnesses for Augusta National, to the surprise of some, turned out to be Roberts himself. Blake Clark, a member of the club who was present at the trial, says, "Northwestern Mutual had a lawyer on its team who was about forty years old. He got Cliff on the stand and asked him a question, and Cliff—as he always did—cleared his throat and gave about a three-second pause while he thought about his answer. Before he could speak, this young lawyer pointed a finger at him and said, 'You haven't answered my question.' Well, Cliff just folded his arms politely, just like that, in Federal Court, and said, 'Well, that was a damn dumb question, and I don't answer dumb questions.' And he didn't. And that was it. The case was over."

The judge's opinion was unequivocal. As a result of the club's efforts, he wrote, "the Masters Tournament has become world-renowned as the epitome of such contests in the field of golf. Whenever the terms 'The Masters' or 'The Masters Tournament,' or 'The Masters Golf

Tournament' are used, they have come to be understood by the *cognoscenti* as well as the *ignoranti* of the game of golf as referring to the plaintiff's golf tournament. This tournament is acknowledged to be one of the greatest sporting events of the year, and because of the manner in which it is staged and conducted, it has come to symbolize, universally, excellence in a sports production." As a result, the judge wrote, "The defendant, its officers, agents, servants, employees, and attorneys, and all those persons in active concert or participation with them, who receive actual notice hereof, are hereby perpetually enjoined and restrained from using directly or indirectly the word or term 'Masters,' or a derivative thereof, in connection with the organization, promotion, sponsorship, advertisement, ticket sales and conduct of any golf tournament or any other golfing event in the continental limits of the United States." He further ordered Northwestern Mutual to reimburse Augusta National for its legal costs.

The lawsuit, despite its outcome, tormented Roberts; some of his friends felt that it hastened his death. In a letter to William Lane toward the end of 1976, Roberts wrote that "the deliberate doings" of Northwestern's president had "damn near wrecked my health." During the final stages of the case, he suffered a mild stroke, and his physical condition deteriorated. He lost weight and was fatigued by mild exertion. Shortly before the 1977 Masters, he checked into St. Luke's Episcopal Hospital in Houston, and remained for nearly a week. He returned to Augusta National in time for the tournament, but was in poor health. Not least of his difficulties was a severe case of hiccups, which lasted a week. During most of the tournament, he was too ill to leave his bedroom.

A few weeks later, shortly after the club had closed for the year, Roberts sent personalized copies of a color photograph of himself to a number of his closest friends. In it, he was wearing his green jacket and one of his favorite caps. Not long after the photographs were sent, Roberts received a thank-you note from Laura Kerr, the wife of William Kerr, who for many years had been the chairman of the club's television and radio committee. She wrote that she had taken the picture to be framed at a gallery in La Jolla, California, and that a saleswoman there had suddenly said, "Why, that's—that's Mr. Clifford Roberts!" The saleswoman turned out to be the wife of a man who had worked with Roberts in New York. Kerr continued, "Then the other day Margie Rader, who is the half sister of Shirley Casper, saw your picture on our wall. She is eighteen. And she also remembered you for a long ago thoughtful gesture. We—and that of course includes you—were at the Caspers' home one Christmas some years ago. While Bill Casper [who won the Masters in 1970] was showing you his house, you went into Margie's room where she had some bills in a little pile on the bed. You asked what she was going to do with them. And when Margie answered that she was saving them up to buy a special something, you added your contribution. She said she had never forgotten your interest and your generosity." Jay Johnson—an Augusta lawyer, who took up golf after Roberts invited him to join the club—also received a copy of the photograph. His wife, upon seeing the picture, said, "You're never going to see him again, Jay. He's saying good-bye."

In late September, Roberts traveled from his wife's home in Beverly Hills back to St. Luke's Hospital. His condition had declined over the past six months. Jane Gosden—whose late husband, Freeman, was one of Roberts's closest friends—says that Roberts had seemed especially frail just before he left for Texas. "We had taken him to see some doctors here in California," she says. "I remember one day when he was visiting us, and he needed to use the bathroom. He was a little unsteady on his feet. My housekeeper, who adored him, said, 'Mr. Roberts, let me help you, sir.' And she took him by the belt and lowered him down the step." Roberts's weight had fallen to less than a hundred and thirty-five pounds; he was easy to lift.

In Houston, Roberts was examined first by a physician who had never met him. The physician noted that Roberts "spoke slowly with slurred speech and difficulty with recall" and made a preliminary diagnosis that included the word "dementia." Later, a different doctor—one who knew Roberts—wrote that he found no sign of dementia and softened the overall assessment by noting that Roberts had always spoken with what to others seemed like difficulty, and that his memory, insight, and clarity of thought were normal for a man of his age. Roberts underwent a CAT scan and various other tests, but no new ailments were de-tected. (He did not have cancer, contrary to accounts of his death in nu-merous articles and books.) On the third day, he asked to be discharged. His doctor said a longer stay would serve no purpose, and Roberts called Jack Stephens in Little Rock. Stephens sent his plane to take Roberts back to Augusta.

"When my pilots got home," Stephens recalls, "they said, 'There's something wrong with Mr. Roberts.' Cliff had jumped all over them for not having that day's newspaper on the plane. But they did have it. Cliff had just lost track of what day it was. He thought the paper on the plane was the one from the day before." In Augusta, Roberts was picked up at the airport by John Milton, one of the club's chauffeurs. As Milton's car turned down Magnolia Lane, the clubhouse came into view, and Roberts leaned back in his seat, sighed, and said, "John, I didn't think I was going to make it home."

The club really was Roberts's home, the only true home he had ever had. He had spent more nights in his bedroom there than he had in any other residence. All his travels had begun and ended there; it was the place he had always come back to. His apartment in New York, his con-dominiums in North Carolina and the Bahamas, his wife's house in Cal-ifornia—all of those had merely been temporary lodgings, places where he had waited out the weeks and months between visits to Augusta. The club and the tournament had been the first important landmarks in his life that had reliably remained fixed in one place from year to year. His friends at Augusta National were the first permanent friends he had ever known.

On his last day at the club, Roberts had his hair cut in the clubhouse barbershop. He asked Bettie Yonker, a receptionist, to go into town and buy him a new pair of pajamas. Late in the afternoon, after his usual snack of tea and toasted pound cake, he asked his regular waiter, Ray Wigfall, to help him walk from his room to the first tee. "He was very, very weak," Wigfall recalls. "As a matter of fact, he almost pulled me down." Standing on the tee, Roberts looked up the fairway, studied the trees at the top of the hill, and assured himself that Montgomery Harison's old house, which for forty years had stood just beyond the first green, had really and truly been torn down. At the end of the previous season, he had told another member, "I don't intend for a guest to come here ever again and ask who lives in that house." Now the house was gone. "We can go back now," Roberts said. He ate dinner alone in his room that night. He had lamb chops, oven-browned potatoes, and carrots—probably his favorite meal. When he had finished, he asked Wigfall if he would mind keeping him company for a little while. Wigfall helped him call his wife in California, gave him a rubdown, and left at about ten o'clock.

Early the next morning, Wigfall picked up Roberts's breakfast in the clubhouse kitchen and took it to his room, as he always did. When Roberts didn't answer his knock, Wigfall let himself in. The bed was empty. The bathroom was empty. There was no sign of Roberts. Wigfall went back to the kitchen and told James Clark, the chef, that the chairman was missing. A receptionist checked with the guard at the main entrance and with the local hospital, and she called Phil Wahl at home. The club's staff dispersed over the property to search.

A housekeeper named Annie Smart was the first to see Roberts's body. It was lying by the side of a service road on the dam at the lower end of Ike's pond, just beyond the southern edge of the par three course. Smart's scream brought others running. James Clark and Homer Jones, another employee, knelt beside the body and saw that Roberts was dead. "I'll remember that as long as I live myself," Clark says. There was a small, neat wound in Roberts's temple. His glasses were hanging from one ear. A pistol lay on the ground near his hand. He was wearing bedroom slippers and the new light blue pajamas that he had sent Bettie Yonker to buy the day before. He had pulled a pair of trousers over the pajama pants. His slippers were on the wrong feet and his shirt was misbuttoned. In his breast pocket was an Augusta National envelope containing a copy of his medical chart, which he had brought from Houston. On a corner of the envelope he had written, in spidery pencil:

> *Dear Betty:*
> *I am sorry.*
> *I love you.*
> *Cliff.*

Those who knew Roberts were not entirely surprised that he had chosen to end his life. "He was a wonderful man," Bill Hibbard, a tournament patron who every year brought Roberts a bag of oranges, wrote to one of Roberts's secretaries. "He just didn't want to go the way of his closest friend, Bob. He didn't want to be a burden to others. He's resting in peace now." For a man whose adult existence had been founded on control, the depredations of age had been intolerable. By placing his medical chart in his pocket he had offered an explanation. At the end, what he feared was not death but life on anyone's terms but his own. He was convinced he would never get better, and he was determined he would never get worse. Against what he had worried were impossible odds, he had made it back to Augusta; once there, he had begun to prepare, with his usual thoroughness, to bring his life to an end. Jack Stephens says that Roberts was characteristically thoughtful even in his choice of location: the embankment on the dam was remote from the course and from all the club's buildings, yet was in a well-traveled area where he knew his body would be easy to find.

Employees who were present at the club at the time of Roberts's suicide doubt that he could have made his way from his room to the dam by himself, especially in the dark, since he had trouble walking on his own and he would have had to negotiate a long, steep, slippery hill in the dark while wearing bedroom slippers. The hill is so steep that the club leaves golf carts parked at the bottom for players finishing rounds on the par three course. (One sportswriter recently wrote that Roberts "strolled down" to the par three course to take his life—an absurdity.) Fred Bennett says Roberts had several brand-new hundred dollar bills in his wallet when he arrived at the club for his final visit, and that the money was no longer in his wallet when his body was found. Bennett thinks Roberts probably paid a night watchman to drive him down to the dam in a golf cart and leave him there. The club's security report for that night said that Roberts had called in the early hours of the morning to report noises outside his room, and that a watchman, at Roberts's request, had helped him load a pistol, which Roberts had owned for many years.

The parallels between Roberts's suicide and that of his mother are

haunting. Like his mother, he had suffered a variety of increasingly de-
bilitating ailments in the months and years before his death. Like his
mother, he had left his bed in the early hours of the morning while
those he cared about slept nearby, unaware. Like his mother, he had
used a gun. Like his mother, he had left a terse note written in pencil.

Roberts had always said that if the Masters ever got out of hand or
became destructive to the club, he would end it immediately. He treated
his life the same way. His suicide was reasoned, deliberate, and unsenti-
mental, and it constituted a sort of ironic proof that his faculties were
intact. He was cutting his losses. With his usual focus and attention to
detail, he chose to die while he was still in a position to dictate the terms.

"The death of Cliff Roberts marks the passing of one of the great
eras of modern golf," Arnold Palmer said when he heard the news. Jack
Nicklaus said, "Mr. Roberts set the tone for tournament golf with his
Masters. The standards and quality with which he conducted the Masters are unmatched anywhere. All of us in golf appreciate what he has
done for the game, and he will be sadly missed." His widow flew to Augusta from California, and a brief memorial service was held for her and
a number of members. Betty Roberts later wrote to Bill Lane, the club's
new chairman, "The Memorial Service was so beautifully done and it
was perfect to hold it at the Club, which he loved, and among friends he
had known for so long." Lane wrote back, "I still feel the same way
about Cliff that you do and every time I have to write about him or
speak about him, I get very emotional. Cliff had become an important
part of my life and I had grown to feel about him as my second father
and the conversations we had are very much missed."

Roberts had left a memo in his files requesting "unmarked interment
on the grounds." Whether his ashes were buried in a single spot or
spread over a larger area is now unknown; the four people who handled
the chore—Jerome Franklin, Bill Lane, Ellis Slater, and Phil Wahl—have
long since died themselves. The most likely spots are probably somewhere on or near his beloved par three course—perhaps near a small
grove of trees where he and Eisenhower had often sat and talked—and
Amen Corner, particularly in the area near the Nelson Bridge, which
crosses Rae's Creek near the thirteenth tee.

At any rate, his grave is unmarked, as he had requested. Had he wanted a gravestone, an appropriate epitaph would have been that of Sir Christopher Wren, the architect of St. Paul's Cathedral in London, whose unassuming tomb in the great building's crypt is inscribed *Si monumentum requiris circumspice*: If you seek his monument, look around you.

At five o'clock in the morning on Thursday of Masters week, a crew of tournament employees is busy making sandwiches in a large food preparation area behind and below the club's press building. The Masters lasts just a week, but feeding the patrons is a full-time job, and it requires the year-round attention of Alex Collie. Planning and purchasing for next year's tournament will begin almost as soon as this year's tournament is over. Collie took over the business in 1968, when his father, who had handled the food and beverage concessions at the Masters since the mid-fifties, suddenly died. "The first year was easy," Collie says, "because I didn't know what to worry about." He is now in his mid-fifties. Until fairly recently, he had to live on the property for a month before every tournament, sleeping in a trailer in the parking lot. "We had old-style tents in those days, and if it rained in the night I had to go out with a broom handle and poke the water out of all of them, to keep the tents from falling down. I would do that all night long, for years and years and years." Collie no longer needs the trailer, because he now has a permanent office at the club; it adjoins the food preparation area, and it opens onto a fully furnished bedroom, where he and his wife live during Masters week.

Ticket holders begin to gather along Washington Road long before the gates are scheduled to open. Most Masters patrons have favorite viewing areas, and they like to stake their claims early. During lulls in the traffic, they can make out the drone of distant mowers, trimmers, and blowers—the low morning music that awakens those members, players, and others lucky enough to be staying on the grounds. When the gates open at eight, the spectators stream onto the course. They don't run. An elderly woman and her grandson place folding chairs beside the eighteenth green. The first twosome won't reach this point for many hours, but they don't mind. "We sit, and we don't move," the grandmother says. "It's a perfect day. There's no way you can get bored. You talk to people, you share stories, you look up old friends." Other patrons leave their chairs as placeholders and wander off to reacquaint themselves with the course. The sky is deep blue, and the weather is expected to hold. "How long have we been coming?" one longtime ticket holder says. "Well, their little boy was four or five years old, and now he's a lawyer. That's how long."

Many changes have been made to the golf course since last April, but even veterans have trouble spotting all of them. Earth-moving crews arrived shortly after the club closed last May; by the time the club opened again, in early October, all the dirt piles, tire tracks, and bare spots had disappeared. Players often fail to notice the subtler changes; nearly as often, they detect changes where none have been made. "The course changes all by itself, too," a member says. The topography of a green shifts in elusive ways through years of rain, wind, the weight of machinery, and the pounding of feet. A mower gradually alters the surface it maintains. Memory plays tricks. Sand thrown from a bunker lifts the ground beneath the fringe. The course evolves.

The sun is still low, but the early morning chill is gone, and the seventeenth green is being mowed. The course superintendent walks half a pace behind the man pushing the mower, eyes downward, inspecting his work. During the weeks before the tournament, the greens are top-dressed repeatedly with minutely thin layers of screened soil. The grass is brushed before it is cut, to make the blades stand up for the mowers. Players and television commentators sometimes talk about the "grain" of one green or another, but the greens crew has studied the matter and determined that the grass on the greens at the Masters is cut too short to lean. A worker with clippers the size of nail scissors trims a high spot in the fringe. Another worker scoops green sand onto the tops of the sprinkler heads, then smoothes the sand to make a surface level with the tips of the grass. A subterranean vacuum system, emitting a hum that can be heard through vents in a greenside mound, draws yesterday's rainfall from the soil, drying the putting surface from underneath.

There are no smudges on the windows in the clubhouse. Marsh Benson, a club employee, says, "In February every year, I'll pick out a scrape or a dark mark on the paint on the side of one of the buildings and keep an eye on it. It will be there and be there—and then in March sometime, I'll look and it will be gone." Last week, two men with cans of green paint spent several hours obliterating tire marks on the concrete curbs alongside the driveway in front of the clubhouse. Today, half a dozen young men and women are slowly working their way up the tenth fairway, using long bamboo poles to sweep away grass clippings the consistency of sawdust. A worker attaches a green garbage bag to a green metal stand. A rules official drives past in a golf cart, on his way to check wooden stakes that mark a lateral hazard not far below the eighteenth tee. The hazard is hard to see. It wasn't staked until a few years ago, when Mike Donald required a ruling after having the misfortune of becoming the first Masters competitor ever known to have hit his tee shot into it.

An amateur player, who stayed last night in the Crow's Nest—the dormitory on the top floor of the clubhouse—heads to the Trophy Room for breakfast. Two nights ago, unable to sleep, he came downstairs to the clubhouse library and studied Alister MacKenzie's first watercolor sketch of the layout of the course, which hangs on the wall. Two members and their guests were standing on the verandah, looking out at the stars, and he joined them briefly before going back up to bed. Now, long tables have replaced the library's furniture. A man holding a portable television camera stands outside near the huge live oak tree just behind the clubhouse. Everything has changed.

Not far below the verandah, a group of old friends is waiting near the practice putting green. One of them says, "We always have lunch at the fountain, and then we go down to the point—the corner—at eleven and twelve, and then come up and sit on the bank at seventeen." When the last players have finished today, the group will return to the northwest parking lot for a tailgate party. One of them says, "We began coming to the Masters thirty-five years ago, and we saw a fancy tailgate party, so we decided to have a tacky one. We've had a tacky tailgate party ever since, and we've tried to make it tackier every year. We've added a parasol and a candelabra and a red carpet and some little fences." When they go out to dinner in Augusta tonight, they will take their candelabra with them. It has garishly colored candles and is decorated with plastic flowers. The oldest drips of wax on the base are ten years older than Tiger Woods.

A committee sets out from Tournament Headquarters to cut the holes. The approximate location of each hole has been marked already with a dab of white paint. "There are no new hole locations," a veteran touring professional, who is a member of the committee, says. "The players sometimes think there are, but there really aren't." Committee members roll putts from the highest point on the green to assure themselves that a speed exists at which a ball will stop within a foot or two of the cup; if none can do it, they move the cup. Al Reid, a retired Class A superintendent who has come to Augusta for more than thirty years to work at the Masters as a volunteer, repairs dents on the putting surface. He carries a large salt shaker filled with a granular synthetic substance that blends with the grass. It contains four parts green granules, two parts orange granules, and two parts brown granules—a combination that, when damp, exactly matches the hue of Augusta National's bent grass. Clarence Stokes, who has worked on the course for more than fifty years, helps to cut the hole and place the cup. A member notices that a slope near a grandstand has become slippery in a place where spectators have been walking, and he uses a walkie-talkie to call for a load of sand. The committee moves to the next green.

A woman sitting near the eighteenth green holds a journal in her lap. She has kept the journal for as long as she has been coming to the Masters. It contains autographs, quotes, observations about the tournament, and entries contributed by other people. Guy Yamamoto, who competed as an amateur in 1995, wrote, "The entire Masters experience has been one that I will never forget. . . . The people of Augusta National have been wonderful to me and my family. On Friday I hit a 7 iron from 171 yards into the cup and made an eagle 2. That became the fourth eagle on #10 in Masters History." Yamamoto shot 84-77, missed the cut, and came in next to last, seven shots ahead of Billy Casper and one shot behind Ian Baker-Finch. He won a pair of crystal goblets for his eagle.

On the far side of the second fairway, a gallery guard points to one of the bunkers near the green and says to a spectator, who has stopped to chat, "Hogan used to try to hit his second shot into the bunker down there. He figured he would either get up and down for birdie or make an easy par." Some of the guards have worked as tournament volunteers for decades. Some plan their work schedules around the Masters, timing their vacations for the first full week in April. Why go to the beach when you can spend a week standing in a ticket booth at Augusta National Golf Club? A guard stationed near the edge of the tenth fairway says, "I've been here for thirteen years. The other guards and I rotate positions, so it always looks different." On the other side of the trees, the grass in a spectator crossing has been trampled to brown straw by the feet of practice round spectators. A smiling member, unconcerned, says, "The grass will all be green again in a couple of weeks." A British photographer spots an unrepaired divot and takes a picture. "A divot at the Masters?" he says. "They'll never believe this!"

Near the sixteenth tee, a man says, "I've been coming since 1955. When my wife was alive, we used to sit down on number six. She loved Gary Player. When he sank that putt on eighteen, in 1961, I thought she was going to have another baby." Another man says, "In thirty-five years, I've seen just one guy skip it across the water and hold the green. It happened right here." He points. Another man says, "A dog ran out and grabbed a ball off the first green once. I saw that. It surprised the heck out of me." Several of the spectators sitting nearby are wearing hats, jackets, or sweaters that are covered with tournament badges, many of them decades old. "I've got a hat like that at home," a man says, "but I don't wear it anymore. It's too heavy." A woman with dozens of badges pinned to the back of her sweater says, "My father loved golf. It was a religion with him. I just wish he could have lived to see Tiger play. He loved to see young players come along." The people sitting here know this green so well that many of them could read the putts as well as most of the players—even though, after so many years, not all of them can see the flag from their seats without the help of binoculars.

In a few more minutes, the first shots in this year's Masters will be struck from the first tee. Parts of the clubhouse are visible from the ob-

servation stands beside the fifteenth fairway, and there are signs of distant commotion. Still, it will be more than three hours before the first
group reaches this part of the course. There is an air of anticipation but
not of impatience. A turtle suns itself on the bank beside the pond in
front of the green. A rules official inspects the edge of the greenside
bunker. "I followed Ben Hogan around," someone says. Nearby, waiting
among old friends, is a woman who has attended every Masters since
the end of the Second World War. Someone asks her which of those
fifty-odd tournaments she liked the best. She thinks back over five
decades of competition—a period that defined the true coming of age
of American golf and encompassed unforgettable performances by
Snead and Hogan and Palmer and Player and Nicklaus and Watson and
Ballesteros and Crenshaw and Faldo and Woods and so many others—
and answers, as Clifford Roberts would have, "I think this one is going
to be my favorite."

Acknowledgments

Henry Longhurst, in an essay about Walter Hagen in 1941, wrote, "[T]hey'll tell you the tale of how Hagen was left with a long putt to tie with Leo Diegel for a tournament in America and insisted that Diegel should be summoned from the clubhouse to see him hole it—to be suitably impressed before the playoff on the following day. Of course, he holed it. The only trouble about this tale, which I have been told by several people who actually saw it happen, is that they saw it happen at several different clubs and the other man was not always Diegel."

Writing about Roberts, Augusta National, and the Masters poses a similar challenge. Most of the best known stories exist in multiple versions, many of them mutually exclusive—a situation not helped by the fact that sportswriters have traditionally assumed substantial creative license in covering their beats: sports anecdotes *evolve*.

Even when factual truth is the goal, first-person sources are unreliable. "Oral history" is often not history at all, because people's memories change over time and leave no trace of having done so. Here is an example of what I mean. Curt Sampson devotes part of a chapter in *The Masters* to the sometimes tempestuous relationship between Augusta National and CBS. His account of the early years of that relationship is based largely on recollections of John Derr, who served as an announcer on the Masters program and whom Sampson describes as "well-met and well-connected." One passage:

"We met at Cliff's office at the Reynolds Company in the fall of 1955, with the head men from Travelers and Cadillac," Derr, now eighty, recalls. "Cliff was very precise in what he wanted. He at first wanted no commercials at all."

This sounds authoritative; Derr, after all, was there. But no such meeting took place. Derr's memory has conflated a number of separate events that occurred over a period of more than a dozen years, and he has added fanciful details of his own. Augusta National did not hold its first meeting with CBS until early 1956; "the head men from Travelers and Cadillac" could not have been involved, because Travelers didn't become a sponsor of the broadcast until 1959 and Cadillac didn't become a sponsor until ten years after that. During the first two years in which the tournament was televised (1956 and 1957), the broadcast had no commercial sponsors, but that was true only because CBS couldn't find anyone interested in filling the role. It was Roberts and the club who found the first sponsor—American Express—as well as all of its successors. The length of commercials didn't become an issue until the club renegotiated its contract with CBS in 1965, a decade after the meeting that Derr believes he remembers.

The point is not to pick on Derr or Sampson; almost no one's memory works much better. For that reason, I have avoided relying on personal recollections as the sole basis of factual assertions, and when I have used recollections I have identified them as such and done my best to back them up. To the greatest extent possible, I have relied on true primary sources, especially letters, contracts, diaries, deeds, and other contemporary documents. Many of these documents are contained in old files at Augusta National Golf Club and until recently were unknown even to the club. I am deeply grateful to Augusta National's officers, who for two years gave me free access to those archives and helped me in innumerable other ways.

This book began in 1995 with Jack Stephens, who was the chairman at the time, and Barbara Spencer, the wife of one of the club's pros. Spencer had persuaded Stephens to let her try to organize a hodgepodge of old historical materials. She and Stephens both believed that published stories about Clifford Roberts had ceased to bear much resemblance to the man they had known as a friend.

Especially helpful was Kathryn Murphy, who worked closely with Roberts during the last dozen years of his life and probably knows more Masters facts than anyone in the world; if I suddenly wondered who had teed off at what time in the sixth Masters, she knew where to look it up. Dozens of Augusta National members, employees, caddies, and others connected with the club gave me many hours of their time. James Armstrong, who is the club's general manager, and Glenn Greenspan, the director of communications, went out of their way to accommodate me. Hootie Johnson, who took over as the club's chairman in 1998, embraced the project as enthusiastically as his predecessor had.

Roberts's early years would still be a mystery if it weren't for the generosity of James Herkelrath and Bill Herkelrath, who are great-nephews of Roberts's, and Madeleine Roberts Hagen, who is a niece. They provided diaries, letters, photographs, scrapbooks, and innumerable other pieces of family memorabilia, which contained information that contradicted widely circulated accounts. Kenneth Roberts, a nephew, supplied one of Rebecca Roberts's suicide notes and helped me gain early access to transcripts of Roberts's Eisenhower interviews at Columbia University. His brother, Clifford, was helpful as well.

Robert Beck, Tom Callahan, Frank Christian, James Knerr, Sidney Matthew, Ron Whitten, and others lent me important documents, shared memories, or directed me to useful sources outside the club. Many past and present Masters competitors were generous with their time. At *Golf Digest*, Jim Moriarty was indispensable as a photo researcher, and Michael O'Malley made excellent suggestions concerning an early version of the manuscript. Jeff Neuman and Frank Scatoni have provided invaluable help at Simon & Schuster. And I will always be deeply grateful to the two men who recommended me for this fascinating project in the first place, Jerry Tarde and the late Peter Dobereiner.

Index

Aaron, Tommy, 252
ABC, 190, 201, 204
ABC Sports, 190, 194
ABC's Wide World of Sports, 188
Achenbach, Gerry, 203*n*
Adams, Sherman, 178
Afrika Korps, 149
A. G. Spalding & Bros., 82, 85
"Alumnus Football" (Rice), 57
Amateur Dinner, 161–62
amateurs:
  Jones as, 30*n*, 82–83
  professionals vs., 157, 161–62
Amen Corner, 14, 116, 124, 189, 198, 269
American Express, 186, 197
American Federation of Television and
    Radio Artists, 203
American Golfer, 57
Amos & Andy, 221
Angott, Sammy, 234
Argentine Golf Association, 253
Arkell, Bartlett, 150
Armour, Tommy, 105
Arrow shirts, 197, 198
Associated Press, 83, 85
Atkinson, Harry M., 54
Atlanta Journal, 92
Augusta (Eubanks), 259–60
Augusta, Ga., 47, 50, 94, 153
  golfing in, 56–57
Augusta Chronicle, 54, 57, 74, 92
Augusta Country Club, 56
Augusta National, Inc., 96
Augusta National and the Masters (Christian
    and Brown), 33, 149–50

Augusta National Golf Club, 208
  average golfers and, 104–5
  beautification committee at, 115
  blacks and, 227–28, 229, 231–36, 241
  board of governors of, 25–26
  caddies at, 238–39
  changes to course at, 109–37
  Closing Party at, 231
  clubhouse at, 53–54, 61, 67, 93, 99, 107,
    109–10, 150–51
  dress code at, 216–17
  dues for, 53, 58, 59
  finances of, 15, 16, 59–61, 65–66, 74–77,
    81, 93–94, 96–97, 144, 150–51
  founding of, 52–59
  the Games at, 212–13
  German POW labor at, 149
  golf hall of fame and, 142–43
  Great Depression and, 55, 56, 60
  green blazers of, 15, 30, 31, 167, 191, 203,
    206, 264
  handicapping at, 122*n*
  history of, 15–17
  Jamboree at, 25, 162, 211–12, 257
  Jones and, 16–19, 20–21, 49, 51, 52, 74,
    142, 151–52, 209
  Ladies Masters lawsuit and, 262–64
  landscaping at, 67
  Masters Tournament and, 13–17, 81–99,
    101–2, 104*n*, 107–9, 110, 111, 112, 114,
    116, 118, 119, 120, 121, 124, 126–28,
    129–30, 132, 133, 134–36, 150–51, 153
  members of, 15, 25–26, 55–59
  official opening of, 74–75
  par three course at, 137–39, 213, 269

Augusta National Golf Club (*cont.*)
  P.G.A. Seniors' Championship at, 141–42
  plans for, 53–55
  professionals at, 209–11
  Roberts and, 16–19, 21, 22, 23–29, 49–50,
    51, 52, 142, 153–54, 210–15
  site of, 49–52
  subdivision for homes at, 67–69
  superior golfers and, 105–8
  television committee of, 196
  World War II and, 145–49
Augusta National Golf Club, golf course at,
    101–39
  Amen Corner at, 14, 116, 124, 189, 198,
    269
  first hole at, 110–12
  second hole at, 112
  third hole at, 113–14
  fourth hole at, 115–16
  fifth hole at, 116–17
  sixth hole at, 117
  seventh hole at, 118–19
  eighth hole at, 120–21
  ninth hole at, 121–22
  tenth hole at, 122–23
  eleventh hole at, 123–26
  twelfth hole at, 126, 189, 190
  thirteenth hole at, 128–29, 189
  fourteenth hole at, 129–30, 190
  fifteenth hole at, 131–33, 190
  sixteenth hole at, 133–34
  seventeenth hole at, 134–35
  eighteenth hole at, 135–36, 201
  nineteenth hole proposed for, 137
  Jones and, 102–8, 109, 113–14, 116,
    118–19, 120–22, 124, 127, 131, 133–34,
    137–39
  MacKenzie and, 62–67, 90, 93, 102–7, 109,
    113–14, 116–17, 118–19, 122, 123, 128,
    131–32, 133–34, 137–38, 272
  Roberts and, 102–3, 109–10, 111, 112,
    113–14, 115, 117, 118–19, 120–22,
    124–25, 127, 128–29, 130, 132, 135–36,
    137–39
Augusta National Invitation Tournament,
  16, 89, 183
Austin, J. Paul, 247–48
Azalea, 128

Bachler, F. S., 56
Bailey, Frank, 56
Baker, Pierrine, 154
Baker-Finch, Ian, 273
Ballesteros, Seve, 102, 275
Banta & Morrin, 45
Barber, Edward J., 151

Barber, Miller, 148
Barber Steamship Lines, 151
Barrett, Louise, 227
Barrett, Robert, 213
Barrett, Thomas, Jr., 52, 94, 213, 227
Beau Jack, 233–35
Beck, Robert, 72
Beman, Deane, 248, 250
Ben Hogan Bridge, 149
Bennett, Fred, 26, 150, 212, 218, 237, 268
Bennett, Lawrence, 49
Benson, Marsh, 272
Berckmans, Louis Alphonse, 115
Berckmans, Prosper, 51, 115
Berckmans, Prosper "Allie," Jr., 115, 141
Bishop, Mary Agnes, *see* Roberts, Mary
    Agnes Bishop
Black, Eugene R., 172
blind trust, 29, 181, 235
Bon Air–Vanderbilt Company, 52
Bon Air–Vanderbilt Hotel, 47, 52, 53, 55, 56,
    63*n*, 64, 153, 156, 210*n*, 233
Bourne, Alfred Severin, 59, 81, 91, 115, 141
Bowden, Ken, 228, 229
Bradley, Albert, 233
Brentwood Country Club, 90
Brewer, Gay, Jr., 202*n*
British Amateur championship, 17, 83, 157
British Open, 17, 86, 92, 105, 106, 154, 156,
    242, 243
Brown, Cal, 33
Brown, Henry, 248
Brown, Stephen W., 215, 257
Buckner Hoseless watering system, 64
Burke, Jack, Jr., 184
Burning Tree Club, 170–71
Bush, George, 79
Bush, Prescott A., 79–80
Butler, Thomas B., 152
Butler Cabin, 152
Byron Nelson Bridge, 149, 269

caddies, 238–39
Cadillac, 197, 198
Camellia, 122
Camp Gordon, 145–46, 149
Canadian Amateur, 251
Canadian Open, 251
Canadian P.G.A., 251
Carling World Open, 190
Carolina Cherry, 121
Carpenter, Frank, 236–37
Casper, Billy, 155, 265, 273
Casper, Shirley, 265
CBS, 20, 152, 183, 184–206, 208, 259–60
Cedar, 118

Champion in a Man's World (Outerbridge), 70
Champion Spark Plug Co., 159
Chase, Salmon P., 19
Cherokee Rose, 110
Chinese Fir, 129
Chirkinian, Frank, 201, 204–6, 208
Christian, Frank, 33, 136, 149–50, 211–12
Christian, Toni, 149–50
Chrysler, Walter, 72
Cities Service Co., 176
Citizens & Southern National Bank, 94
Citizens for Eisenhower, 175–76
Civil War, 229, 230
Clark, Blake, 217, 263
Clark, Eural, 241
Clark, James, 24, 267
Closing Party, 231
Cluett, Peabody & Co., 197
Cobb, George W., 138
Coca-Cola bottling plants, 216*n*, 252
Coca-Cola Company, 247
Coe, Charles, 203–4
Coleman, Merritt, 185
Collett, Glenna, 72
Collie, Alex, 270
Collier's, 158
Colt, Harry S., 62
Columbia University, 165, 166, 172
    Oral History Research Office at, 47, 166*n*,
        177, 230
Contractors and Engineers Monthly, 64–65
Cooley, Denton A., 224
Cooper, Harry, 105
Couples, Fred, 14, 101, 130
Cox, James Middleton, 142–43
Cox, James Middleton, Jr., 142–43
Crash of 1929, 18, 45–46, 59, 99, 147
Crawley, Leonard, 86, 107
Crenshaw, Ben, 151, 275
Crowell, Henry P., 59–60, 115
Crow's Nest, 150–51, 272
Crusade in Europe (Eisenhower), 171, 181
Crystal Downs (golf course), 119
Curtis Cup Match, 70
Cypress Point (golf course), 61, 62, 71

Deere & Co., 151
Del Monte Golf and Country Club, 61
Demaret, Jimmy, 120, 156, 157, 184, 188
de Soto, Hernando, 50
de Vicenzo, Roberto, 90, 252–54, 260
Dey, Joe, 248
Dickinson, Gardner, 112
Diegel, Leo, 88
Dirksen, Everett, 178
Dobereiner, Peter, 22, 199

Dogwood, 123
Dolph, Jack, 190, 203
Dorado Beach Resort, 221
Dudley, Ed, 118, 127, 209–10, 219, 221
Durslag, Melvin, 199
Dutra, Mortie, 91
Dutra, Olin, 90–91

Eisenhower, Dwight D., 37, 165–82
    at Augusta National Golf Club, 28,
        134–35, 165–69, 178–80, 234
    background of, 169
    bridge and, 171
    death of, 258
    as golfer, 30*n*, 111, 127, 134–35, 170–71
    heart attack of, 180–83
    personality of, 169–70
    popularity of, 165–67
    presidency of, 127, 173, 178–80, 223, 230
    presidential candidacy of, 28, 165–66,
        168–69, 171, 173–79, 185
    Roberts as financial adviser of, 29, 171–73,
        180–82, 235
    Roberts' friendship with, 23, 28–29, 47,
        48, 169–70, 171–73, 180–83, 258, 269
Eisenhower, Mamie, 167, 168, 172, 180–82,
    223
Eisenhower Cabin, 142, 152, 179–80
Eisenhower Tree, 135
Elder, Lee, 240, 246–49, 250
Emerson, Edward L., 213–14
Emmet, Devereux, 70
ESPN Classic, 188
Esquire, 171
Eubanks, Mark, 238
Eubanks, Steve, 259

Faldo, Nick, 14, 108, 130, 275
Farewell to Sport (Gallico), 47
Faubus, Orval E., 229–30
F. A. Willard & Co., 45, 74–75
Fazio, Tom, 138
Federal Communications Commission
    (FCC), 195
Ferguson, Francis E., 262
Finger, Joseph S., 120
Fire Thorn, 131
First National Bank of Chicago, 46*n*
Fletcher, Pat, 251
Flowering Crab Apple, 115
Flowering Peach, 113
Floyd, Ray, 261
Fontainebleau Hotel, 235
*Forbidden Fairways: African Americans and the
    Game of Golf* (Sinnette), 241
Ford, Doug, 124, 188

Ford Motor Co., 225
Forest Hills Hotel, 231
Founders Circle, 16
Fownes, Henry C., 105
Fownes, William, 105
Franklin, Jerome, 127, 217–18, 219, 259, 269
Fruitland Manor Corporation, 52, 96, 97n
Fruitland Nurseries, 51, 115
Fry, Roger, 219
Fulcher, William, 26

Gabrielsen, Jimmy, 248
Gallery, Tom S., 184
Gallico, Paul, 20, 47
gambling, 155–57
Games, the, 212–13
General Electric Co., 22, 135
General Motors, 197, 233
Georgia Power Co., 115–16
Georgia Railroad Bank & Trust Company,
    52, 96–97
Glen Head Country Club, 71
Glenn, Rhonda, 70
Goalby, Bob, 250, 252, 254
Golden Bell, 126
golf:
    amateur vs. professional status in, 83
    blacks and, 241, 245–47
    Great Depression and, 55, 56, 60, 73
    influences on, 30n
    social milieu of, 46
    television and, 185–86
    women in, 69–74, 208
Golf, 247
Golf Architecture (MacKenzie), 106
golf balls, 214
Golf Channel, 188
Golf Digest, 152, 228, 257, 261
Golf Is My Game (Jones), 19, 83, 104, 206–7
Golf Story, A (Price), 33
Golf World, 33, 189, 252
Goodman, Johnny, 61
Goodner, Ross, 33
Goodson, Arthur, 248
Gosden, Freeman, 221, 265
Gosden, Jane, 221, 223, 265
Gould, Alan, 85
Graffis, Herb, 84–85
Grainger, Isaac, 253
Grandfather Golf & Country Club, 217, 218,
    222
Grand Slam, 13
    Jones and, 13, 84
Graves, Johnny, 117
Great Depression, 15, 16, 55–56, 59–61, 63,
    73, 76, 84, 94

Greater Hartford Open, 240, 245, 246
Griffen, E. F., 55
Guldahl, Ralph, 156, 209
Gwin, Wilda, 254

Hackbarth, Otto, 141
Hagen, Walter, 88, 92
Haggin Oaks (golf course), 62
Hamilton, Thomas J., 57
Hardin, Hord, 208
Harison, Phil, 120–21
Harison, W. Montgomery, 68–69, 120, 266
Harlow, Robert, 85
Harmon, Claude, 188
Harris, Charles, 215
Harris, Helen, 251
Hastings, Val, 214
Hatch, Edwin, 115–16
Hawkins, Fred, 124, 188
Hibbard, Bill, 268
History of Cypress Point Club, The, 71n–72n
Hobby, Oveta Culp, 223
Hogan, Ben, 86, 92n, 101, 112, 130, 132, 144,
    146, 149, 154–56, 157, 170, 192n, 204,
    255, 275
Hollins, Harry P., 70
Hollins, Marion, 69–74
Holly, 135
House of Representatives, U.S., 246
Hutchison, Jock, 141, 142n, 259

Illustrated History of Women's Golf, The
    (Glenn), 70
indigo, 50–51
Information Please, 145
Irvin, Willis, 54
Ishida, Reisuke, 250–51

Jacobs, Tommy, 202n
Jamboree, 25, 162, 211–12, 257
Japan Golf Association, 250
Jaques, Herbert, 80, 81
Jenkins, Dan, 205
Johnson, Hootie, 30, 154, 244n
Johnson, Jay, 265
Jones, Ernest, 71
Jones, Homer, 267
Jones, Robert P. "Colonel," 52, 96, 125–26,
    127–28, 135
Jones, Robert Trent, 133, 221
Jones, Robert Tyre "Bobby," Jr.:
    Amateur Dinner and, 161–62
    amateur vs. professional status and, 30n,
        82–83
    Augusta National Golf Club and, 16–19,
        20–21, 49, 51, 52, 74, 142, 151–52, 209

Augusta National golf course and, 102–8, 109, 113–14, 116, 118–19, 120–22, 124, 127, 131, 133–34, 137–39
black golfers and, 245, 246–47
finances of, 46, 76, 82, 216n, 234
golfing career of, 61, 65, 72, 82–86, 91–93, 105, 106
Grand Slam of, 13, 84
illness and death of, 152, 160–62, 224, 257–60, 261
Masters television broadcasts and, 206–7
Masters Tournament and, 17, 82–86, 87–89, 91–93, 152, 157–63, 202, 245, 246–47, 252–53, 259–60
membership campaign of, 55–59
personality of, 17–18
physical appearance of, 18
popularity and legendary status of, 16, 17–18, 19–20, 30n, 47, 55, 61, 82–86, 91, 92, 94, 96, 142, 151, 165–66, 167
Roberts's friendship with, 17–19, 22, 29, 33, 46–48, 77, 258–60
U.S. Open and, 80
and World War II, 145, 146, 147
Jones, W. Alton "Pete," 176–78
Jones Cabin, 151–52, 253
Joroberts, 216n, 251–52
Juniper, 117

Keeler, O. B., 20, 83, 89, 92, 103, 131, 133–34, 210n
Keiser, Herman, 16, 154–57
Kempton, Murray, 171
Kendall, Theodore R., 64–65
Kerr, Laura, 264–65
Kerr, William, 196, 264
Key, Maria Lyman, 43
kinescopes, 188
Kirkwood, Joe, 91
Klein, Willie, 90
Kletcke, Robert, 210–11, 213, 214
Knollwood Country Club, 46

Ladies British Amateur, 70
Ladies Masters, 161–64
Ladies Professional Golf Association (L.P.G.A.), 261–63
La Gorce Golf Club, 90
Lahey Clinic, 224–25
Lane, William, 261, 264, 269
Lema, Tony, 132
Life and Times of Bobby Jones, The (Matthew), 216n
Lister, Betty, see Roberts, Betty Lister
Littler, Gene, 92n, 248
Locke, Bobby, 154

Lodge, Henry Cabot, 174
London Daily Telegraph, 86
Longhurst, Henry, 21, 199–200, 201, 204, 207
Long Meadow Country Club, 234
Los Angeles Open, 250
Louis, Joe, 241

McArthur, Jim, 200
McClintock, Frank G., 261
Macdonald, Charles Blair, 70, 128
MacFarlane, Willie, 88, 209
Machrihanish (golf course), 119
McKay, Jim, 136, 188, 191, 199, 200, 207
MacKenzie, Alister:
    Augusta National and, 62–67, 90, 93, 102–7, 109, 113–14, 116–17, 118–19, 122, 123, 128, 131–32, 133–34, 137–38, 272
    Cypress Point and, 61–62, 71
    Pasatiempo and, 61, 69, 71–73
MacKenzie, Hilda, 63n, 66, 93
McKim, Mead, and White, 71
McLeod, Fred, 141, 142n, 259
MacPhail, William, 184–85, 192, 196, 203, 204, 260
Magnolia, 116
Magnolia Lane, 14, 29, 49–50, 150
Mandate for Change (Eisenhower), 169
Mangrum, Lloyd, 126
Marshall, George C., 170
Marshall, Walton H., 52, 59
Masters, The (Sampson), 33, 96n–97n, 216n, 251
Masters Classics, 188
Masters Club, 26
Masters on Monday, 188
Masters Tournament, 13–15, 270–75
    advertising and, 30
    Amateur Dinner and, 161–62
    Augusta National Golf Club and, 101–2, 104n, 107–9, 112, 114, 116, 118, 119, 120, 121, 124, 126–28, 129–30, 132, 133, 134–36, 150–51, 153
    black golfers and, 228–29, 240–50
    early years of, 86–99
    gambling and, 155–57
    honorary starters at, 142n
    international golfers and, 249–54
    invitation criteria for, 240, 241–45
    Jones and, 17, 82–86, 87–89, 91–93, 152, 157–63, 202, 245, 246–47, 252–53, 259–60
    major status of, 86
    members of, 259
    origins of, 81–99
    prestige of, 13–15
    professional golfers and, 81, 90–91

Masters Tournament (*cont.*)
  Roberts and, 17, 20, 22–23, 29–31, 81–85, 87, 89, 97–99, 155–63, 202, 243, 245, 246–47, 252–53, 259–60, 275
  special events at, 88–89
  sportswriters and, 14
  success of, 260–61
  television broadcasts of, 20, 30, 152, 183–208, 259–60
  as well-run event, 86–87, 97–99
  World War II and, 145–46, 153
Masters Tournament Committee, 22
Matthew, Sidney L., 20, 216n
Maxwell, Perry, 119, 123
Maxwell rolls, 119
Mays, Willie, 255
Maytag, Lewis B., 119
Maytag Company, 119
Mellon, Eleanor, 70
Metropolitan Golf Writers, 247
Mezzrow, Milton "Mezz," 124
Miami Biltmore Hotel, 91
Miami Biltmore Open, 81
Middlecoff, Cary, 193
Miller, Wendell, 72, 117, 131, 138
Milligan, Bowman, 25, 224–25, 231–36
Milton, John, 25, 231, 266
Miss America Pageant, 196–97, 198
Mitsui & Co., 250
Moaney, John, 171
Monroe, Jay R., 93
Monsanto Open, 240, 247
Morris, Old Tom, 119
Morse, Samuel F. B., 70, 71
Moss Creek Plantation, 262
Murphy, Bob, 250
Murphy, Kathryn, 17, 254, 259
Murray, Jim, 246
Museum of Television and Radio, 188

Nandina, 134
National Baseball Hall of Fame and Museum, 142
National Capital Open, 82
National Guard, 230
NBC, 183, 184, 194, 195–96, 262–63
Nelson, Byron, 17, 19, 24, 86, 120, 125, 142n, 144, 146, 149, 155, 156, 157, 186, 209, 255
New England Baptist Hospital, 225
New Yorker, 14, 33, 98–99
New York Herald Tribune, 165, 234, 235
New York Post, 247
New York Sun, 17
New York Telegram, 158
New York Times, 127, 248

Nicklaus, Jack, 102, 116, 126, 130, 132, 136, 151, 192n, 202n, 204, 255, 260–61, 269, 275
Nixon, Richard M., 180
Norman, Greg, 102, 108
Norman, Moe, 92n
North Atlantic Treaty Organization (NATO), 172, 173
Northwestern Mutual Life Insurance Co., 261–64

Oakmont Country Club, 105
Observer, 22
Official World Golf Ranking, 245n
Oglethorpe, James Edward, 50
Old Course at St. Andrews, 64, 106–7, 116, 118
Olmsted, Frederick Law, 67
Olmsted Bros., 67, 69, 72, 74, 97, 143
O'Meara, Mark, 151
On the Ball, 248
Oosterhuis, Peter, 247
Ouimet, Francis, 61, 74
Outerbridge, David E., 70

Palacios Beacon, 42
Paley, William, 185, 203
Palm, 115
Palmer, Arnold, 14, 24, 30n, 124, 144, 188, 192, 193, 199, 204, 208, 255, 260, 269, 275
Palmer, Johnny, 156
Pampas, 118
Par 3 Contest, 138–39
Pasatiempo (golf course), 61, 69, 71, 72, 73–74
Patton, Billy Joe, 203–4
Pearl Harbor, Japanese attack on, 145
Pebble Beach (golf course), 61, 70
Peek, Burton F., 151–52
Peek Cabin, 151–52
P.G.A., *see* Professional Golfers' Association
PGA, The (Graffis), 84–85
P.G.A. Championship, 86, 90, 95, 242, 243
P.G.A. Seniors' Championship, 141–42
P.G.A. Tour, 240, 241, 244, 246, 248
Phoenix Open, 241
Picard, Henry, 88
Pine Valley (golf course), 62, 209
Pink Dogwood, 112
Pinkertons, Inc., 87, 166, 179
Player, Gary, 14, 261, 274, 275
Preferred Lies and Other Tales (Whitaker), 203
Price, Charles, 20, 33, 152, 257–58

Professional Golfers' Association (P.G.A.),
    81, 82, 84–85, 87, 95, 209, 239, 241, 250,
    253
    proposed golf hall of fame of, 142–43
professionals, amateurs vs., 157, 161–62

Rader, Margie, 265
radio, Masters Tournament broadcast on,
    183
Rae's Creek, 101, 107, 117–18, 123, 125, 128,
    133, 149–50, 269
Ravenscroft, Gladys, 70
Raynor, Seth, 62, 70, 71
RCA, 187, 195
Reagan, Ronald, 215
Red Bud, 133
Red Cross, 145
Red Lead Pencils, 58
Redmond, Dennis, 51
Reed, Philip, 22, 135
Reed, Ralph, 186
Reid, Al, 273
Reilly, Rick, 126
Reynolds, Robert, 231
Reynolds & Co., 33, 75, 147, 216n
Reynolds Securities, 216n
Rhodes, Ted, 241
Rice, Grantland, 57, 74, 80, 85, 87–88, 89,
    137, 148, 234
Rice University, 120
Richardson, Sandy, 228
Road Hole, 116
Roberts, Alpheus, 34, 35, 40, 43–44, 45
Roberts, Betty Lister, 219, 222, 265, 266, 267,
    269
Roberts, Charles DeClifford, Sr., 35, 36–37
    death of, 45
    wheeling and dealing of, 36–37, 38, 40, 41,
        229
Roberts, Clifford:
    Amateur Dinner and, 161–62
    Augusta National Golf Club and, 16–19,
        21, 22, 23–29, 49–50, 51, 52, 142,
        153–54, 210–15
    Augusta National golf course and, 102–3,
        109–10, 111, 112, 113–14, 115, 117,
        118–19, 120–22, 124–25, 127, 128–29,
        130, 132, 135–36, 137–39
    background of, 18, 169, 228
    black golfers and, 245
    blind trust invented by, 29, 181, 235
    childhood of, 34–43
    clothes and, 216–17
    determination of, 16, 17, 44
    driving of, 217–18
    early career of, 18, 38, 41, 43, 44, 47
    as Eisenhower's financial adviser, 29,
        171–73, 180–83, 235
    Eisenhower's friendship with, 23, 28–29,
        47, 48, 169–70, 171–73, 180–83, 258, 269
    and Eisenhower's presidential campaign,
        28, 173–79
    finances of, 33, 45, 46, 76–77, 215–16, 234
    fire in childhood home of, 41, 43, 99
    gifts given by, 26–28
    as golfer, 46, 213–15
    illness of, 224, 264–68
    international golfers and, 251–54
    Jones's friendship with, 17–19, 22, 29, 33,
        46–48, 77, 258–60
    and Ladies Masters trial, 263–64
    management style of, 25–27, 63, 65, 66,
        72, 74, 99
    marriages of, see Roberts, Betty Lister;
        Roberts, Letitia; Roberts, Mary Agnes
        Bishop
    Masters television broadcasts and, 184,
        185–87, 189–93, 194–95, 198–208, 255
    Masters Tournament and, 17, 20, 22–23,
        29–31, 81–85, 87, 89, 97–99, 155–63, 202,
        243, 245, 246–47, 252–53, 259–60, 275
    medicine and health as interest of, 223–26
    membership campaign of, 55–59, 74–75,
        80, 143–44, 151, 259
    personality of, 16, 20, 22, 23–25, 38–40,
        152–53, 169–70, 220, 224, 226
    P.G.A. golf hall of fame and, 142–43
    physical appearance of, 21, 39–40, 216–17,
        220
    public image of, 20–23
    race and, 227–55
    real estate of, 216n, 217, 218–19, 266
    relationships with women of, 222–23
    religion and, 39, 41
    suicide of, 23, 69, 267–70
    U.S. Open and, 80–81
    as Wall Street stockbroker and investor,
        18, 33, 45–46, 56, 75, 76, 91, 147,
        153–54, 172–73, 215–16, 235
    in World War I, 44–45
    World War II and, 145–49
Roberts, Dorothy, 34, 35, 37, 39, 40, 41, 42,
    43–44, 45, 166, 220
Roberts, John "Jack," 35, 36, 38, 40, 41,
    43–44
Roberts, Julian, 69
Roberts, Kenneth, 216n
Roberts, Letitia, 220–22, 223
Roberts, Mary Agnes Bishop, 219–20
Roberts, Rebecca Key, 37, 40, 41, 229
    diary of, 34–35, 38, 39, 40, 41, 42
    ill health of, 18, 35–36, 37–38

Roberts, Rebecca Key (*cont.*)
  personality and appearance of, 34, 39
  suicide of, 18, 34, 37, 41–43, 99, 268–69
Roberts, Robert Key, 34, 35, 37, 40, 41, 43–44
Roberts & Co., 45
Robinson, William E., 165, 171, 174, 234
Rodriguez, Chi Chi, 240, 250
Rommel, Erwin, 149
Royal and Ancient Golf Club of St.
  Andrews, 53, 92, 154, 161, 253
Royal Canadian Golf Association, 251
Royal Lytham & St. Annes (golf course),
  105
"Rubber Ducky," 212
Runyan, Paul, 82, 88, 92
Ryan, J. Richard, 197, 254, 258
Ryder Cup, 242, 243

Sabin, Charles H., 79, 80
St. Andrews (golf club), 66
St. Luke's Episcopal Hospital, 224, 264,
  265
Sampson, Curt, 33, 96*n*–97*n*, 216*n*, 251
Sarazen, Gene, 86, 91, 96, 112, 142*n*
  double eagle of, 16, 89*n*, 95, 101, 151
Saturday Evening Post, 37, 38, 47
Schenkel, Chris, 193, 199, 201
Schoo, Clarence J., 111–12
Schooie's Gulch, 111–12
Scotland's Gift: Golf (Macdonald), 128
Scott, Carl, 225
Scudder, Louise Fry, 219–20, 223
Searle, James, 154, 183, 237–38
Secret Service, 127, 179–80, 215
Senior P.G.A. Tour, 142, 238
Shippen, John, 241
"Shouting at Amen Corner," 124
Shultz, George, 215
Shute, Denny, 92, 156
Sifford, Charles, 240, 241, 245, 246, 249, 250,
  251, 252
Signal Corps, 44
Silver, Betsey Fry, 219–20
Silver, Tom, 220
Singer Sewing Machine, 59
Sinnette, Calvin H., 241
Slater, Ellis, 235, 269
Smalley, Ben, 231
Smart, Annie, 267
Smith, Horton, 16, 92, 119, 154, 155, 156
Smith, MacDonald, 88, 209
Snead, Sam, 14–15, 17, 86, 112, 138, 139,
  142*n*, 144, 155, 156, 204, 275
Southern Hills (golf course), 119
Spalding, 82, 85
Spalding Dots, 214

Spanish Dagger, 129
Spencer, Barbara, 225–26
Spencer, David, 210–11, 213, 215, 225–26
Spirit of St. Andrews, The (MacKenzie), 66,
  71, 119
Sport, 234
"Sportlight, The" (Rice), 57
Sports Illustrated, 33, 108, 124, 126, 205,
  247
Stadler, Craig, 151
Stephens, Jackson, 33, 132, 152–53, 266,
  268
Stephens Cabin, 152–53
Stevenson, Adlai, 178
Stirling, Alexa, 70
Stoke Poges (golf course), 133
Stokes, Clarence, 273
Stoltz, Commodore J. Perry, 51
Storer, George B., 25
Story of Augusta National Golf Club, The
  (Roberts), 23, 46, 79, 124, 125, 227–28
Stout, Gene, 210
Stranahan, Frank, 157–60
Summerall, Pat, 199, 205
Supreme Court, U.S., 230
Surlyn, 214
syringomyelia, 258

Taft, Robert, 175, 176
Tam O'Shanter Country Club, 184
Tea Olive, 110
television:
  advertisers for Masters Tournament and,
    30, 197–99
  color, 194–96
  early golf coverage on, 183–84
  early technology of, 183, 184
  first broadcast of Masters on, 184–85
  Jones and, 206–7
  live, 187–88
  Masters Tournament broadcast on, 20, 30,
    152, 183–208, 259–60
  Roberts and, 184, 185–87, 189–93, 194–95,
    198–208, 255
Texas Heart Institute, 224
Three Pines, 126
Tillman, Claude, 227–28, 231
Time, 16, 86
Tolley, Cyril, 72
Travelers, 197, 201
Traylor, Melvin A., 46*n*
Trevino, Lee, 246
Trevor, George, 17
Trophy Room, 151, 258, 272
Truman, Harry S., 165, 172
TV Guide, 199

United Golfers Association, 249
United States Golf Association (U.S.G.A.),
    46n, 79, 80–81, 82, 84, 96, 146, 154, 161,
    186, 208, 209n–210n, 239, 241, 253
    handicapping method of, 122n
U.S. Amateur championship, 17, 46, 61, 72,
    79, 83, 84, 154, 204, 242, 243, 250, 254
U.S. Open, 16, 17, 61, 79, 84, 86, 90, 95, 96,
    105, 107, 126, 154, 184, 186, 241, 242,
    243, 244, 250
U.S. Women's Amateur tournament, 69,
    70

Venturi, Ken, 142n, 184
Verdet, Suzanne, 220
Vidmer, Richards, 234
Volpe, Ray, 262
Von Elm, George, 46

Wadkins, Lanny, 250
Wahl, Phil, 210, 224, 269
Walker, George H., 79
Walker, Sidney, see Beau Jack
Walker Cup, 79, 242, 243
Wall, Art, Jr., 250
Wallace, Fielding, 52, 210n
Warner Bros., 82
Washington Road, 50, 150
Watrous, Al, 88
Watson, Tom, 261, 275
Weiskopf, Tom, 126
Werden, Lincoln, 127, 248
Wergeles, Chick "Hercules," 234
Whitaker, Jack, 199–204, 207

White, Paul Dudley, 180
White Dogwood, 123
Whitman, Ann, 180, 223
Whitney, Payne, 72
Wigfall, Ray, 266–67
Willard, Frank, 74–75
Williams, Joe, 158
Willingham, William A., 55–56
Wind, Herbert Warren, 14, 17, 19, 20, 33, 86,
    98–99, 124, 189, 260
women, in golf, 69–74, 208
Women's National Golf and Tennis Club,
    70–71
Women's Open, 208
Wood, Craig, 95
Woodbine, 112
Woods, Earl, 15
Woods, Tiger, 14, 130, 254–55, 273, 274, 275
    Masters victory of, 15, 102, 114, 151, 255
World Bank, 172
World Championship of Golf, 184
World War I, 44–45, 52, 62, 220
World War II, 58, 83, 95, 120–21, 143,
    144–50, 153, 170, 215, 243, 275
Worsham, Lew, 184
Wren, Christopher, 270

Yamamoto, Guy, 273
Yates, Charles, 25–26, 83, 132, 147–48,
    161–62, 217, 258–59
Yates, Dorothy, 147–48
Yellow Jasmine, 120
Yonker, Bettie, 266, 267
Young & Rubicam, 197

Photo Credits